James W. Wilson

Money vs. Products

Why Times are Hard

James W. Wilson

Money vs. Products
Why Times are Hard

ISBN/EAN: 9783337338992

Printed in Europe, USA, Canada, Australia, Japan

Cover: Foto ©Suzi / pixelio.de

More available books at **www.hansebooks.com**

—or—

Why Times Are Hard

*A Complete Exposition of the Causes Which Led
the Prevailing Industrial Depression, and
the Remedy Therefor*

By JAS. W. WILSON

CHICAGO
HOWARD & WILSON PUBLISHING CO.
1895

THE following is the substance of two lectures delivered by Jas. W. Wilson before the Austin Economic Circle, Austin, Ill., February 5 and 11, 1894, on the causes of the prevailing industrial depression:

CHAPTER I.

INTRODUCTION.

Before entering into a discussion of the subject for the evening, allow me to congratulate you on the successful organization of the Austin Economic Circle. Its large muster roll and the many intelligent people here present bespeak for it a career of usefulness. We cannot thus early forecast what benefits will grow out of these studies, or how far the usefulness of the Circle will extend. One thing is certain, however: if a sovereign people are to govern themselves intelligently, and administer the affairs of a government "of the people, by the people and for the people" in such a way as to bring the greatest good to the largest number, it is of the utmost importance that they understand and apply those economic principles which underlie all good government.

I am particularly well pleased to see so many of our school-teachers present, and to note the growing interest among public educators in economic questions. It is unfortunate that the study of the science of government is

neglected in the high school course, and only approached
in colleges.   As a consequence, as the Hon. David A.
Wells says in the January Forum, "The most appalling
ignorance prevails in respect to economic subjects, not
only among the masses but among many who are filling
important stations as legislators, editors, and as educational directors and teachers."

In view of these facts it is time our public educators and
educational institutions shook off some of the fossil Latin
and Greekisms of bygone ages, and devoted more of
their energies to fitting our young men and women to
grapple with the every-day problems of modern civilization.
On the threshold of our work, however, we are confronted
with a serious question involving danger. "When," as
David A. Wells further says, "professed teachers of political economy need to be retaught and when institutions of
learning claiming high character accept endowments of
chairs of this department of knowledge with the agreement that their occupant shall teach only such political
economy as the donor thinks will subserve his private interests." to which we may add, and when the majority of
the works on political economy are written in the interests
of the fund-holding classes and lay down principles which
when applied are against the interests of the masses of the
people, especially the producing classes, the question of
broad and sound teachers and authorities becomes one of
serious import.

The organization of such circles as this for the study
and free discussion of economic subjects is, therefore, a
step in the right direction an example which could be
followed to advantage by the organization of a similar
society in every town, village and hamlet in the nation. I
am sure if this could be done the progress of our people
into the happier life of a higher civilization would be rapid
and soon accomplished. At least the better education

which would result would enable us to steer the ship of
state clear of such shoals as those with which she is now
confronted.

On the authority of the Chicago Tribune and other papers of its stripe, if we dig too deep into these questions
we shall be classed with the genus "crank." Like the
priests of religion during the dark ages, our high priests
of finance do not want the people to know too much.
With them financial knowledge outside their own circle is
sin. As they cannot burn the sinners at the stake they
have to content themselves with calling names.

It is a case where "too much learning" will make the
people "mad," and when they "get their mad up" they
will be sure to administer some vigorous kicks, and somebody will get hurt.

"Cranks" are very useful in their way, however. They
"turn things" and the machinery of the world is moved
by them. The word from an ephithet of derision has
come to be synonymous of progressive ideas. To be a
member of the "crank" fraternity is now an honor. It
indicates a person who does his own thinking.

In view of their unreliability or the inspired character
of many of the writings on economic subjects, if we
would reach the truth it will be as well not to lean too
much on so-called standard authorities or accept without
question the editorial dictum of public journals. What
we want is plain facts from which to draw our own
conclusions. Such I shall endeavor to lay before you.

After a brief excursion into the formidable subject
which you have assigned me, I am inclined to agree with
the young man down in Georgia. This young man was
born and raised on one of those seven by nine clearings
common among the poor whites in that State, and had
never been very far out of it. On the occasion of his
twenty-first birthday his father gave him a treat by tak-

ing him to Atlanta, twenty miles away. After his return on recounting his experiences and adventures to his associates he remarked, "If the world is as big t'other way as it is that, she's a whopper." That's about the conclusion I have come to after examining the causes of the prevailing industrial depression. I have been investigating along the financial lines, and can safely say if it is as big some other way as it is that, "she's a whopper."

In presenting my case I shall endeavor to follow a different course than did the Star of Bethlehem as described by an old negro preacher whom I heard down in the piny woods of Louisiana. "Dat dar stah," said he, "rose in de yeast an' flew right straight zigzag across de hebbens." I shall try to travel "right straight," but should I get warped let those who follow in the debate knock the "zigzags" out of the argument.

THE CONDITION OF THE COUNTRY.

To use the words of his eminence, President Cleveland, "We are confronted with a condition, not a theory." The condition in which we find the nation to-day is indeed deplorable. Looking at it from many points of view, I believe we are passing through the worst crisis of our national existence. As there is no effect without a cause, there is a cause lying under this condition. To discover that cause, and if possible find a way to remove it, and thus cure the evil, is the purpose of this discussion.

Like causes produce like effects. As the effect is an evil condition, the cause must be of like nature. Such conditions of distress in national life can be brought about in three ways: By a failure of crops, by prolonged and devastating war, or by unwise legislation or governmental policy. There is no war, and we are at peace with ourselves and all nations. And so far as nature is concerned, and the bountiful hand of nature's God, we are in the midst of abundance. The barns and storehouses of the nation are filled to overflowing with grain, and the sleek cattle and fleecy sheep roam over a million hills. So far as the nation's food products are concerned, except, perhaps, in a few drouth-stricken sections, her "vats are overflowing with fatness." Yet in the midst of this seeming great prosperity we hear the daily wail of tens of thousands crying for bread, while hundreds of thousands do not know where the next meal is coming from. The ready hand of charity is strained to the utmost.

It is estimated that three millions of workingmen are out of employment, which with those dependent upon them make indeed a vast and appalling army. Many of these during better times have laid by them in store against this rainy day and are now drawing on their resources; but the majority, either through imprudence or necessity on account of many mouths to feed, have nothing to live upon but what their hands can earn from day to day. The condition of such is pitiable indeed.

Here is abundance of skilled labor willing and anxious to produce the necessaries and luxuries of life for others who may need or want them, willing to exchange the product of their craft for food, but who find no demand for their labor and therefore must suffer. Why?

On the other hand, we find millions of food-producers with their barns full of the products of the soil, which they are willing and anxious to exchange, who are suffering for the other necessaries of life; whose wives and children are half clad and shod, or housed in scantily built and half furnished houses; who are unable to surround themselves with those home comforts to which every industrious citizen of this republic is entitled, or to give their children the education which every child beneath our flag has a right to demand. Why?

The manufacturer and the artisan are anxious to supply the farmer with the necessary articles he lacks, and the farmer in turn is anxious to fill the hungry mouths of the family of the artisan. Why cannot this exchange be made so that both can be made comfortable and happy? Why are the mills and factories closed? Why the wheels of commerce clogged? Why are intelligent and willing workingmen walking the streets and their children crying for bread? Why are the farmers' wives and children compelled to go half clad? There is no war. The hand of the Almighty has been bountiful. We cannot charge this trouble to an all-wise God. To what must we attribute it but to man's blundering stupidity, born of ignorance of the rudiments of political economy? Or perhaps more likely, but let us be charitable, to man's cunning craftiness born of his abnormal greed?

Why cannot the farmer get a sufficient price for his products to enable him to pay his debt and have something left with which to buy the necessaries and comforts of life? When we have found a correct answer to this last question we shall have found a solution to the problem why times are hard, and an answer to all our other questions.

To unwise legislation, to a wretched policy of government, to the application of unsound principles of political economy, then, we must attribute the cause. Let us see if we can discover what are these unsound principles, when they began to work, and trace their effects, culminating with the present condition.

SOME MISTAKEN THEORIES.

To account for the panic and the subsequent depression many theories have been advanced from time to time, some because their advocates believed in them and others to distract public attention and lead the people on a false scent. Some of them have already been exploded while others remain at the front, strenuously upheld by their advocates. The first of the former we shall call

THE CLEVELAND THEORY.

The President in his message calling the special session of Congress last August stated in substance that the panic was due to the purchasing clause of the Sherman act, and that its prompt repeal would cure the evil and set again in motion the wheels of industry.

This was the doctrine of the high priests of finance in Wall street. It was re-echoed by the Bankers' Association, Petitions were sent out by the latter to the banks through-y out the country demanding that Congress repeal the hatead clause forthwith. These the bankers were asked to circu- late and cajole their customers into signing. When as many signatures as possible were obtained the petition was to be forwarded to the Congressman representing the district where the petition originated and pressure used to influence his vote in line with the bankers' wishes. The monometallist press teemed with acrimonious editorials in which all manner of abuse was heaped upon those who knew and dared to say that the Sherman act was innocent of the huge crime with which it was charged, and that instead of being an evil was in fact, so far as it went, a blessing, in that it stood in the way of the bankers' and fund-holders' dearest wish—the single gold standard. It was one of the remaining bulwarks which stood between the people and the omnipotent power of the bankers over the currency of the country. The bankers are fighting the principle established in the greenback—the right of the Government to issue paper money directly to the people without the intervention of banks. The Sherman act was in line with this principle. Under it the Government was issuing treasury notes directly to the people. It maintained and increased the circulating medium to keep pace with the increased demands of commerce and the increase in population. For this reason, although imperfect in itself, it

was a good thing for the producing classes. The fund-
holders want money with a high purchasing power, so
that the interest from their bonds will buy more of the
products of labor. It did not, therefore, suit the Wall and
Lombard street high priests of finance, so it must be cruci-
fied, and hence the cry, "Away with it! Away with it!
Release unto us the gold, Barabbas!"

The long contest in Congress over the repeal of the act
is too recent and fresh in our memories to need recount-
troing. During its progress both parties were repeatedly
it given the opportunity to carry out the declaration of the
financial planks of the platforms on which they were elected. In these platforms the people expressed their wishes.
On the principles set forth in them their representatives were elected and should, if they are honest and true
to the people, carry out as far as practicable the platform declarations. On the question of silver involved in
the Sherman act the Democratic platform declared:

We hold to the use of both gold and silver as the standard
money of the country and to the coinage of both gold and silver without discrimination against metal or charge for mintage.

The Republican platform in the same relation declared:

The American people from tradition and interest favor
bimetallism, and the Republican party demands the use of
both gold and silver as standard money.

The House, as a substitute for the Sherman act, was
given the opportunity of carrying out the wishes of the
people of both parties as expressed in their declaration by
adopting a measure for the free coinage of silver at any
ratio from 16 to 1, to 20 to 1, but it rejected all. The Senate also had like opportunity, but the majority, either
seduced or whipped into line by the tremendous patronage of the presidential office, voted down all substitutes, and finally a bill for unconditional repeal passed
both houses.

It is said that when this great wrong against the producing classes had been accomplished some of the noble band of Senators who had withstood the tremendous tide of abuse turned upon them and had made such a prolonged fight in the interests of the people, actually shed tears. They had measured the consequence and knew full well the size of the disaster which had befallen the nation. It was indeed a time to weep. The dark, prophetic forebodings of the martyred President of the people, Abraham Lincoln, were being fulfilled. A triumph of the money power over patriotism was accomplished, and liberty had received a dangerous wound in the back. If there is a producer in the land who, when voting time comes again, does not remember the noble band of Congressmen and Senators who stood by the people and their party platforms during that bitter contest, he will not be doing his duty by his nation, himself or his family.*

The act was repealed.

WHAT WAS THE ANSWER OF COMMERCE?

Let me read you an extract from the market reports as they appeared in the daily papers next day. The Chicago Tribune market report, Oct. 31 issue, said:

The sharply downward course of the wheat market was an unquestioned surprise to most of the people in the trade,

---

*The following is a list of the members of the House who voted for the free coinage of silver at a ratio of 16 to 1 as a substitute for the purchasing clause of the Sherman act. It should be preserved as a roll of honor:

Abbot,	Conn,	Hundson,	Pence,
Aitken,	Cooper (Tex.),	Hunter,	Pendleton(Tex.),
Alexander,	Cox,	Hutcheson,	Pickler,
Allen,	Crawford,	Jones,	Post,
Arnold,	Culberson,	Kem,	Richardson
Bailey,	Curtis (Kas.),	Kilgore,	(Mich),
Baker,	Davis,	Kyle,	Richardson
Bankhead,	DeArmond,	Lane,	(Tenn.),
Bell (Col.),	Denson,	Latimer,	Robbins,
Bell (Tex.),	Dinsmore,	Lawson,	Robertson,
Black (Ga.),	Dockery,	Lester,	Sayers,
Blanchard,	Donovan,	Livingston,	Sibley,

as the price slid off two and three-quarters cents from Saturday's close. The bulls had long been hoping for silver repeal in the Senate, believing this would result in higher prices.

The FARM, FIELD AND FIRESIDE, Chicago, of the issue of the week following the repeal, said:

Dun's Weekly Market Review, which throughout the great silver debate has been industriously trying to uphold the monometallist side, now devotes considerable space to explain how it happened that in the face of its roseate prophecies the prices of all commodities took a sudden tumble on the passage of the act. The following extract from its report of Saturday should open the eyes of any financier whose brain is not lop-sided: "The action of Congress had less visible influence upon speculative markets for products, in part because foreign markets obstinately refuse to accept the higher valuations which speculators here tried to establish. Though people across the water award unstinted praises to those who secured the passage of the repeal bill there is not much disposition to pay higher prices on that account for wheat or cotton." Most assuredly the foreigners will not pay higher prices for staple commodities on account of the act. They are not such fools to work for the passage of the bill and praise those who passed it if the result of such action were going to make them pay higher prices for raw material for their factories and food for their people. It was

Bland,	Doolittle,	Lucas,	Simpson,
Boatner,	Edmunds,	Maddox,	Stallings,
Boen.,	Ellis,	Maguire,	Stockdale,
Bower.	Enloe,	Marshall,	Stone (Ky.),
Bowers,	Epes.	McCullough,	Strait.
Branch,	Fithian,	McDearmon,	Swanson,
Bretz,	Funston,	McKeighan,	Sweet,
Broderick,	Fyan,	McLaurin,	Talbert,
Brookshire,	Geary,	McMillan,	Tarsney,
Bryan,	Goodnight,	McRae,	Tate,
Bunn,	Grady,	Meredith,	Taylor (Ind.),
Burnes,	Hall (Mo.),	Money,	Terry,
Caminetti,	Harris.	Montgomery,	Turpin,
Cannon (Cal.),	Hartman,	Morgan,	Tyler,
Cannon (Ill.),	Hatch,	Moses,	Wheeler,
Capeheart,	Heard,	Murray,	Whiting (Mich.)

because they were far-sighted enough to see that such action would lower prices by making gold dearer, so that the interest on their foreign investments would buy more commodities, that they praised those who passed the bill. Alas! such praise, and that we have legislators who will receive it to their glory instead of shame. It does look as if some of our financial writers who are looked upon as authorities have plenty of vacant space in the upper part of their craniums.

Wheat immediately went down three cents a bushel, iron slumped off two dollars per ton, and other products of labor went down in price in like proportion. They have since become lower still and the end is not yet. This means that the purchasing power of money has advanced; that the bondholder's dollar collected for interest will buy from five to ten per cent more of the products of labor; that as a consequence of this action of Congress the debtor will have to expend from five to ten per cent more labor to pay his interest and debts.

The act is repealed but the business horizon shows no signs of the coming day so strongly predicted. The wheels of industry are still clogged. The workingman still walks the streets. Those who are fortunate enough to remain at work will have to take less pay. Strike, riot and resist as they will, eventually they will have to submit to the inevitable. While the farmer has to sell three

Clark,	Henderson	Neill,	Williams (Ill.),
Cobb (Ala.),	(N. C.),	Newlands,	Williams (Miss.)
Cockrell,	Holman,	O'Ferrall,	Wilson (Wash.),
Coffeen,	Hooker (Miss.),	Paynter,	Woodard.—125.

The following is a list of Senators who voted against unconditional repeal:

Allen,	Colquitt,	Kyle,	Roach,
Bate,	Daniel,	Mitchell (Ore.),	Shoup,
Berry,	Dubois,	Martin,	Stewart,
Blackburn,	George,	Pasco,	Teller,
Butler,	Hansbrough,	Peffer,	Vance,
Call,	Harris,	Perkins,	Vest,
Cameron,	Irby,	Pettigrew,	Walthall,
Cockrell,	Jones (Ark.),	Power,	White (Cal.),
Coke,	Jones (Nev.),	Pugh,	Wolcott—36.

bushels of wheat for a dollar he cannot buy the other products of industry. Money cannot get into circulation, but will remain congested in the banks, and the mills and factories will remain idle.

The President has had his way. It has proved a failure. The Cleveland theory of the cause of the prevailing industrial depression has exploded.

THE BOND THEORY.

After the Cleveland comes the bond theory. Finding that a revival of industry did not follow the repeal of the purchasing clause of the Sherman act as had been so abundantly predicted, some other cause for the continued depression must be found. This the high priests of finance, ever alive to the interests of the fund-holding class to which they belong, found in the rapidly vanishing gold reserve.

It is perhaps known to you that our total stock of paper currency amounts to over eleven hundred million dollars.* On the construction of President Cleveland and his Secretary of the Treasury any of this paper money, no matter under which act it is issued, is redeemable in gold at the option of the holder. It does not signify that the silver certificates say "Pay the bearer so many silver dollars;" the President says that in order to keep all the various forms and issues of money at a parity all must be redeemable in gold.

The original intent of the gold reserve of one hundred million dollars was to serve as a basis for the redemption of the three hundred and fifty millions in greenbacks. It

---

*From the report of the Secretary of the Treasury, Aug 1, 1893, the following was then the total stock of paper money issued and outstanding:

Gold certificates................................. ....$	87,704,739
Silver certificates...........................	333,031,504
Treasury notes under Sherman act....................................	148,286,348
Greenbacks.......	346,681,016
Currency certificates.............	8,340,000
National bank notes...	183,755,147
Total..$1,107,798,754	

mattered not to the financial doctors that a much larger issue of greenbacks had been floated and successfully served the business requirements of the country without any gold reserve, the country must be bled and this vast sum withdrawn from circulation and stowed away in the treasury vaults.

Under the Cleveland regime this comparatively slender shaft of gold is made to support a structure eleven times its size. It must not only uphold the three hundred and fifty millions of greenbacks, but all the other forms of paper money, and even the silver dollar itself. I have a diagram here (page 14) from which you can see the character of the financial structure our financial architects and builders have reared.

But the rats began to eat away the base. The Jews of London and New York, who fatten on panics and hard times, and revel in bonds, were not slow to grasp the situation. Under a single gold standard, which the policy of the Administration had made a fact, they held the key to the situation. The United States Treasury and the finances of the country were within their power, and through its finances the whole country. They could get up a corner on gold at any time and then raise its purchasing power, and with it the purchasing power of all money, stocks and bonds. This would give them and the others of the fund-holding class a larger percentage of the products of labor for their holdings and interest dues. They also had it in their power to depress the prices of stocks at any time it suited their purpose, or to buy up a lot of paper money, take it to the Treasury and deplete it of its gold, and then compel the Administration to buy gold with bonds to replenish the reserve. For years the gold clique and fund-holding class, of which the Jews are the brains and ringleaders, had been working to get into this position. The innocent professors of political econo-

$$$
$ $
$ $

$ Gold $
$ Certifi- $
$ cates, $
$ $87,704,739. $
$ $

$
$ Treasury $
$ Notes, $
$ $148,286,348. $
$ $

$ National Bank $
$ Notes, $
$ $183,755,147. $

$ Silver Certificates, $
$ $333,031,504. $

$ Greenbacks, $
$ $346,681,016. $

Gold
Reserve.

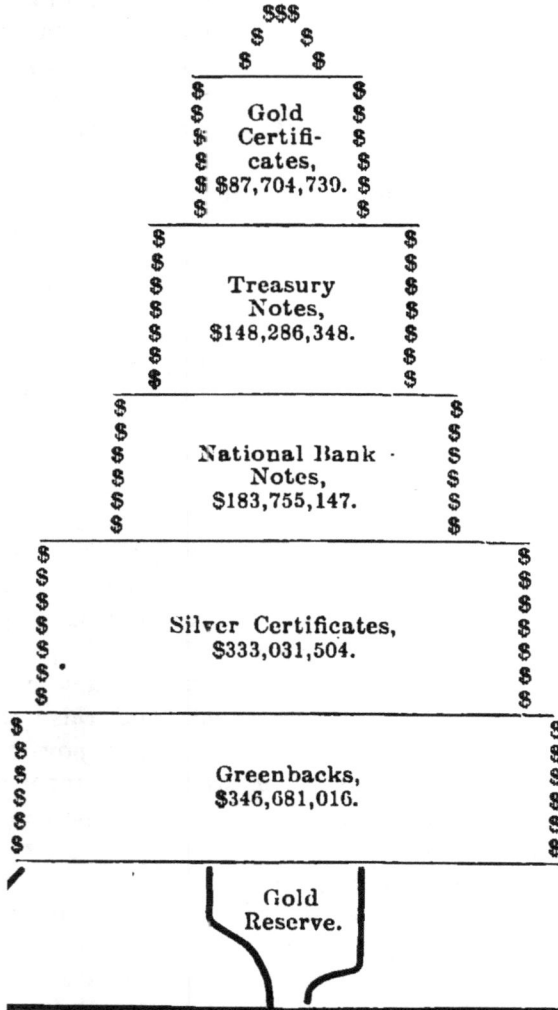

OUR FINANCIAL PYRAMID.

my from English-written text-books had been teaching the doctrine of so-called "sound money." The great economic monthlies—the Arena, Forum, North American Review, American Journal of Politics—and other journals of a similar character, teemed with inspired articles filled with dire predictions of disaster to come if we did not get on a gold basis forthwith.

The news and editorial columns of the great metropolitan journals, which are largely owned or controlled by monometallists,* have been filled for two years past with the same kind of literature. The country weeklies were sent tons of "boiler plates," accompanied by wily letters asking the editors to publish the matter as "news for the good of the country." If the country editor was found "not so green as he looked," he was allowed to publish the matter at advertising rates.

This tremendous amount of energy was not expended for nothing. These men, whoever they are, were not spending their money for the "good of the dear people." They were not philanthropists, but were inspired by a common interest of selfish greed. They were spending their money because they expected to get it back again with tenfold interest on the investment. To this end the people must be educated in line with their wishes. Dangerous heresies were abroad. Their promoters must be silenced. The heretics had the best of the argument, therefore discussion must be stopped by the purchase of editorial dictum. Those who knew the truth and warned the people of the rocks ahead, onto which the ship of state was being steered so the wreckers might plunder the car-

---

It is time that we should assert our Americanism and not be guided solely by the dictates of Lombard street or Wall street. The press of the country form to a great extent public opinion. It takes large sums of money to establish and run the leading papers of the land. The backing necessary to establish and maintain such enterprises naturally comes from those who favor a single standard, because they are the ones possessed of the gold. Therefore it is not to be wondered at that the leanings of many of our prominent daily papers are to a single standard.

go, were branded as "calamity howlers" and "cranks," so that people would not listen to their warnings.

We have all been hedged in, more or less, on our seven by nine economic farms by this educational timber of the money power. Let us climb over the fence and see if the world does not contain some better pastures. Let us cast out the beam of prejudice thus put before our eyes and then we shall clearly discern the mischief-makers.

This thorough educational system was designed to influence votes in such a way that an Administration and Congress should be elected who would be subservient to the money power, or to influence or excuse their acts after they were elected. They cared not which party won so long as the winner was friendly to their interests.

After Harrison had been nominated at Minneapolis, twelve of the representatives of the fund-holding class met in Chicago—six Republicans and six Democrats—and then and there decided that Grover Cleveland must head the other ticket. He was accordingly nominated and elected, and as we see by every-day evidences both he and the majority of all parties in Congress have proved willing tools.

These educators of the people builded different than they knew, however. I hardly think they intended to precipitate a panic, but only to get absolute control of the finances of the country through the narrow basis of gold standard. But the continued predictions of coming disaster charged to silver had the effect of making people apprehensive and nervous. They had been told that silver would drive gold out of the country and the loss of gold would be followed by dire disaster.

When, therefore, the rats began to eat away the base, when the Jews began to exchange currency for treasury gold and ship it abroad, the operation was watched with the keenest anxiety.

A voice: "Why do you charge this upon the Jews?"

If you will consult the public documents you will find that those who bought and shipped gold abroad at that time were all of that nationality.

Herdelbach, Ichlcheimer & Co., L. Von Hoffman & Co., Lazard Freres, Kuhn, Loeb & Co., etc., are not American names. At the other end was the great house of the Rothschilds. These men paid their premium of $2,000 on each million of gold and then took advantage of the effect which they knew would follow in the depreciation of stocks by going into the stock market and selling that market a vast amount of stock short. It is said they made a million profit on the first deal.

The movement of gold under their manipulating hands is shown by the following table culled from official reports:

Total exports of gold from July 1, 1892, to July 1, 1893... $98,228,705
Total imports for same period.......................... 21,466,525

Total loss of gold................................... $76,762,180
The total loss of gold for the fiscal year ending June 30,
1892, was.. 142,654,000

This gold was drawn from the Treasury and paper money exchanged therefor, evidently on a concerted policy of action looking to a common purpose.

As the gold reserve got nearer and nearer to the $100,-000,000 mark the anxiety of the people became greater. Somehow the idea had got out that when it should fall below that mark, disaster would follow. The papers, as you remember, were full of it. The amount of every ship. ment of gold sent abroad was wired over the country and published with editorial comments. The Western banks, apprehensive of danger, exchanged gold for currency to prop up the reserve, hoping in that way to stem the tide. This only increased the apprehensions of the people, however, and the more cautious began quietly to withdraw their deposits from the banks and hide the money away in

safety vaults.   The effect was that some of the weaker
banks closed their doors.   Then began the mad scramble,
and the panic with its fearful consequences was under full
headway.

Whether the high priests of finance designed to have
a panic or not we cannot say; all we know is, they took
exactly the right course to bring it about.

Everything that could be done to stampede the people
and create distrust and lack of confidence was done.   Nor
are the United States officials free from guilt, but from the
President down joined in the attack and used every effort
in their power to create distrust and financial chaos.

That this was done intentionally both by the banks and
officials is evident from their utterances at the time.   The
Inter Ocean, of Chicago, Republican, in an editorial said:

There was perhaps no organized conspiracy against the
West in the great financial centers of the East, but there
was a general understanding all along the line that the
West should be forced into line to help the East accomplish
what it long desired.   Early in the winter a bank president,
cornering a Chicago business man, said to him, "Mr. Jones,
we are going to make the West pay up this summer."

"But why should you press the Western creditors this
summer?" asked Jones.   The reply was:

"Well, we think it would make you a little more thought-
ful on currency matters and drive you from your foolish ideas
about silver."

President Cleveland had not been inaugurated a week
before he gave utterance to the following astounding prediction, which in the light of the utterances of bankers and
others or read by the light of subsequent events bears
evidence of a conspiracy whose magnitude, heartlessness
and criminality cannot be measured by words:

"This country is going to have the hardest times during
the next six months it has experienced in many years.   Time
will be exceedingly hard, money will be close, and it will be

withdrawn from banks and hoarded up in such a way as to create great distress. I expect to see many banks fail. There will be many factories and shops closed, and there will be thousands of men who will go into bankruptcy. I shall be sorry to see individuals suffer, but I don't intend to raise my hand to prevent it. What this country needs and must have is an object-lesson. We must have hard times and business failures and bankruptcy and a certain amount of distress before Congress will realize its duty and perform it. I propose to give the country an object-lesson."

This declaration clearly shows a criminal knowledge of a conspiracy to bring about the identical conditions named, and a criminal intent to aid and abet the conspirators. Otherwise there is no meaning in words. We are now experiencing the Cleveland object-lesson. A further evidence of conspiracy is found in the following extract from an editorial in the New York Sun, Friday, April 28. After reciting some of the incidents of the enjoyable conference between Secretary Carlisle and the Wall street bankers, in which "all shook hands and there was harmony all round," the Sun says:

President Cleveland's advisers have told him that the only way to induce the Western and Southwestern Senators and Congressmen to consent to the repeal of the Sherman law is to demonstrate to their constituents that they are losing money every day that this law is in operation. The missionary work in that direction has been started by a number of the banks in the solid communities of the East. They are daily refusing credit to the South, Southwest and West. * * * The Chicago banks, it is said, are carrying out the same line of policy.

As showing the unity of purpose between the President and bankers as parties to the great conspiracy, is the following from the financial column of the New York Sun of Saturday, April 20:

The statement of Mr. Carlisle to the New York bankers

makes it clear that, while Mr. Cleveland works in **Congress,**
the bankers will be expected to work not in New York only
but throughout the country, doing their utmost to pinch
business everywhere, in the expectation of causing a money
crisis that will affect Congress powerfully from every quarter. There is an explicitness in these declarations and a
boldness in making them that would be astounding were
not the country too familiar with Mr. Cleveland and his
methods to be astonished by anything from him.

The money-lenders and coupon-clippers, with the powerful assistance of the incumbent of the White House,
have carried out their purpose. The crisis came and there
is ruin and suffering everywhere. We are receiving our
"object-lesson." Tremendous pressure has been brought
upon Congress, and the Sherman act has been repealed.
Another burden has been laid upon the shoulders of the
producing classes. ·

Are they content now? No. Will they ever be? No.
Their next move was for more bonds and more coupons to
clip, so the parasites still kept on eating away the base. They
were after a bond issue and were in position to command
it. To overcome the scruples of the people against increasing the public debt, the organs of the fund-holders
said that as soon as the gold reserve should be replaced
the wheels of industry would again turn. The only way
to replace the gold was to buy up a stock of the precious
metal with bonds. The parasites were greedy. They
wanted $200,000,000 issued, but finally compromised on
$50,000,000, well knowing that they had it in their power
to compel another issue later.

The bonds are now sold and the gold reserve is re-
plenished. What is the result? Have you watched the
effect on the markets? If not, look at the papers for the
past few days. The same result has followed as after
the repeal of the purchasing clause of the Sherman act·

Wheat has gone down in price, and with it all the primary products of labor.

The purchase of so much gold has had the same effect on the gold market that the purchase and withdrawal from market of 50,000,000 bushels of wheat would have on its price. Gold being now the sole measure of values, the effect of dear gold is manifested in the higher purchasing power of money, which means cheaper products and more labor on the part of the producer to pay his debts, interest and taxes.

Under such circumstances I claim that it is impossible for business to revive. Unless the primary producer can get a sufficient price for his products to give him a surplus he cannot buy the products of the mills and factories, and therefore they must remain idle.

The bond theory, like the Cleveland theory, has therefore exploded. It leaves us worse off than we were before.

The end is not yet, however. The rats will keep on gnawing and by and by our financial pyramid will need a prop on the other side. More bonds will have to be issued to buy more gold.* The purchasing power of money will be still higher and products cheaper.

I have recounted to you well known facts, and drawn some conclusions. There are more to follow.

THE DAVID A. WELLS THEORY.

Another theory of the cause of the panic and hard times, for want of a better name, I will call the David A. Wells theory, suggested by the reading of a somewhat amusing article in the January Forum, written by that ardent economic apostle of the bankers. Otherwise it may be denominated Lack of Confidence. Said one recently imported American citizen to another:

"Pat, vat ish dot Irishmon vat dose bapers calls Lack

*How well this prediction was fulfilled the two succeeding bond issues and the still precarious condition of the Treasury reserve will show.

O'Confidence, vot gicks oop so mouch devilment in dish goonthry."

"I donno," said Pat, "I think he racently cum over. I heard av him in the ould coonthry. He was always up to some divilmint in ould Ireland."

In this case, as I have already intimated, this much talked of fellow was begotten of the Rothschilds, born of Wall street, nurtured by such economic writers as the Hon. David A. Wells and his clients the bankers, equipped by the President of the United States and sent on his mission of "divilment."

But "ould Lack O'Confidence" was an independent fellow, and when once loose with his shillaleh, like the typical Irishman at the Donnybrook Fair, wherever he saw a head he hit it. He was sent out to smash the paper money of the United States, crack the skull of the Sherman act, and "clean out" the gold reserve to make way for a bond issue. But the erratic rascal "thwacked" his blackthorn on the heads of those who nurtured him.

The American bankers at least did not intend there should be a panic. What they wanted was to bring discredit upon the people's money, accomplish the repeal of the hated Sherman act, and thus strengthen their power. But old Lack O'Confidence, with his "bit of a stick," was no respecter of persons. Once let loose, instead of distrusting the currency, he "cleaned out" the banks.

David A. Wells in the aforesaid article makes haste to set him right, and tries in vain to turn his attention to the bankers' hated foe—a national currency. He says:

"It is capable of demonstration that the cause of this disturbance (the panic) was mainly artificial and a wholly unnecessary and unnatural distrust on the part of the people of the United States of the future of the money of their country, which distrust in turn was created by an artificial, unnecessary and unnatural fiscal policy. This proposition

OULD LACK O' CONFIDENCE.

finds curious illustration and proof in the fact that the large withdrawals of deposits from banks did not seem to be influenced or occasioned by a suspicion of unsoundness or mismanagement on the part of the banks, but rather by an almost universal sentiment on the part of the depositors that it was expedient for them to get their money as quickly as possible into gold or its representative, and then bring it more under their individual control by placing it in safety deposit vaults or in other secure hiding places."

During the period between May 4 and Oct. 3, 1893, old Lack O'Confidence compelled the national banks alone to yield up $378,000,000, and from State banks enough more to undoubtedly raise the amount to above $500,000,000. This vast sum was withdrawn from the banks and hid away in safety vaults and other places of safe keeping. Why? Mr. Wells says not because of "a suspicion of unsoundness or mismanagement on the part of the banks." That is, the people had no fear the banks would fail, but on account of "a distrust on the part of the people of the United States of the future of the money of their country." That is, they thought the money unsound.

I submit to you, my friends, if that is not about the most peculiar piece of logic you ever heard? Like the little girl speaking of something her mother had told her, on its being questioned, said: "It's so because mother said so, and so it's so if it ain't so." So coming from so great an authority as the Hon. David A. Wells, we are expected to accept this economic teaching as so even if it ain't so.

It reminds me, however, of a boy who once worked for me. On one occasion the lad had about him a disagreeable odor. I thought it was feet and said to him:

"Johnnie, when you go home to-night, give those feet of yours a good soaking; their odor is exceedingly disagreeable."

"Oh, ho," said Johnnie, "dot ain't feet, dot's Switzercase I brought fer my lunch."

I think Mr. Wells has mistaken the odor. It was not unsound money but rotten banks the people were afraid of.

People do strange things in panics, but I can hardly credit that they would be so insane as to withdraw $500,-000,000 of unsound currency, because they were afraid of its future, from sound banks, and hide it away. A sound bank credit is certainly to be preferred to a lot of unsound currency in a safety vault.

It is true Mr. Wells says they wanted to get it into "gold or its representative," all of which is the veriest bosh. Not one depositor in a thousand looked at his money after he had withdrawn it, except to count it. Gold, greenbacks, silver certificates or treasury notes were all the same to him. What each wanted was to get his money as quickly as possible before the bank should close its doors. The total amount of all the gold in the country did not equal the amount of money withdrawn.

As Lincoln well said: "You can fool some of the people some of the time, but you can't fool all the people all the the time." The efforts of this coterie of conspirators to create lack of confidence in the people's money reacted with terrible force on the banks.

The panic itself was a fear for the security of banks which suddenly possessed the people. It manifested itself in a common impulse to get their money out as quickly as possible. This simultaneous withdrawal coming unex-pectedly at a time when the conspiring metropolitan banks had decided to cause a stringency of money, especial-ly in the West, by the withdrawal of credits, caused a sud-den suspension of credits, with the resultant stringency and failures.

It is true the purchasing clause of the Sherman act has been repealed and the bond issue has been made. The money power thus far has had its way, but the victory was

obtained at a fearful cost. It was one of those victories
which presage overwhelming defeat. The fierce struggle in
the Senate and the action of the President in using the tremendous patronage of his office to bribe Senators and Congressmen and make them subservient tools of Wall and
Lombard streets has opened the eyes of the people. Another such victory, which will come with the next issue of
bonds, will certainly bring trouble to the money power and
will result in its downfall.

We were confidently told when the Sherman act should
become a back number and the bonds were issued, that
erratic wild Irishman, Lack O'Confidence, would at once
become a decent citizen, but he is still abroad with his
"bit of a stick" and his "divilmints."

The facts of the case are, neither in the lack of confidence nor in the panic is to be found the true cause of the
prevailing industrial depression. They are incidents connected with it, it is true, and have greatly aggravated the
case; but the great underlying cause lies deeper and
further back. I have hinted at it and before I get
through shall bring it under the calcium light of truth,
so that you can behold it in all its hideous aspect. Before doing so, however, I shall clear the lens of truth of
a few more of the false causes which obscure its bright-
ness.

THE REPUBLICAN THEORY.

The theories already canvassed are those born of Wall
and Lombard street financiers and echoed by their follow-
ers. Their mission was to hide, excuse or justify the doings and methods of those who control the money bags of
the world. Let us get the idea well into our minds that
the country and, we may say, the world, is in the begin-
nings of a tremendous war. "Capital and labor" they
call it, only unfortunately the laborer has mistaken his

employer for the capitalist. The contention should be well defined.

On one side are the fund-holders of the world, keen, cunning, crafty, actuated by insatiable greed, already with the world by the throat, yet determined to strengthen their power and hold by compelling the world to adopt for the world's measure of values the single gold standard. This means severe and continued contraction of money, contracted to such proportions as to be absolutely under their control, falling prices for the products of labor and the commodities of commerce.

This is what they are seeking. They want to make the bond and mortgage eternal and that the holders of them shall receive money whose purchasing power is twice as great as the money they loaned. They want to double the value of their coupons as represented in the products of labor. It means that the workers must produce and sell twice as much of the products of labor to meet the billions of monetary obligations of the world in excess of what the holders are rightfully entitled to.

On the other side we find the great body of producers of the country, both primary and secondary, a mighty force slowly but surely awakening to a realization of their position. With them and laboring in their cause are the friends of civilization, hope and progress. These know that the money of the people—a money which shall be equally just to both the debtor and creditor alike, to the employer and employed, and to the banker and producer—must have a broader, safer, more stable, more equitable and sounder base than gold alone. Gold is insufficient in quantity, too fickle, dependent upon the uncertainties of the mines or the whims of rulers of nations, or worse still on the powers of confederated greed to manipulate. They would have money on the broader base of both gold and silver, without discrimination as to metal, or better still,

on the still broader base of the nation's credit growing
out of the quality of full legal tender for all payments.

Let us keep this everlasting conflict in view as we progress with this discussion, for somewhere within its lines
will be found the cause we are seeking.

The doctors of finance having failed to correctly diag-
nose the disease and prescribe a cure, we shall turn to the
politicians.

I fear I am now treading on dangerous ground. Already I forecast some of your thoughts and see you pulling
on your armor of political prejudice. Don't, please. This
question is much greater than party, and must be viewed
not through smoked party spectacles but with the clear
eyes of American citizenship. I give you fair warning,
however, I am no party man, but stand on the higher
platform of an American citizen with an independent vote
to cast where humanity and patriotism dictate is best for
the good of the whole people.

Those of my partisan friends who see only good in their
own party and all that is bad in the others, remind me of
a little incident that occurred when I was a lad on the
farm, before I fell from grace and became a newspaper
man.

A village cousin was making a visit and went out with
me into the hay-field. At that time the aforesaid cousin
was a small boy of limited experience, and one of the experiences he had yet to encounter was a skunk. Sure
enough, as we were crossing a stubble-field one of these
pretty little innocent-looking disagreeable creatures came
into view. As it happened, we were to the windward of it
with a strong breeze blowing.

"Hi!" said Sammy, "what's that? "Stop! let me run and
catch it."

"Don't be in a hurry, Sammy," said I; "better let that
animal alone."

SAMMY AND THE KITTEN. A STORY WITH A MORAL. SEE PAGE 29.

"What for? It looks like a pretty little kitten."

"Yes, but all the same it is a skunk."

Sammy's ideal skunk was very different from this seeming reality. He seemed disappointed. In some way that pretty creature did not fit the ideal.

"Skunk!" said he, "I thought skunks stunk!"

Said I, "Just get out and run around him and nose around a little on the other side."

This Sammy proceeded to do with results which may be better imagined than described.

If some of you dyed-in-the-wool partisans, if indeed there be any here, will nose around on the other side a little you may find the creature not so innocent as it looks.

The Republicans tell us the hard times are due to a change in the administration, and the consequent fear of a change in the tariff policy of the Government. Undoubtedly this fear, like the panic, has aggravated the cause, and when the Democrats settle on a line of tariff policy there will be a small recovery. This fear operates only on such industries as will be materially affected by tariff changes, and as compared with the great original cause of the depression exerts but a small disturbing influence.

If the Republicans had remained in power we should have had hard times. The cause which produced them was in operation long before Cleveland was even nominated or before the McKinley bill was thought of.

The years 1890, 1891 and 1892 are looked upon and pointed to with pride by the Republicans as years of great prosperity. Democratic policy, they now say, has changed this prosperity, and is responsible for the present condition. This will be the future campaign cry of Republican orators, and it will prove effective with those who do not look beneath the surface. The blame for the prevailing condition is, however, no more chargeable to the Democrats than to the Republicans. In fact, the latter were in responsible power when the greater part of the mischief was done, and are equally responsible with the Democrats in allowing the money power to manipulate legislation in its own interest and control the policy of its rule. The Democrats were indeed unfortunate in getting into power just at the fag end of this seeming prosperity, when the collapse was impending, and thus caught the blame. They are blameworthy, however, in that instead of applying the remedy which they have it in their power to do, and which their own party platform prescribed, they are greatly aggravating the disease.

Instead of "Democratic times" these should be called "goldbug times," as they are the direct results of the manipulations of the money power.

The years mentioned, so far as the workingmen were concerned, such as I shall call secondary producers—the mechanics, workers in factories, etc.—were indeed years of prosperity. The wheels of industry and commerce were busy and wages were steady and good. But it was that prosperity which comes of borrowed capital and extended credit. When the power to borrow and buy on credit reached its limit a collapse was inevitable.

The manufacturer sold to the jobber and wholesaler on a gradually extending credit, the wholesaler to the retailer, and the retailer to the consumer. Gradually, it became more difficult to make collections, especially from agricultural communities. The manufacturers of farm implements sold on gradually extending time and took farmers' notes, at first on short time, then longer, until it was no uncommon thing to sell a harvester on a year's time. Then when notes came due in many cases perforce they were compelled to extend the time of payment through sheer inability on the part of the farmers to pay. I am in the agricultural newspaper business. We advertise farm

implements quite extensively, and it was no uncommon
thing for large manufacturers rated highly to ask extension of their accounts. The reason given for asking such
extension was invariably inability to collect accounts from
farmers.

The real facts of the case are that while others were
enjoying a measure of prosperity, the great wealth-producing class, whose welfare underlies all prosperity in
this nation, were being pinched. They were compelled to
face a falling market for products which year by year were
bringing them less money for their labor. The price of
their products was falling below the cost of production,
at the same time their expenses were growing but little
if any less. Under such circumstances they were unable
to buy the products of the labor of others or pay their
debts and, therefore, the collapse of the seeming prosperity of others was inevitable.

You are familiar with the great complaint of the farmers, coming first from the Western agricultural States.
Being well fed yourselves you paid no heed to it. The political papers called them "calamity howlers," and you
smiled and acquiesced.

When Kansas, with 80,000 Republican majority, turned
to a new party whose existence was due to farmers, the
papers said the farmers were being misled by a lot of
cranks, and you believed it.

Next, Iowa, another stronghold of Republicanism, turned
its colors and elected a Democratic Governor. This
through farmers' votes. The papers said it was due to
Prohibition fanatics, and you believed it.

Next, Michigan, Nebraska and other strong Republican
States got on the other side. Then came the great landslide of 1892, due also, not to the votes of prosperous mechanics, but to the pinched and desperate farmers. It was
not the manufacturing States where the landslide occurred,

but in the agricultural States. It may be true that they slid from the frying-pan into the fire, but when men get angry they sometimes do foolish things.

The farmers knew they were suffering a great wrong, and rightfully held the party in power responsible. Legislation produced the wrong, and legislation could have cured it; therefore the party which had the power to legislate and execute was twice guilty, and must bear their share of the odium of their guiltiness. It will not do to charge it to the Democrats. Each party must be held accountable for its just share of responsibility.

THE DEMOCRATIC IDEA.

The Democrats, on the other hand, charge the prevailing condition to the Republican policy of protection. "The McKinley tariff law is the great and cruel monster which is crushing the life out of the American farmer and workingman." Just how they make the connection I am unable to see.

There is much nonsense about this old straw of the tariff. It is an important question, it is true—important to certain special industries—but to the great masses of the common people it sinks into insignificance as compared with the great financial question which underlies all this mischief, and to which both now and heretofore the great panics and industrial depressions which have afflicted this nation are due. The Government must have its revenues, and these the wealth producers of the country must furnish. It makes but little difference to them whether they pay them on a tariff laid upon sugar or woolen goods, on iron or on tin, or on all of them; the tariff is a tax, and in order to support Government taxes must be paid. Congress cannot levy a direct tax, therefore must find the bulk of its taxes through tariff taxation. Instead of keeping up such a powwow about protection and impossible

free trade, the efforts of Congress could be better directed
in arranging such equable distribution of this tariff tax
that its burdens shall fall on all classes alike, and such
benefits as arise through the incidental protection offered
shall be shared alike by all industries.   The money power
is back of this interminable debate. It is kept to the front
to detract the attention of the people from the real issue.

If the great depression was confined exclusively to the
United States there would be some reason for charging it
to the McKinley law, but it is world-wide.   At least, it
extends through all the single gold standard countries.

The English and Irish farmers, who are not afflicted
with a McKinley law, are complaining just as bitterly as
our own.   They also have an intelligent understanding of
the cause.   They attribute it to monometallism, and are
strongly petitioning the English Government to adopt bimetallism and protection against foreign competition as
their only salvation.

The organized German farmers, also, to the extent of
some eight hundred lodges, have petitioned the Emperor
for a restoration of bimetallism as a means of restoring
prosperity to their farms.

News also comes from India of great distress among the
farmers of that great country as the direct result of the
English policy of forcing the gold standard upon them.

On the other hand, on the authority of the Hon. David
A. Wells, "Mexican farmers are prosperous, in spite of
the depreciation of silver." Not for the same reason which he
gives, however, but because Mexico conducts her finances
on a silver basis.   Her silver has not depreciated
except as measured by gold.   An ounce of Mexican silver
will buy just as much of other products of labor to-day
as formerly.   The advantage a Mexican farmer has over
a farmer in the United States is, he sells his products and

pays his taxes and debts on a silver basis and pay our
debts on a gold basis.

The Democratic doctors have not correctly diagnosed
the disease. We predict their remedy of free trade or
tariff reform will not cure the evil. They now have the
power in their own hands. Let them apply their rem-
edies and see if the patient mends.

In coming elections, especially in the next Presidential
campaign in 1896, a tremendous effort will be made by
the money barons to again relegate the financial question
to the background and keep the people blinded and set
class against class by again stirring up the interminable
tariff debate.

The high priests of Shylock well know that if the people once get their eyes opened as to the real cause of the
prevailing hard times and the frequently occurring panics
which afflict the nation they will demand a change and
enforce their demands at the ballot box. The policy,
therefore, will be to keep the politicians and political
press pounding away at the old partizan tariff straw;
thus to keep up the senseless fires of partizan strife and
hatred over a question which, while of importance to certain industries, individually concerns the majority of the
people but little. Anything to divide the people into
party lines and prevent the discussion of or making an
issue of the greater financial question.

It will be a troublesome thorn in the flesh. however.
So many people are becoming enlightened that it will not
down. The light is spreading. It is dangerous to old
party supremacy, and unless suppressed will rend both
old parties asunder. It will tax the skill of the wiley
politicians to the uttermost to keep them together. With
the rank and file of both hopelessly divided on the financial question, and the money powers dictating the policy
of both, their only salvation will be to evade or straddle

the financial question and come out strong on the tariff issue.

The average practical politician is not patriotic, but will be found in line with the fattest pocketbook. He belongs, therefore, body and soul to the money power, and as its tool will get in his work in behalf of harmony in party platforms. He cannot wholly ignore the financial question, but will in both party platforms concoct some meaningless straddlebug, good Lord, good devil plank which can be construed to every man's liking.

If he is a Republican his platform will in vehement thunder tones denounce the brainless incompetence and villainous depravity of the Democratic party, to which will be charged not only all the sins of the decalogue, but the additional tremendous sin of having been the cause of the great industrial depression.

In like manner if he is a Democrat the Republicans will in his platform be sinners even greater than those on whom the tower of Siloam fell, and will in like manner be charged with the enormous guilt of bringing about hard times. The important question is how much longer will the people allow themselves to be deceived by such methods?

CHAPTER II.

THE REAL CAUSE.

Having disposed of some of the principal alleged causes which are or have been held up to the public as accounting for hard times, I will now endeavor to make plain the real cause, that which underlies all others.

I now find myself in the position of the old darky preacher down South.

"Bredren," said he, "Ise gwine tah tak my texus f'om de Bible dis mawnin'. I ain't gwine' tah tak' ut f'om Generusus n'r f'om Revehlations n'r f'om eny ov dem yuther books wot jines Generusus an' Revehlations, but Ise gwine' splash er roun' somewhar wah de' Postle Paul got mad and pinted his pistle at the Pheaseans. My texus am 'We's feahfully an' won'erfully mad (made).' So yah bettah look out. Ise gwine preach a powehful sahmon an' somebody's gwine get hut."

I shall not pick my text from the dry bones of the tariff issue nor from the visionary theories of Henry George, but shall "pint my pistle" at the great underlying financial question.

The great apostle before mentioned says "The love of money is the root of all evil." In line with this great truth we shall find that the abnormal love of gain is the root of the evil condition under which we are now suffering. I shall show, also, before I get through that it has been brought about deliberately by the cunning craftiness of men with intent to increase their wealth and live at ease and luxury on the products of the labor of others.

This corrupt and wicked ambition, which has inspired evil-minded persons from the earliest ages to acquire wealth to consume upon their lusts at the expense of the labor of others, is the root of nearly all the man-born evils which have afflicted the world.

That monstrosity, human slavery, which in this nation was crushed out at the expense of so much blood and treasure, was a growth from this root.

The root is still alive. The crushing of black slavery did not crush human greed nor crown the rights of labor, nor bring righteousness, equity and justice to the forefront as the dominant virtues of the nation. On the contrary, the very necessities of the people's government in its efforts to crush the slave power, brought to the front and into the saddle another power, whose slavery is even farther-reaching and more disastrous to humanity than negro slavery could ever be.

We have simply made an exchange of rulers. The limited slave power formerly dominated the nation. We crushed and deposed it by the power of arms, to install in its place that which arms cannot reach, the unlimited money power, which has for ages been the God-defying power of the world.

With superb effrontery the men of the old regime, the slave-holders, claimed to be the especial champions of the flag of their country and the liberties of which "Old Glory" is symbolic. Those who opposed them were called "fanatics," "disunionists," etc. This, too, at a time when they were plotting to overthrow the Republic should the time come when they could no longer control it.

History is again repeating itself. The same root of mischief has sent up other shoots, dangerously masked as before—plotting mischief while charging conspiracy upon others—by cunning craft manipulating the finances of the country to make products cheap and the purchasing power of money, mortgages, bonds and coupons great; hypocritically assuming to be the champions of sound money and liberty, while accusing the real champions of freedom who oppose their methods, with conspiracy to rob them; calling the liberty-loving people who would restore prosperity by undoing the mischief their greed has wrought, "cranks," "fanatics," "fiatists," "dishonest debtors who want to pay their debts with fifty-cent dollars," etc. Such are the men who are responsible for the present condition of the country.

The fact is conveniently overlooked and kept in the background—masked, in fact—that the primary producer has to expend twice as much labor to-day to earn the price of a dollar as would have been necessary on the day the debt was contracted.

When President Jackson put his big honest foot on that vile octopus, the United States bank, and crushed, as he supposed, the life out of it, Senator Benton said:

Jackson has not killed the bank. She is a wounded tigress, and has escaped to her jungles. By and by she will return and bring her whelps with her.

The war was her opportunity. The tigress has returned with her brood, which now have their fangs in the throat of the nation, sucking the life blood of the producing classes.

To meet the enormous expenses of the Government in maintaining the war, paying soldiers, etc., Congress at the suggestion of President Lincoln and his Cabinet created the greenback, which was issued directly to the people with whom the Government was dealing and made full legal tender for the payment of all debts. This was true American policy and in conformity with the Constitution, which delegates to Congress the sole right to issue money. Congress, however, has no right to exercise this power except in the interests of the whole people.

The greenback was born of patriotism and at once became popular with the people and saved the life of the nation.   The money power, however, is not patriotic.   It is
simply greedy.   War with its direful carnage and appalling horrors is to it as incense to the nostrils, a pecuniary
feast.   Other men's necessity is its opportunity.   The
mangled bodies of the slain are the harbingers of millions
to be reaped from war's necessities and excessive taxes.
The capitalists and bankers did not like the greenback,
and from the day it was first issued until the present
have ever been its uncompromising enemies, and have ever
and are still waging a ceaseless war upon it, not because
it is not good money, nor that they have any fear that it will
ever become depreciated, but because they cannot control
it or make it serve their selfish ends as is possible with
the national bank currency.

A money issued directly to the people is beyond their
control.   As soon, therefore, as they could get together
and formulate a plan of action they made their demands
upon the Government.   As necessity knows no law, and
the necessities of the Government were pressing, it was in
a measure compelled to yield.

Their demand was the scream of the tigress coming back
from the jungle with her whelps.   It materialized in the
present national banking system and national bank notes.

The latter is purely a concession to the banks—a special
privilege wrenched from the Government in the hour of its
dire necessity as the price of their assistance.

The banks are fighting to gain absolute control over the
currency.   The national bank note was a step in that
direction.   It enables them in a measure, by acting in
concert through the bankers' association, to contract or
expand the currency at will.   At the same time it gives
them a chance to collect double interest: First. on the
bonds deposited at Washington as a basis on which to

issue notes, and second, by loaning out the said notes
to the public.

Except as a special concession to the banks there is no
excuse whatever for the issue of these notes. There is not
a single purpose they serve which could not be equally
well filled by the greenback. It is customary for the
bankers and their organs to sneer at the greenback as
"fiat," meaning that it has no other basis behind it than
the national credit. Granted; but the national bank note
is even more so. It is not based on the credit of the
bank issuing it. The bank is not responsible for the redemption of the issue but simply controls it; the national
Government guarantees it. The safety of the notes is
based on the Government bonds deposited at Washington for their redemption. The security of these bonds
rests purely on the national credit, therefore the bank note
based on the bond has no other security than that afforded by the national credit. The greenback, on the
other hand, has an additional basis of security in the now
slender thread of gold kept in the treasury for its redemption.

Previous to the present administration this redemption
fund was kept at $100,000,000, but is now much less.

We need no other guaranty behind the greenback, however, or any other form of paper money issued by the
Government, than full legal-tender power for the payment of all debts, taxes and custom dues, and the credit
of the nation. The credit of such notes would never be
questioned.

Not content with this concession the money power next
began a warfare on the greenback. They demanded its
demonetization and destruction. The fight was carried to
the Supreme Court, which haply decided that the issue
was constitutional. This fight gave birth to the much
abused Greenback party.

Although backed by the Supreme Court the bankers
have still kept up the fight. It is still on, and they have
been in a measure successful. In line with the policy of
contracting the currency they have succeeded in greatly
reducing the greenback issue from what it was at the time
of the war, and, in part, have offset the remaining issue
by another scheme not thought of at first, that of withdrawing one hundred millions in gold from circulation and
storing it in the treasury vaults, presumably, although un-
necessarily, as a redemption fund.

Not succeeding in entirely getting rid of the greenback,
another more brilliant plot was laid, or rather imported
from England—a plot in which the money power of the
world could clasp hands and work to a common purpose.
To accomplish the demonetization of silver and thus contract the money of the world to a gold basis was indeed a
brilliant undertaking worthy of his satanic majesty himself. This would give them a magnificent opportunity for
speculation, and as years rolled by the chances for accumulating wealth would multiply like the stars at eventide.
It was the most colossal plan of robbery ever thought of.
There were billions on billions in it. More than this, it was
a plan to set at naught the fundamental principles of
liberty and the Constitution, and enslave all the people
to the power of the moneyed class.

How far it has succeeded I will now show you from facts,
figures and statistics. I trust you will follow them closely.
Such things are considered dry, I know, but they are vital
to the question, and to a student of political ecoonmy are
full of interest.

THE CO-RELATION OF WORKERS.

I am trying to make plain some economic principles
which may be and doubtless are new to many of you.
I myself until very recently got my political economy
from the strongly biased editorials of the daily press. It

is not strange, therefore, if there are others who have not taken time to study the great financial question from the other side. I hope you will excuse me, then, if I adopt some of the methods of the pedagogue. As there are about a dozen of the teachers of our public schools in the room, they at least cannot complain of such methods.

I have here a number of charts containing facts and figures collated from various official sources. I use these because figures seen are much easier comprehended than those heard only.

In chart No. 1, I have divided humanity according to their various occupations so as better to show their co-relations.

CHART NO. 1.

PRIMARY PRODUCERS.	SECONDARY PRODUC-	CONSUMERS.
Farmers.	ERS.	Merchants,
Miners.	Manufacturers of all	Railroaders and all
Lumbermen.	kinds and their Em-	Carriers,
Fishers.	ployes.	Ministers,

PARASITES.	Teachers,
Capitalists, who live on incomes derived from loaned money, bonds, rents, etc. All who live off the products of the labor of others without themselves contributing anything for the good of humanity—speculators. gamblers, thieves, tramps, etc.	Doctors, Lawyers, Public officials, Military, and all engaged in useful but non-productive occupations.

The primary producer is also a consumer of the products of the secondary producer, and the secondary producer in turn consumes the products of the primary producer: therefore, both these classes are producers and consumers at the same time. My third class are only consumers. They produce nothing, yet have a useful place to fill. They are equally necessary to the body politic. My fourth class, however, have no place in an ideal community. No one has the moral right to live off the products of the labor of others without contributing something useful in return therefor. From this rule I except the unfortunate and those who have lived a useful life until the infirmities of age overtake them or until they have earned by honest labor and saved by honest thrift sufficient to keep them through life's remaining years.

For every idler otherwise supported the workers become to that extent slaves.

In a properly organized and regulated society the civic relations between the first three classes are mutually advantageous and equitable. The farmer, miner, etc., sell their products to the secondary producer and consumer, receiving therefor something called money. This money is again exchanged for the products of the secondary producer, the merchant and carrier acting as the medium of exchange.

The minister attends to their spiritual wants, the teacher instructs the young, the doctor tries to repair the ills of the flesh, while the lawyer waxes fat off their quarrels. Every one has his niche to fill.

If money is plenty so as to be readily had in exchange for labor and products and crops are good and no foreign influence intervenes, prosperity reigns. Each receives a just recompense for his labor. Whenever this ideal co-relation of workers is disturbed, which it may be in various ways, to the extent of the disturbance some one class or all or some subdivision of a class are made to suffer loss, or are compelled to labor for the benefit of others without just compensation.

A NATURAL DISTURBANCE.

There may be a failure of crops; such often happens. In that case the farmer has less produce to exchange, consequently he gets less money and buys less. The merchant and the carrier have, therefore, less trade, and the manufacturer loses for the time being his best customers and is compelled to reduce his output and discharge a part of his working force.

Thus the whole body politic suffers with the farmer. It is an old saying that when the farmer prospers all prosper, but when the farmer is in adversity all suffer loss. All business prosperity is linked with that of the farmer.

This is a natural cause of disturbance, which to the extent of the calamity would cause industrial depression. No such condition exists at the present time, however, to account for the prevailing depression, but, as before said, the vats of the nation are overflowing.

ARTIFICIAL DISTURBANCES.

The artificial causes are due to man's desire to take dishonest advantage of his fellow man, to enslave him and live off the products of his labor without returning a just equivalent therefor.

The manufacturers of a certain staple product, for instance, combine and organize what is known as a trust, the object being to contract the output of the said staple and raise its price. Thus an unfair advantage is taken of the primary producer who furnishes the raw material, and the consumer who is compelled to pay an excessive price for one of the essential articles of consumption. This is a common practice. In fact, a large portion of the staple manufactured articles of commerce are controlled in this way.

A notable example is seen in the great sugar trust now so conspicuously before the nation by its efforts to dictate legislation in its favor. Every time we sugar our coffee we are contributing to the wealth of this iniquitous monopoly.

Again, the primary producers in a certain line may combine to control a staple output of the mines. Such, for

example, as the great coal combine, which now controls
every pound of anthracite coal consumed.

Every ton of coal we burn puts a dollar or two of
unearned dividends into the pockets of the coal barons.

Again, the merchants may, and sometimes do, combine
to take advantage of both producer and consumer by buying products cheap and selling them dear, or to prevent
competition.

A notable example is seen in the meat combine at the
stock yards. Every time we buy a pound of meat at the
Chicago or Austin butcher shops we contribute a mite to
the ill-gotten gains of this combine. This is the reason
why, while cattle and hogs are cheaper than they have
been for years, we pay no less at retail for our meat.
Somebody is taking an unfair advantage of us. The great
packers combine to keep down the price of hogs and cattle, and hold up the price of meat. All who eat meat in
Chicago, poor and rich alike, must contribute to their cof-
fers. Is it any wonder, under such circumstances, that
these packers have become multi-millionaires?

The retail implement dealers recently tried to effect a
combine to fix the price of all farm implements and machinery and to compel the farmer to buy of them exclusively.

The railroads form combinations and traffic associations
to destroy competition and fix the price of freight and
passenger traffic, which naturally is fixed at as high a
rate as the traffic will bear. In this way an unfair advantage is taken of both producer and consumer. Trades-
unions are also formed among workingmen in special lines
of trade, and higher wages demanded and received. The
manufacturers, who are then compelled to pay these higher
wages, have to reimburse themselves by charging more
for their wares, so that the consumer has to pay more for
his goods than he otherwise would; while the farmer, who

alone cannot combine or control the price of his products or retaliate by charging a higher price for them, must pay the bill and suffer the loss.

These are some of the notable artificial disturbing elements which tend to interfere with the proper co-relation of the various classes of society and injure the prosperity of the body politic.

Through some of these instrumentalities a few are made immensely rich at the expense of the many, and a moneyed aristocracy is created whose dominant sway and greedy exactions are far more oppressive than is chargeable to the titled aristocracy of Europe.

A protective tariff would affect the different classes in this ideal body politic as it might be wisely or unwisely applied. Wisely applied. while furnishing revenue to the Government. it would at the same time prove beneficial to all classes by shutting out the disturbing effects of foreign cheap labor. But unwisely applied it would become an instrument of oppression by favoring one class as against the other, or one group of industries at the expense of the rest of the body politic.

The policy of free raw material and protected manufactured articles, for example, discriminates against the wool-growers and miners in favor of the manufacturers. While a policy of free manufactured articles would discriminate against the manufacturer in favor of the importer and merchant class.

GREEDY PARASITES.

We have to deal with a still greater disturbing element than these, however. While human greed as manifested in trusts and combines and selfish tariff legislation is bad enough, their injurious influence on society is insignificant as compared with that of my fourth class, the parasites. Some of our pompous bond-holding capitalists and wealthy speculators who corral the finest cushioned pews in the synagogues, or the dudish sons of wealthy fathers like unto whom Solomon in all his glory was not arrayed, may not like the name, but it is appropriate. All who live upon unearned increment, of whatever nature or however acquired, are parasites upon society.

As before stated, none of my fourth class have any moral right in a well regulated body politic. Wherever they exist they are a disturbing element. Whatever of wealth they acquire is taken by morally unfair means from the products of the toil of the workers. Of what use to a community is a speculator on the Board of Trade of Chicago? He contributes nothing to the welfare of others. What money he gets in his operations some one else worked for. By sharp practice, "fleecing the lambs," as it is called in Board of Trade parlance, he has acquired it. He is considered much more respectable, I know, in the eyes of the community and he doubtless is admitted to membership in some high-toned church, but in the eyes of the Almighty how much better is he than the vulgar thief who demands your pocketbook on the highway, or the common gambler who "bucks the tiger" in the ordinary way? Perhaps he has combined with his fellow speculators, and with an aggregation of capital buys up some specialty, or in other words, conducts a corner. As a result the price of that product is forced up, and, as has often been the case, a harvest of millions of dollars in profits is reaped. Somebody has this to pay, and who else are the victims but the producer, who alone creates wealth and ultimately pays for all?

Many of Chicago's millionaires and wealthiest citizens have made their money in this way. What they have gained the producers of the country have lost. I have an old and experienced Board of Trade operator for authority that the farmers of the country are losers to the extent of one hundred million dollars a year directly charge-

THE WARDS OF PRODUCTIVE INDUSTRY.

able to the operations of Board of Trade speculators.
This immense unearned increment is then probably
invested in lands, buildings, stocks and bonds, from the
rents, dividends or interest on which the owner lives at
ease and luxury. He reaps and enjoys while others toil
and spin. To the extent that the people contribute to
his support and luxury, I maintain the workers are slaves.

A voice: "I cannot understand how the operators on
the Board of Trade should cause such a great loss to the
farmers. It is true, the bears on the Board force prices
down when they can; but to counterbalance this adverse
influence, the bulls are at work bolstering up prices. It
seems to me one about offsets the other, so that between
the two influences prices are kept at fair equilibrium.
Will you please explain?"

Certainly. The explanation is simple. I have a chart
here which I intended to refer to later, which will materially
assist in making the matter plain.

This chart, taken from the New Year's number of the
Chicago Tribune, shows the fluctuation of the three
leading Northern farm products, wheat, corn and mess
pork, during the year 1893. These fluctuations are caused
by the gambling operations of the speculators on the Board
of Trade, who make a football of prices. The bulls, as they
are called in Board of Trade parlance, make it their business
to force prices up, while the bears crowd them down.

In Board of Trade language, when prices are low the
bears are "on top," and when they are high the bulls are
under holding them up. It is reasonable to suppose that
the natural supply and demand price would be the mean
between the extremes shown on this chart.

Please take notice that the trend of prices has been
downward. That is, they were much lower at the end of
the year than at the beginning, a fact which I shall recall
and explain later.

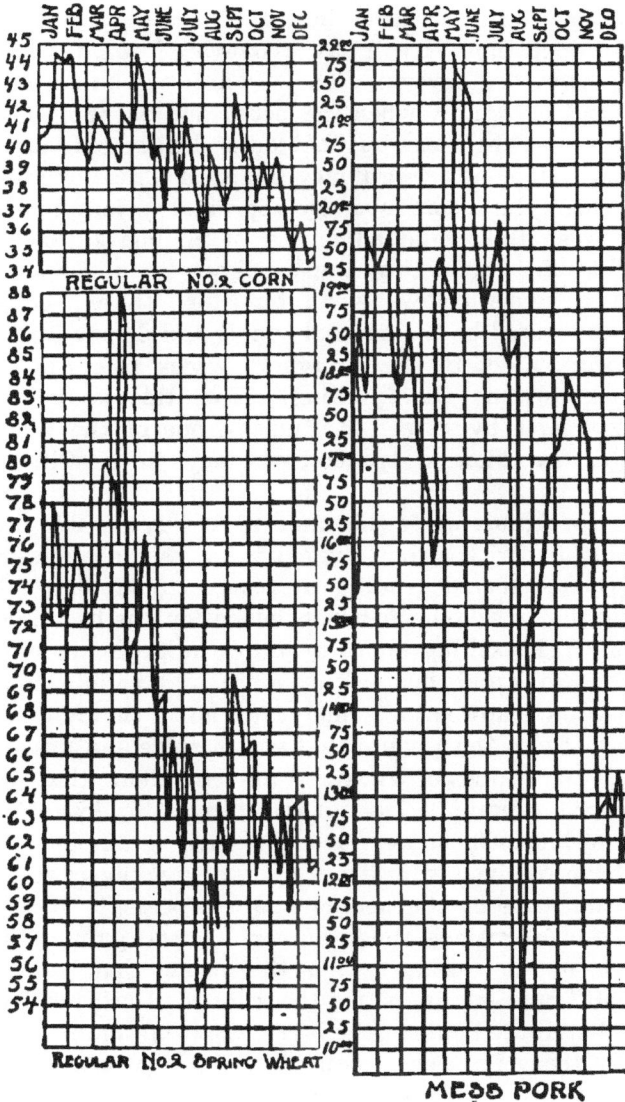

REGULAR NO. 2 CORN

REGULAR NO. 2 SPRING WHEAT

MESS PORK

CHART NO. 2.

In answer to the question how the farmers are losers
by these operations, I will say that the foreign buyers
and exporters are shrewd.   They do not buy on a bullish
market but invariably when the bears are on top.   They
are bears with the bears, but instead of dealing only in the
fictitious article as the ordinary Board of Trade operator
does, when the bears are on top and prices are at
their lowest they take advantage of the market to buy
the real stuff.   In this way the foreigner gets our products at a figure below what but for these bearish
operations would be the natural supply and demand price.

The bears aided by the foreigners wreck prices by the
process known as short selling.   How this is done is
well explained by Israel P. Rumsey, one of the oldest
and most experienced traders, who says in the Chicago
Post:

"The foreigners up to this time were buyers, but they
were educated with great difficulty by our commission
men, who preferred trading in futures to handling the
actual grain, to sell short, which education has been most
effectual.   This selling short by a few in large amounts,
calling margins and then selling more and calling more
margins was followed for some years, until the few had
sold many times the amount that was in store and actually
wrecked the values of wheat.   I am confident that the
agricultural community has not received within from $50,-
000,000 to $100,000,000 as much for their grain as they
would have received were it not for the wrecking of values
during that time by the 'selling short' process."

By these operations the foreigners are the gainers and
our farmers the losers, while the worse than useless
Board of Trade gamblers are the cause.   That hundred
million distributed among the farmers, to be again spent
spent by them for the products of other workingmen,
would have given work to many who now walk the streets.

THE BOARD OF TRADE ILLUSTRATED. SEE PAGE 51.

WATERED STOCKS.

Those who speculate in stocks are no better. Whatever of wealth they accumulate or live upon comes ultimately from the producer. That class of stock jobbers who are responsible for the watered stock found in nearly all our corporations have many sins to answer for. Watered stock is an over-issue of stock beyond the real cost of construction. Take the Western Union telegraph as an example. If I am correctly informed, its lines could be duplicated for twenty million dollars, yet it is capitalized and made to earn dividends upon eighty millions.

Somebody has been made immensely rich with this sixty millions of unearned increment, while the producers are taxed to pay dividends upon it. On the proceeds of this rascality somebody is living in luxurious ease, while the producers pay the bills. This is only a sample. There are untold millions of such stock issued on railroad and other corporations on which the public are paying dividends, all of which ultimately comes out of the producers. I am satisfied that the annual dividends paid on watered stock alone in this country would pay a large part of the taxes.

All these evil instrumentalities mitigate against the prosperity of the country, and contribute their part toward the prevailing condition under which we are suffering.

THE FEW ARE ABSORBING THE WEALTH.

In my ideal community the co-relation of workers and traders is regulated and adjusted wholly by the natural law of supply and demand. In such a community abundant crops, abundant supplies from the mines, lumber camps and fisheries and an abundance from mills and factories would mean increased prosperity and happiness. Increased production would mean increased consumption and more of the comforts of life for each worker. Im-

proved machinery and the development of the natural
forces of nature would lighten labor, shorten labor's hours
and add to the comforts of life and the pleasures of living.

Such influences as those narrated which interfere with
or set at naught this natural supply and demand co-relation to the extent of their power and magnitude tend to im-
pair the prosperity of the country. Instead of the grand
and beneficent inventions, the light and education and the
wonderful natural resources of our country benefiting
the many, lightening their burdens, dispensing intelligence,
culture and the happiness resulting therefrom and adding
to the material comforts of all industrious workers, the
few are seizing upon the blessings resulting from these
advantages. By morally dishonest methods vast fortunes
are accumulated and a large army of idlers is maintained
in luxury at the expense of the workers. To such an extent is this evil growing that already, according to the
eminent statistician, Thomas G. Shearman, in 1891, 40,000
families owned half the wealth, and fewer than
250,000 families had in their possession three-fourths
of the wealth of the country, or $46,500,000,000, or an aver-
age of $186,000 each. On the basis of $62,000,000,000, the
total estimated wealth of the country at that time, this
would leave $15,500,000,000 for the remaining 12,350,000
families, or an average of $1,225 each.

According to another statistician, Geo. K. Holmes,
special census agent on mortgage statistics, ninety-one
per cent of the families of the country own no more than
twenty-nine per cent of the wealth, while nine per cent
own seventy-one per cent.

Again, the United States census reports show that in
1860 the workers owned seven out of every sixteen dollars
of the wealth of the country. This was bad enough, the
Lord knows, but in 1890 this proportion had been reduced
to seventeen out of sixty dollars. Again, in 1880 the

workers owned $9,600,000,000 of the $40,000,000,000 of the wealth of the nation, while in 1890, after ten years of what the politicians call great, unexampled prosperity, in which it is claimed the workers were especially prosperous, during which period $20,000,000,000 was added to the supposed wealth of the country, the workers got for their share $600,000,000 and the parasites pocketed $19,400,000,-000. What wealth was produced the workers carved out and retained for their share, a paltry six hundred million, while the idlers pocketed the nineteen thousand four hundred million. That is not the worst feature. By methods named above, this vast sum of wealth has naturally created a vast additional fresh army of idlers, who now propose to continue to live in idleness and luxury off the interest, taxes and dividends which they have it in their power to exact from a suffering public though the agency of this accumulation of wealth so that not only ourselves but our children and our children's children will be bound in the toils of this plutocratic slavery.

In chart number three I have tabulated these statistics so that you can study them at your leisure. They are not the imaginings of some alleged calamity howler but are reliable statistics gathered from official sources. You can draw your own conclusions. To me the showing is appalling and makes me tremble for our liberties.

CHART NO. 3.

Total estimated wealth of the country Jan., 1891	$62,000,000,000
Total population in round numbers	63,000,000
Average wealth per person	984

HOW DISTRIBUTED.

Total number of families, 12,600,000.

40,000 families own $755,000 each	$31,000,000,000
12,560,000 families own $2468.15 each	31,000,000,000
Total	$62,000,000,000
250,000 families own $186,000 each	$46,500,000,000
12,350,000 own $1,255 each	15,500,000,000
Total	$62,000,000,000

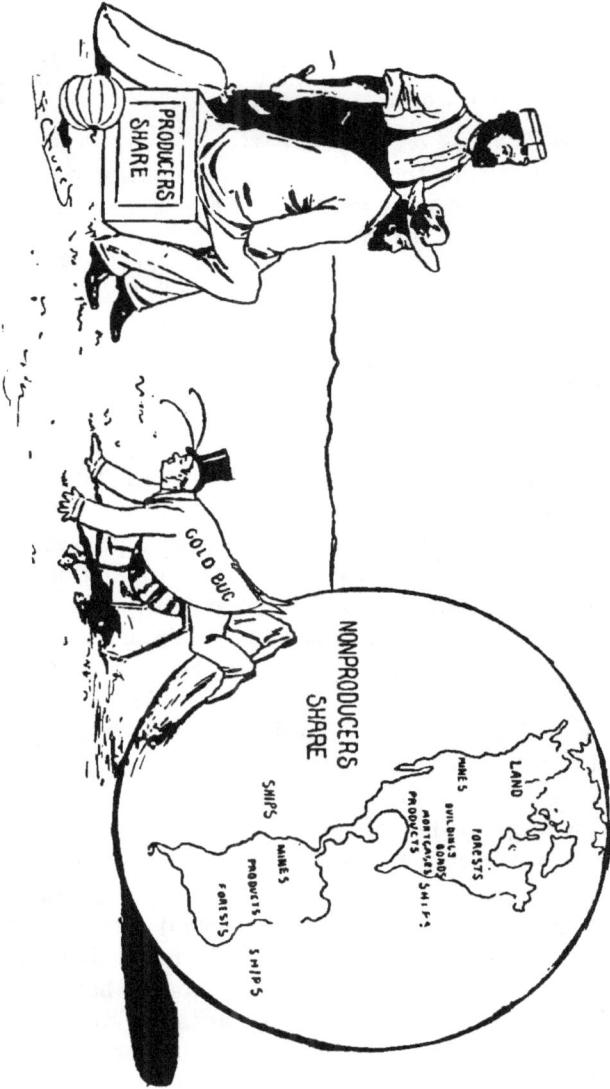

PRODUCERS' SHARE OF THE WEALTH OF THE UNITED STATES IN 1891, $15,500,000. NON-PRODUCERS' SHARE, $46,500,000.

GEO. K. HOLMES'S STATISTICS TABULATED. BASED ON U. S.
                    CENSUS, 1890.

    4,047 families own...$12,000,000.000
    926,516 families own.................................. 30,600,000,000
    11,593,887 families own.............................. 17,400,000,000

        Total.. $60.000,000.000

Table showing the decrease of per cent of wealth owned
by workers between 1860 and 1890. From U. S. census
reports in round figures.

Year.	Population.	Workers' share Of wealth Per cent.	Non-Producers (Parasites) Per cent.
1860	16,000,000	43¾	56¼
1870	30,000,000	32⅜	67⅝
1880	40,000,000	24	76
1890	60,000,000	17	83

Taking as a basis the increase of wealth for the decade we find that while the net increase of wealth above
consumption for 1890 was about $2,300,000,000, the
workers got for their share, $80,000,000, while what is
vaguely called capital absorbed the residue or $2,220,000,-
000. It is reasonable to suppose the proportion continued
until the panic caused a shrinkage of all values.

If this condition is allowed to continue how long will it
be before the parasites absorb all the wealth of the nation
and the workers become slaves? Free in name, but
slaves in fact, compelled to sow while others reap. The
vital question with the producers of the country is, "How
are these results brought about?"

This aggregation of wealth in the hands of the few is
slowly but surely accomplishing the slavery of the common people—not, indeed, chattel slavery, but another
kind which is equally ruinous and demoralizing, the
slavery of tenantry of farm or home or hopeless wage
servitude, with no hope of getting above that condition.

The rapid increase of farm tenants during the last decade is indeed alarming. According to a careful comparison
of the census reports of 1880 and 1890 in forty-seven

States and Territories, while the number owning farms increased 158,957, largely due to Uncle Sam's generosity in giving away farms, the number of tenant farmers increased 599,337. This means the transmission of many a farm from the hands of the struggling owner, to the hands of the capitalist, through the agency of mortgage foreclosure—a condition not due to shiftlessness or lack of thrift on the part of the owner, but to the increased burden of the debt, due to the enhanced purchasing power of money as exhibited in falling prices. It is true the goldite politicians and press tried to fool him into thinking that falling prices did not injure him because the things he had to buy were falling in like ratio, but he found the burden of his debt and interest together with his taxes growing constantly heavier each year, taking more of his hard-earned products to pay, until finally the evil day could no longer be postponed and another was added to the rapidly growing list of tenant farmers.

In 1880 25.62 per cent of the farms in the United States were cultivated by tenants, while this year (1894) shows 34.13 per cent to be tenant farmers. Now that the Government lands are exhausted so that there are no more free farms to be carved out of the public domain, we predict that unless the financial policy of the Government undergoes a radical change the next census will show half the farmers of the country reduced to an even worse condition than Irish tenantry.

The condition of the people in the cities is much worse. Surprising as it may seem, the census bulletin for 1890 shows that 93.67 per cent of the population of the city of New York are tenants—people who do not own their own homes, but who pay a monthly toll of rent to the capitalist.

In comparison with the other nations of the earth, the United States is only exceeded by one other nation in the

proportion of tenants to population. That exception is
the nation from whom we have borrowed our financial
policy. Great Britain alone exceeds the United States in
the proportion of tenants to population. This does not
speak well for our glorious republic. There is a screw
loose somewhere.

The onward march of the cruel oppressor, manifested
in the absorption of wealth by the few, is also seen in the

INCREASE OF BUSINESS FAILURES.

In the years 1863, 1864 and 1865, with a sufficient currency, the people were practically out of debt. The country was supplied with plenty of money and so did not
have to do business on the credit system, consequently
there were but few business failures in those years.

I have here another chart showing the business failures
from 1863 to 1894, as exhibited in Dun's commercial reports. I call your attention to it here as showing how,
under this process of the aggregation of wealth in the
hands of the few, the big fish have been swallowing up
the little ones: CHART NO. 4.

Year.	Failures.	Amount of Liabilities.	Year.	Failures.	Amount of Liabilities.
1863.....	495	$ 7,899,900	1879.....	6,658	98,149,053
1864.....	520	8,579,000	1880.....	4,735	65,752,000
1865.....	530	17,625,000	1881.....	5,582	81,155,932
1866.....	1,505	53,783,000	1882.....	6,738	101,547,564
1867.....	2,780	96,666,000	1883.....	9,184	172,874,172
1868.....	2,608	63,694,000	1884.....10,968		226,343,427
1869.....	2,799	75,054,054	1885.....10,637		124,220,321
1870.....	3,546	88,242,000	1886.....	9,834	114,644,119
1871.....	2,915	85,252,000	1887.....	9,634	167,560,944
1872.....	4,069	121,056,000	1888.....10,679		123,829,973
1873.....	5,183	228,499,900	1889.....10,882		148,784,337
1874.....	5,830	155,239,000	1890.....10,907		189,856,964
1875.....	7,740	201,000,000	1891.....12,273		189,868,638
1876.....	9,092	191,117,000	1892.....10,344		114,044,167
1877.....	8,872	190,669,936	1893.....15,242		346,779,889
1878.....10,478		234,383,132			

Calendar year.	Total business population in United States.	Total No. dropping out each year.	Net total No. added each year.
1879	703,000	100,000	. . . . .
1880	733,000	110,000	30,000
1881	780,000	110,000	47,000
1882	820,000	105,000	40,000
1883	855,000	110,000	35,000
1884	875,000	120,000	20,000
1885	890,000	145,000	15,000
1886	920,000	165,000	30,000
1887	933,000	170,000	13,000
1888	955,000	178,000	22,000
1889	978,000	209,000	23,000
1890	989,000	229,000	11,000

I want to use this chart also as illustrating the agency
which has brought about these results, and which, if permitted by the freemen of America to continue its drastic
work, will surely destroy our republic or change it to a
republic in name only, while its people are slaves to the
despotism of plutocracy. The agency is the contraction
of the primary money, first, from an elastic legal tender
paper to a coin basis by the refunding and the resumption
acts, and the act of 1873 demonetizing silver and making gold alone primary or redemption money. Temporary relief was afforded by the Bland act passed in
1878. If that act had made silver full fledged primary
money and opened the mints to its free coinage instead of
making it half fledged money our prolific mines would have
given full relief to the country and saved it. As with the
farmer who could not pay his debt because of falling
prices, these business failures may likewise be attributed
to the same cause, the constant enhancing of the purchasing power of money. I will fully explain this with
the other charts later.

CAPITAL AND LABOR.

In discussing the labor problem it is customary to consider capital and labor as the two contending interests.
The employer of labor is treated as the capitalist. This
is largely a mistaken idea. There should be a distinction.
There should be a triple classification, the capitalist, the

employer of labor and the laborer. In many instances the classes intermingle, it is true. Sometimes the employer of labor owns the whole of his own plant and sometimes he also works at the bench with his men. But the distinction is sufficiently marked to admit of the above classification.

The employer is rarely the capitalist (counting the capitalist and landlord together) and the laborer is rarely his own employer. On the one hand the laborer asks for wages; he takes no risk but when Saturday night comes he expects his pay. He consents to labor only for a stipulated sum guaranteed in advance. Whether the business is prosperous or not his pay must be forthcoming.

The capitalist, also, takes no risks. He rents the lands or buildings or both, as the case may be, for a stipulated sum guaranteed in advance. Or he loans his money for a stipulated amount of interest, payable at certain stated intervals, and to secure payment of both principal and interest he takes a mortgage or trust deed on the plant or is otherwise secured so that in case of failure he can get his own, with usury.

The employer is the third party. He is sometimes a capitalist and sometimes a laborer, but more often stands between, belonging to neither class but required to bear alone all the risks of both. Between these two, the secured capitalist and the guaranteed laborer, the employer —the man who endeavors to organize industry, to manage business, to make production possible—must stand alone and take all chances.

If there is a strike, it is not a war between capital and labor, as is commonly supposed, but a war between employer and employed. The capitalist is unconcerned. He is secured; the strike does not affect him. If there is a fall in prices it does not affect the laborer; his wages are guaranteed. The employer must bear the burden.

If he fails, as statistics show from seventy-five to ninety per cent do sooner or later, the capitalist forecloses and the farm or the workshop passes into other hands. The laborers change masters and the overworked, harrassed employer is ruined or driven into an insane asylum.

The iron hand of the security-holder bears even heavier upon the employer than upon the workingman. It is not the manufacturers and employers of labor, great and small, who are robbing the country, as some of the addled brained politicians would have us believe, but the parasites who suck the blood from all forms of industry. The workingman should make a distinction and learn who are the real enemies of labor. If they will do so a large part of the animosity which now exists between the employer and employed will disappear, and all producers will unite to crush the growing power of the security-holder and thus restore prosperity to farms and workshops.

THE SECURITY-HOLDERS.

The resources of the country are so great that even while bearing the many burdens which I have enumerated the country could still enjoy a measure of prosperity were it not for the still heavier hand of the security-holder.

Not content with a pound of flesh, these cormorants have deliberately shaped the financial legislation of the country, and not only that of this country but of the commercial nations of the world, to give them two pounds.

Nothing will more quickly or surely bring disaster upon one class or another than to disturb the relations existing between money, the measure of price and products. Modern business is largely done on the credit system. Out of this credit system has grown stocks, bonds, notes, mortgages, etc.

Two classes are created called debtors and creditors. The relations existing between these two are measured by money. The dollar in this country is the standard of measure.

Formerly this unit of value was made of a certain number of grains of silver; in 1873 for reasons well known to the fund-holding classes it was changed to gold.

If for any reason the exchangeable price of a dollar as measured by products is increased, or, to state it in another way, if the purchasing power of money is enhanced so that it takes more of the products of labor to buy a dollar, the debtor is placed at a disadvantage. He must spend more labor to pay his debts. If, on the other hand, the exchangeable price of money is diminished, the creditor is placed at a disadvantage. The money returned to him by the debtor will not buy as much of the products of labor as when the debt was contracted.

It is an old rule of political economy, based, by the way, on the use of metallic money, that plenty of money means good prices and is to the advantage of the debtor and producing classes, while a scarcity of money means low prices for products, and is, providing the contraction has taken place since the debt was made, to the advantage of the creditor class.

This rule holds good as applied to metallic money, and would hold good on what we might choose to call an irredeemable paper money. That is, a paper money which is not made redeemable in metallic money. Under our present system, however, as applied to paper money, it does not hold good. A paper money made redeemable in metallic money cuts no figure in this rule. It has no more influence in fixing the purchasing power of money than an issue of redeemable gold bonds, mortgages or notes would.

As I have before stated, it is not the volume of paper money which fixes the relations between money and products or its purchasing and debt-paying power, but the volume of the metallic money on which it is based or in which it is redeemable.

This rule the security-holders would like the public to conveniently overlook, for in it lies their power. They understand it well, and to apply its principles to their own advantage have secured legislation adopting the single gold standard.

By this one stroke of cruel, selfish policy, the purchasing power of money has been doubled and the producers and debtors of the country have been taken at a tremendous disadvantage. By this act alone the holdings of the creditor or security-holding class, as measured by labor and its products, is doubled in value.

This is the reason why the life is crushed out of all industrial enterprises. This is why workingmen walk the streets, while the farmer's wife and family go half clad. This is why times are hard. A restoration of prosperity can only come by a removal of the cause. By a change in our financial policy which shall restore the parity between the purchasing and debt-paying power of money, and thus deprive the security-holder of his ill-gotten advantage, and restore to the producer a fair price for his products.

In order that we may fully understand the relations between debtors and creditors. wealth and its representatives and money. I will go a little more into detail. To help make the matter plain I have prepared another chart (see next page). classifying the different articles of value, to which your attention is invited.

Lands and some of the products of labor when not used by the owners yield rents. And articles of legislative value, a value fixed by law, yield interest and dividends.

The class known as securities which I have labeled articles of artificial value are representative only of articles of real value.

CHART NO. 5.

WEALTH AND ITS REPRESENTATIVES.

ARTICLES OF REAL VALUE.	BASIS OF EXCHANGE Money consisting of	ARTICLES OF ARTIFICIAL OR LEGISLATIVE VALUE.
Land,	Paper,	Stocks, Bonds, Notes,
Mines,	Silver,	Mortgages
Forests and	Gold,	and all forms of
All Products of	Minor coins.	Indebtedness.
Labor.		

The face value of the security, with the annual interest which it says on its face the giver must pay, is secured by some article of real value, which is usually worth from double to two-thirds more than the number of dollars the face of the security demands.

A mortgage or trust deed is secured by the real estate described in it, and unless paid the holder has the legal right to cause a public officer to seize the real estate and sell it at public auction to satisfy the debt.

A bond, if on a railroad or other corporation, is secured by the property of the railroad, and the interest must be taken care of before any dividends on the stock can be paid. A State, county, city, village or school district bond is a lien on all the taxable property in the territory on which it is levied.

Stocks are not properly securities, but represent, or are supposed to represent, money invested in the industry or property they represent, and are a lien only on the surplus earnings of the corporation by which they are issued.

All debts are a lien on the property of the debtor and can be collected by legal process.

Money, which in this chart is placed between the articles of real and artificial value, is the medium of exchange and the measure of price.

It is supposed that primitive man had neither money nor securities, but exchanged one article of value directly for another. As time progressed, however, and man became more civilized and commerce increased, a convenient basis of exchange became necessary. To meet the needs this medium of exchange must be some commodity or commodities of little bulk, so as to be easily carried, yet of high value. The precious metals, therefore, gold and silver, by the law of natural selection, came to be used as money. First in bulk by weight and afterwards by the fiat of constituted authority which by stamp fixed its price as a measure of the prices of other commodities. As men and nations entered into a still higher civilization and commercial exchanges covered a wider range, and the stability and faith of governments and commercial business houses became established, it was found unnecessary to use gold and silver in ordinary transactions, but that the government stamp on paper, coupled with the legal quality of full legal tender, answered all purposes, was much more convenient, and tended greatly to the expansion of commerce and the growth of prosperity. Various forms of commercial paper, drafts, checks, postal money orders, etc., come to be used in place of money.

The wonderful commercial supremacy of the Republic of Venice maintained for eight centuries was conducted on what our security-holding friends would call a "fiat," or irredeemable paper currency. An eye witness of the great commercial prosperity of that little model republic, Petrarch, a resident of Venice, says:

"From this port I see the vessels departing which are as large as the house I inhabit, and which have masts taller than its towers. These ships resemble a mountain floating on the sea; they go to all parts of the world amid a thousand dangers; they carry our wines to the English, our money to the Scythians, our saffron, our oils and our linen to the Syrians, Armenians, Persians and Arabians; and wonderful to say, they convey our wood to the Greeks and Egyptians. From all these countries they bring back in return articles of merchandise which they diffuse all over Europe.

"They go even as far as Tanais. The navigation of the seas does not extend further north; but when they have arrived there they quit their vessels and travel on land to trade with India and China, and after passing the Caucasus and Ganges they proceed as far as the Indian Ocean.

"The paper money of the Republic, which we may say begot this great prosperity, rested solely on confidence in the Government and the quality of legal tender in the usual transaction of business. Strange as it may seem, this paper currency was at all times above par as compared with coin, while the interest-bearing bonds of the Government were never at par."

In many instances great national emergencies have been met by the issue of paper money.

England met the demands on her financial resources engendered by the Napoleonic wars, by the issue of non-interest-bearing legal tenders, which became twice as valuable as the three per cent gold-bearing bonds of England.

The paper money of the Revolution aided us to throw off the yoke of British oppression and establish this republic, and the "fiat" greenback furnished the sinews of war to crush the great rebellion.

Our more modern financiers, for selfish reasons, are taking a step backward. Paper money issued by the Government directly to the people is out of their control. It enables the producers of the country to transact their business without so much of the proceeds sticking to the greedy fingers of the bankers. Therefore they insist that the only "sound" money is metallic money, and that the only real sound metallic money is gold money. The quantity of gold is so limited they can control it, "corner" it when they will, as a board of trade operator does wheat or corn, and fix its price and through it the purchasing power of money to suit themselves. They can kick it up and down as the board of trade men do farm products, and enrich themselves enormously in the operation. Silver is too heavy for them to kick. They don't like it, and paper money has no "sound."

THE VALUE OF SECURITIES DOUBLED.

Keeping in mind that the relative volume of money fixes its price as measured by the products of labor, we can readily see that if the Government were to adopt any financial system which would contract the volume of money, it would result in enhancing the value of securities as compared with articles of real value. That is, it would take more of the latter to pay off or cancel the former. Such an act on the part of Government would result to the profit of the creditor as against the debtor, to the profit of the security-holder who lives on the proceeds of the labor of others, and to the injury of all producers, who would be compelled thereby to expend more labor to pay debts, taxes, interest, etc.

The security-holders of the world are not philanthropists. On the contrary, history shows the money power to be unscrupulous and exacting and, in fact, is the root and cause of more evil and misery, both national and individual, than any other human agency.

With the past experiences of the race before us, is it not reasonable to suppose if the money power could either openly or by stealth secure such legislation they would do it?

To openly pass a law which would double the face value of all debts and securities would lead to revolution. The debtors would be up in arms at once. It was necessary, therefore, if this mean and cruel advantage was to be secured, that it be done by stealth and gradually, so that while the debtors and producers should feel the pinch of

the screws, they would at the same time be blinded as to
the cause and not recognize the hand which turned them.

We are now confronted with the fact that within the
past twenty years the value of securities, or their exchangeable value as compared with the products of labor, has
been doubled.

A man who has held a Government or any other good
bond continuously for twenty years can exchange it to-
day for twice as much silver, iron, copper, lead or farm
products or other products of labor as he could have done
twenty years ago.

In fact, a security-holder who has held a good mortgage
on a farm for three years continuously can now exchange
it for nearly one-third more of the products of the farm
than it would have purchased three years ago. This unearned increment the security-holder receives in addition to
the annual interest which in itself is also greatly increased
in value. Thus the security-holder is enriched at the expense of the debtor, and the old adage "The debtor is
slave to the lender" is doubly verified.

This enormous increase in the value of securities has
been just as surely accomplished, and by legislation, too,
as if Congress had the power and had enacted a law
doubling the value of all debts and securities.

HOW IT WAS DONE.

Keep in mind that not so well understood economic
law, that the purchasing power or exchange value of redeemable paper money is not fixed by its volume but by
the volume of the metallic money in which it is redeemable, and you will have the key to the situation.

This law is well known to the practical high priests of
finance, but the people are largely ignorant of it and have
been kept so for reasons which are apparent. By the
application of this law and through legislation in conformity with it, the present unequal relations between

debtor and creditor, between security-holder and producer, have been directly brought about.

Formerly silver and gold both had equal privileges at the mint for free coinage, both were standard money, and paper money was redeemable in either at the option of the Government.

In 1792 Congress thus defined a dollar:

Dollars or units, each to be of the value of a Spanish milled dollar as the same is now current and to contain 371 4-16 grains of pure or 416 grains of standard silver.

Thus the silver dollar was made the unit or measure of prices.

In regard to the relative value of gold to silver for coinage purposes, the law said an eagle of 247 grains fine or 270 grains standard gold should be "of the value of ten dollars or units." That is, of the value of ten silver dollars.

The ratio of the coinage value of gold and silver was fixed at fifteen to one, the coinage ratio in Europe is fifteen and one-half to one. In 1837 the ratio was unwisely changed to sixteen to one.

The reason why silver was made the unit instead of gold was because, being the more abundant and more stable metal, it was not so much given to fluctuations in value as gold and could not be so readily hoarded and thus taken out of circulation or "cornered" by wealthy speculators. As a further precaution against dear money and to make it impossible for wealthy conspirators to victimize the debtor and producing classes by its manipulation, our fathers were also very careful to establish by law the free and unlimited coinage privilege at the mint for both metals, regulating by law only the ratio, weight and fineness.

This wisdom and forethought, however, was destined to be completely undone by conspirators of a later day. In 1873, when there was comparatively no coin in circulation and consequently the people and Congress were not on the alert, the following little clause was inserted in a lengthy bill of sixty-seven articles regulating the mint:

That the gold coins of the United States shall be a one dollar piece, which at the standard weight of twenty-five and eight-tenths grains shall be the unit of value.

Some say it was inserted after the bill had passed, before it was enrolled. At any rate it was not noticed by the Congressmen who voted for it, nor the President (Grant) who signed it, yet its effect has cost the country far more than the late war, and has been more disastrous than any foreign war could possibly have been.

That seemingly little clause made the gold dollar the unit of value, denied the free use of the mints to silver, and relegated silver to the commodities. Not content with operating in the United States, the same influential band of conspirators, inspired by a common impulse of greed, during the same year succeeded in securing the demonetization of silver in both France and Germany, and in closing the French mints, which for seventy years had maintained the parity of the two metals, against the free coinage of silver. They have since that time been steadily at work against silver, securing the adoption of the single gold standard wherever they can. The effects of their work are seen in the tremendous fall in prices as against a lessened production and increased demand.

By the light of the aforesaid economic law, that the exchangeable price of paper money is not fixed by its volume but by the volume of the metallic money in which it is made redeemable, the object of the demonetization of silver is apparent. The coin of ultimate redemption is now narrowed to gold.

As all the leading commercial nations have adopted the same policy, the natural result is an enormous increase in the demand for gold. The supply being limited, under the workings of the natural law of supply and demand,

Its exchangeable value as compared with other commodities has been greatly enhanced. And having been made the only coin of ultimate redemption, the exchangeable price of all other money, so long as it remains at a parity with gold, is increased in purchasing power with it.

To show the gradual fall in price of all commodities except gold since 1872 as a direct result of the demonetization of silver, I invite your attention to the carefully prepared tables on

CHART NO. 6.

Year.	Per Capita Circulation	Av'rage price of 47 Commodities	Average of Food Products.	Wheat per Bushel.	Average of Textiles.	Cotton per Pound.	Average of Minerals.	Price of Silver in a Dollar.	Value of a gold dollar as measured by 47 commodities.
1872.....	$18.19	$1.03	$1.02	$1.47	$1.14	.193	$1.27	$.992	$.97
Silver Demonetized.									
1873.....	18.04	1.03	1.07	1.31	1.03	.188	1.41	.974	.97
1874.....	18.13	1.02	1.04	1.43	.92	.154	1.16	.958	.98
1875.....	17.16	.96	1.00	1.12	.88	.15	1.01	.933	1.04
1876.....	16.12	.95	.99	1.24	.85	.129	.90	.867	1.05
1877.....	15.58	.94	1.01	1.17	.85	.118	.84	.902	1.06
1878.....	15.32	.87	.96	1.34	.78	.111	.74	.864	1.15
Bland Act.									
1879.....	16.75	.83	.90	1.07	.74	.009	.73	.842	1.20
1880.....	19.41	.88	.94	1.25	.81	.115	.79	.850	1.13
1881.....	21.71	.85	.91	1.11	.77	.114	.77	.85	1.16
1882.....	22.37	.84	.89	1.19	.73	.114	.79	.849	1.19
1883.....	22.91	.82	.89	1.18	.70	.108	.76	.831	1.20
Cleveland's 1st Term.									
1884.....	22.65	.76	.79	1.07	.68	.105	.68	.833	1.30
1885.....	23.02	.72	.74	.86	.65	.106	.66	.790	1.41
1886.....	21.82	.69	.72	.86	.63	.009	.67	.746	1.45
1887.....	22.45	.68	.70	.89	.65	.095	.69	.733	1.47
Harrison Elected									
1888.....	22.88	.70	.72	.85	.64	.098	.78	.704	1.43
1889.....	22.52	.72	.75	.90	.70	.099	.75	.702	1.41
1890.....	22.82	.72	.73	1.08	.66	.101	.80	.784	1.41
Sherman Act.									
1891.....	23.41	.72	.77	.85	.59	.10	.76	.741	1.41
Cleveland's 2nd Term.									
1892.....	24.44	.68	.73	.80	.56	.087	.72	.654	1.47
1893.....	25.57	.60	.60	.54	.48	.072	.63	.565	1.66

This table, which has been carefully compiled from official sources and is authentic and reliable, will bear careful study. It is an eye-opener in many ways. How shall we account for this tremendous fall in the prices of the products of labor as measured by gold, which, taking into consideration the still further reduction since this table was compiled, amounts to fully fifty per cent? As I have before said, in this great reduction in the purchasing and debt paying power of the products of labor is the key to hard times.

As a result we have the present condition. On account of its high purchasing power money cannot get into circulation, but remains idly congested in the banks. When it takes three bushels of wheat to buy a dollar, or sixteen pounds of cotton, and other products in proportion, it takes but little money comparatively to move the crops; consequently it cannot get into circulation.

The body politic, of which money is the blood, is like a diseased person whose blood is congested at the heart and lungs.

It is argued that as the reduction applies to all the products of labor it ought not to affect the prosperity of the farmer, because while he gets less for what he produces he pays less for what he buys of other producers, so that one offsets the other; he handles less money for his products. but the little he handles goes just as far in purchasing what he consumes.

Such reasoning would be sound if all other things were equal, and all forms of indebtedness, taxes, etc., were reduced in price in the same comparative ratio with products. Such is not the case, however.

Of all the producers the farmer alone has no control over the price of his products. They are, therefore, the most sensitive, and are the first to feel the effects of any legislation affecting the purchasing power of money. The manufacturers can and have combined to bolster up prices so that while there has been a reduction in the price of tools, machinery, clothing, etc.. such reduction is not so great as that of primary products. The farmer is compelled to expend more products to-day to buy a plow or harvesting machine than he did ten years ago.

It is in the power of railroads, also. to combine and check the fall in the price of freights. This they have done, so that it takes a larger portion of the products of the farm or mine to-day to get the balance to market than it would have done a few years ago. It will be noticed by this table that while the average price of forty-seven commodities has fallen a little over forty per cent, the price of wheat has fallen from $1.47 a bushel in 1872 to fifty-four cents, the average farm price during 1893; and cotton from nineteen and three-tenths cents a pound to the average farm price for 1893 of seven and two-tenths cents, or to the present price of a little over six cents a pound. Also while there has been a great reduction in the price of textile fabrics it is not so great as that of the raw textiles. You will therefore readily see that the farmer, who is the greatest wealth-producer of the nation, the one on whose prosperity it is acknowleged the prosperity of all other classes depends, has suffered the greatest loss of income. The dominant party in Congress also, with singular perversity and short-sightedness, proposes to still further reduce the income of the farmers and other primary producers by removing the tariff from raw materials, thus opening them up to the competition of the world, while still retaining a protective tariff on manufactured articles. While sustaining a loss of half their income the other burdens of the producing classes have not been lightened in the least degree.

It must be borne in mind that the producers of the country alone make wealth. and therefore all the burdens of government, all interest and dividends paid capitalists, all wages paid employes. etc., eventually have to

be paid by the producers.   While their incomes have been
cut down one-half, there has been no reduction in fixed
incomes.   You school-teachers are drawing even more
salaries than you were a few years ago when the farmer
was getting a dollar a bushel for his wheat.   The salaries of public officials have not been reduced, but on the
aggregate increased.   The expenses of government are
no less.   Taxes have not diminished but rather increased.
The minister still gets his old salary, the doctor the same
old fee.   And if you ride on the railroad the same three
cents per mile is demanded, and the same nickel a ride on
street-cars.   I have traveled back and forth between
Austin and Chicago for twenty years. I still pay the same
eight cents a ride which was demanded twenty years ago.

TABLE OF ASSETS AND LIABILITIES.

The following table, showing some of the debts of people and corporations in the United States during the year
1890, tells a tale every producer will do well to ponder:

Railway debts of 163,420 miles of railroad as stated in Poor's Manual for 1891. Introduction, page 1...	$5,753,541,572
Loans from 3,640 national banks, as shown by Statistical Abstract of the United States for 1891, page 31	1,986,100,000
Loans from 5 579 State, saving, stock, and private banks and trust companies, as shown by United States Statistical Abstract.....................	2,201,764,292
National debt (Treasury report).....................	891,960,104
State, county, municipal, and school district debts, as stated by Statistical Abstract of the United States for 1891, page 9...........................	1,135,351,781
Mortgages on farms and homes, not including those occupied by tenants	2,500,000,000
Mortgage indebtedness on real estate used in business and all other realty not including the farm and home mortgages as stated above..................	3,500,000,000
Indebtedness of street railways, manufacturers, business enterprises, etc., as shown by the census of 1890....................................	1,500,000,000
Chattel mortgage estimated.......................	1,500,000,000
Private interest-bearing notes estimated...........	1,000,000,000
Total...	$21,468,816,709

This estimate is made from statistics gathered in 1890
and 1891.   This debt has probably increased twenty
per cent since that time, making a grand total in
round numbers of................................... 25,000,000,000

Population...	65,000,000
Debt per capita in round numbers	404
Average wealth per capita, see chart No. 5	1,000
Net assets per capita.....	600
Producers' share of wealth at present about seventeen per cent...	10,500,000,000
Producers' indebtedness (all debts must ultimately be paid from the products of labor),............	25,000,000,000
Excess of producers' liabilities over assets.....	14,500,000,000
Estimating producers at 40,000,000 the per capita liabilities over assets would be	365
Net liabilities over assets per producer's family.......	1,815
Interest on $25,000,000,000 at five per cent.............	1,250,000,000
Annual interest tribute each family of producers pays to non-producers....................................	155

The tendency towards gold monometallism has increased the burden of this indebtedness at least one-fourth since 1890 on account of falling prices.

HOW THIS INTEREST TAX IS PAID.

While you, dear producer, may have no mortgage on your farm and house and owe no interest-bearing debt, if this is your situation you are lucky. The majority of the producers of the country are not so fortunate. Still you are just as surely contributing to this interest tax as if you had a mortgage on your farm or house. You pay it in this way:

1. By your State, county, village or school district tax which goes to pay interest on the bonds they owe.

2. The railroads over which your freight is shipped is mortgaged to the bondholder. The interest on these bonds you help to pay in freight and passenger traffic charges.

3. The manufacturer who makes the machinery or utensils you use or the clothing you wear or any of the various articles of household economy is doubtless working largely on borrowed capital and must add interest charges to the price of his wares. Thus, in various indirect ways which add to the expense of living, you are compelled to contribute your share to the support of the parasites.

To illustrate how this great reduction in the wages of the farmer clogs the wheels of industry and throws working men and women out of employment and thus causes general distress, we will bring the matter home by supposing

that the Board of Education of Austin should cut down
the salaries of you teachers one-half.   Indeed there
would be a howl.   You would not be as patient in
submitting to injustice as the hard-working farmers.
But suppose the board should perpetrate such an unjust
act, and you could not do better but had to submit to the
reduction, what would be the consequences?   Instead of
buying four new bonnets a year you would have to be content with two.   Therefore, the milliner would have less
trade and would be compelled to curtail expenses by discharging the now unnecessary help.   The milliners' help-
ers, therefore, would be out of employment.   Instead of
buying four new dresses a year, you would have to make
two answer, and also go without that new spring cloak
you intended to buy.   Perhaps, as is very likely, your
landlady would be obdurate and charge you no less for
room rent and board.   In that case you would have to
still further curtail expenses in other directions, and instead of attending the Austin Economic Circle, or your
Shakespeare Club or similar educational institution, in all
probability you would have to stay at home evenings to
make over your old hats and dresses and cloaks.   As a consequence the milliners, dress and cloak makers would have
to shut up shop, and their employes go to soup-houses to
get sustenance.   The mills which made the fabrics for
your hats, dresses and cloaks would have to lessen production and discharge employes; and the primary producers who grow the raw material would find a lessened sale
for their products.

In the case of the latter, according to the characteristic
unwisdom of the editors of the partisan press, there
would be a case of overproduction, but as you will readily
appreciate, or at least would appreciate if such a calamity
as I have outlined should befall you, it would be a case of
underconsumption.

We will go a little further and suppose one or more of you with commendable thrift had bought a home and was paying for it out of your earnings on the instalment plan. You did not anticipate such a reduction in your income but thought, as you had a right to do, that things would continue as they were, and made your calculations accordingly. Instead you are now brought face to face with the problem. Your wages are one-half less, but the instalments and interest on your purchase remain the same. They must be met or you lose all your savings for years.

If you meet the payments you cannot buy even one bonnet and dress a year, or if you do they must be of the poorest quality. You would have to stay at home, go poorly clad, scrimp and half starve yourself to keep up payments, which when the debt was contracted were easy to make. After a brave effort to save your property, privation and worry bring on sickness or something else happens and your earnings and savings of years are absorbed by the capitalist, who, to make this hypothetical case fit the real one, we will suppose influenced the board of education to reduce your salary so that he might in this way secure your accumulations.

"No man would be so mean," you say. There are some mighty mean men in this world, but if history and Biblical authority are to be believed there are none meaner than the money-changers. Of all the classes of men the Savior came in contact with on earth, the money-changers were the only ones who so aroused his indignation as to lead him to use violence. On them he used a whip of cords and upset their tables and charged them with making his Father's house a den of theives. Human nature is much the same to-day. Those fellows who were thus summarily driven out of the temple were evidently, as the world goes, respectable, otherwise they could not have had access to the temple. There are many such who

sit in the best cushioned pews of God's Temple to-day.
Will the Savior when he comes again use the whip of
cords?

Go to now, ye rich men, says the Apostle James, weep and
howl for your miseries that shall come upon you.

Your riches are corrupted, and your garments are moth-
eaten.

Your gold and silver is cankered; and the rust of them shall
be a witness against you, and shall eat your flesh as it were
fire. Ye have heaped treasure together for the last days.

Behold, the hire of the laborers who have reaped down
your fields, which is of you kept back by fraud, crieth; and
the cries of them which have reaped are entered into the
ears of the Lord of Sabaoth.

Ye have lived in pleasure on the earth, and been wanton.

The possible case which I have thus brought home to
you has its exact counterpart in the condition of the
farmer and the country to-day. As you will see by this
table, the wages of the farmer have been reduced even
more than one-half. Consequently his power to purchase
other goods has been reduced in like proportion. His
landlady, the Government, has refused to reduce his expenses, which curtails his power to purchase still more,
and if he has a mortgage on his farm, as one-third of those
who own their farms have, his condition is just as deplorable as yours would be under the conditions I have outlined.

The mean man has also got in his work, and conspired
to get for himself the fruits of the labor of others and the
hard-earned accumulations of the wealth-producers. His
work is seen in financial legislation which has doubled the
purchasing power of money through the adoption of the
single gold standard, the effect of which is to reduce by
one-half the purchasing power of all products, which represent the wages of the farmer.

When we come to measure the loss to farmers resulting from this fall in prices the figures are appalling. In
the past ten years the loss on the single article of

wheat alone measured by former gold prices would amount to nearly two thousand million dollars, while on the five staple articles, cotton, wheat, corn, oats and dairy products, the loss would be from seven to eight thousand million dollars. That vast sum received and spent by the farmers in clothing, home comforts, farm conveniences and for the education of their children, would have kept the wheels of industry turning to their utmost capacity. Under such conditions there would have been no calamity-howlers, no panics or hard times, but the producers of the country would be reaping the fruits of their own labor and enjoying a degree of prosperity to which they are entitled and which the abundant resources of our country amply warrant.

AN IOWA FARMER'S EXPERIENCE.

A recent conversation which I had in my office with an old farmer from Iowa, a sturdy veteran of the war, who owns four hundred acres of land free from debt, well illustrates the condition to which gold monometallism has brought the producers of the country. He said the pinch had been felt some time ago by those farmers who were owing money on their farms, but now its severity was reaching farmers like himself. With four hundred acres of the best land in Iowa he barely paid expenses last year, let alone living as a white man is entitled to live. If he had the value of his farm and stock in securities, he said, even at a low rate of interest, his income, without doing a stroke of work, would be larger than it now is.

Asked if his taxes were any less, he replied no, they were higher. He had just paid them. They amounted to $156. Formerly, he said, he could sell a good three-year-old colt and pay his taxes. Now it takes three. Also he formerly could pay his taxes with 150 bushels of wheat. Now it takes 450 bushels. It is unnecessary to say he is a bimetallist.

Iowa is one of the richest agricultural States in the Union. I recently read in a goldbug daily paper that the farmers in Iowa were prosperous, contented and happy. The Des Moines Register, however, the leading Republican organ of the State, owned by General Clarkson, late chairman of the Republican State Central Committee, tells a different story. I quote:

With a decrease in the production of all the cereals last year in the United States and in the world, the average value is the lowest on record, and nearly every week adds to the decrease in their values. The world's hog crop is lighter, but prices are about twenty per cent lower than last year at this date. Chicago's annual report on receipts and sales of horses states that the average price of horses per head, received during 1893, was $30 below the average of 1892—a loss of $2,490,000 on the 83,000 horses received in that market. The same statement shows that thirty per cent of those 83,000 horses were shipped from Iowa, which makes the portion of the loss which fell on Iowa farmers $747,000 on the 24,900 horses shipped to Chicago last year. So it is with all other farm products and the aggregate loss on the farm products of Iowa for 1893 exceeded $100,000,000 as compared with 1892. These facts should be studied by every farmer with an intent to solve the problem and return to general prosperity.

This is one year's contribution only to the security-holders from one agricultural State. If the farmers of Iowa had that $100,000,000 to spend. that sum alone spent in the products of other producers would have kept many of the wheels of industry turning and saved much suffering.

As you know, I am connected with the FARM, FIELD AND FIRESIDE. In behalf of its readers it is a hard fighter for the restoration of silver and prosperity. We sometimes get letters from readers who do not understand this question, whose minds have been warped by the sophistry and demagogue statements of the goldite organs. One in particular I have in mind which accused us of being in the pay of the mine-owners, that the free coinage of silver would be for their benefit exclusively.

This was accompanied with a wrathful "Stop my paper."
All people are not wise and some never will learn wisdom.
If this biased stopper could clear his eyes of partisan
cobwebs he would see that the benefits to the farmer as a
result of free coinage, as compared with those to the
mine-owners, are as one hundred to one. While Iowa
alone lost one hundred million dollars last year on account of the depreciation of the price of farm products, the
total loss on all the silver mined for the year 1893, through
depreciation in price as compared with gold, would
not exceed one-tenth that sum. In fact, the total difference between the present price of silver bullion and its
coinage value on all the silver mined in 1893 would not exceed fifty millions.

Another old farmer from Elgin, Illinois, who owns a
large and valuable farm, and who milks morning and
night forty head of cattle, shipping the milk to Chicago,
said to me in a recent conversation, if he could sell his
farm and stock at a fair valuation and loan the money at
three per cent interest, his income without any work on
his part would be larger than it is now. I believe that is
the case generally. The prices of products are so low as
compared with expenses that the best farmers are barely
making a living.

RELATION OF SILVER AND PRODUCTS.

To refer back to the table on Chart No. 6:

Please to carefully note the close relation between
silver and other products of both the farm and mines.
The table shows the average yearly price of forty-seven
commodities. The average prices of food products, minerals and textiles are taken from a table prepared by Augustus Sauerbeck, Esq., of London, a statesman accepted as
authority by both the British and United States Governments. It is published in a pamphlet prepared under the
direction of the Committee on Finance, United States

Senate. The per capita circulation is taken from the report of the United States Treasurer and the price of silver in a dollar from the report of the director of the mint. The other tables have been compiled from reliable sources.

You will notice how closely the relative price of silver bullion and that of forty-seven commodities have kept together. An ounce of silver will buy as much as the average of forty-seven commodities or of food products, textiles or minerals, except gold, to-day as it would have done twenty years ago. Silver, therefore, as measured by other products, has not depreciated in value. Of what import, then, is all this talk about the depreciation of silver on account of alleged overproduction? Have the whole line of human productions included in this table, except gold, been overproduced? The same argument will apply to each. In fact, in the case of wheat and cotton it is so used. We are told that in each of these cases the low price is due to overproduction. If that is the case, if there has been such an abundant yield of the products of labor as to depreciate the price of all one-half, how is it that stark want is staring the producers in the face? Why is it the farmer's wife goes half clad and the mill worker's wife cannot get sufficient food for her children? It is strange such a condition should exist when the market is so overglutted with products, as our goldite friends claim, that the prices have been reduced one-half. If lower prices are due to overproduction, how is it that gold bullion does not get lower? On the authority of the director of the mint the production of that precious metal is largely on the increase. Yet its price as compared with other commodities is steadily rising.

THE THEORY OF OVERPRODUCTION.

The foolishness of the overproduction theory was well illustrated by an old farmer out in Iowa.

A partisan political orator was discussing the financial question. To illustrate his point he held up a ten dollar gold piece, and said: "I will show you the kind of money I believe in. Has any one here a greenback he will exchange for this?"

Some one in the audience, prepared beforehand, produced the greenback. Holding it up, he said:

"Has any one a silver certificate he will exchange for this?"

The silver certificate was forthcoming, then that was in turn held up and exchanged for ten silver dollars, and the dollars in turn exchanged for the ten dollar gold piece. "That is the kind of money I believe in," he said. "The one kind exchangeable for the other, each on a parity with the other. That is what I call sound money."

The old farmer then arose and said:

"I would like to ask a few questions."

"All right; fire away."

"I will give you ten bushels of wheat for that gold piece."

"Oh, I can't do that. That would not be fair. Wheat is only forty cents a bushel."

"No, I suppose not. Ten years ago you would have given me ten dollars for ten bushels of wheat. Why is it not worth that now?"

"Simply because of foreign competition in the wheat market. India, Russia and the Argentine Republic have been growing and exporting a largely increased quantity of wheat, which has come in competition with ours. The world has been growing more wheat than consumption warrants, and by the natural law of supply and demand prices have fallen. It is a case of overproduction."

"Will you give me that ten dollar gold piece for thirty-five pounds of best Iowa wool?"

"Certainly not. The best Iowa wool is only worth fifteen

cents a pound. I do not care to speculate that way.'

"Ten years ago you would have been glad to make such a trade. Why is wool worth only half as much now?"

"I suppose for the same cause. They are growing large quantities of wool in Australia, Southern Africa and South America. Doubtless the present extremely low price is due to the certainty of the repeal of protective duties."

"But a great fall in price took place before it was known the Democrats would win the election of 1892, while we were protected against foreign wool by a prohibitive tariff. How do you account for that?"

"By the law of supply and demand, which alone affects prices. There must have been an oversupply."

"Another case of overproduction?"

"Yes. What are you trying to get at, anyway?"

"I will give you 100 pounds of A, No. 1 cotton for that gold piece."

"Not to-day, thank you; cotton is only worth about six cents a pound."

"Ten years ago you would have made a good thing by buying it at ten cents a pound and twenty years ago at eighteen cents a pound. Why has this great staple, upon which our brother farmers of the South so largely depend for their income, suffered such an enormous depreciation in price compared with gold, or money?"

"Same rule, I suppose—overproduction. The Southern farmers should grow less cotton. They should diversify their farming more."

"Grow more sugar, eh?"

"Yes, and save importing so much. Only one-eighth of the sugar we consume is grown here."

"Just so. I will give you 100 pounds of refined sugar for that ten dollars."

"What are you getting at? I can buy all the sugar I want at five cents a pound at retail."

"I suppose so. Twenty years ago you would have made two cents a pound at the price I name. Why not now? Is it another case of overproduction?"

"Machinery for the manufacture of sugar has been greatly improved, which probably accounts for it."

"I will exchange you some choice steers for the money at $6.80 per hundred."

"We can't trade on any such basis. This is getting monotonous."

"Ten years ago you would have been glad to. Why not now? Has there also been an overproduction of steers?"

"Evidently, or the price would not have fallen."

"I will give you 900 pounds of pig iron for your ten dollars."

"Certainly not. The exchange would not be fair. Iron is not worth such a price. This must stop; I'll answer no more questions. The greatly increased facilities for mining iron have increased the output and cheapened it."

"How about silver?"

"The same rule applies."

"And copper and lead?"

"Yes."

"I find from an examination of Sauerbeck's reports, as published by the English and United States Governments, that an average of forty-seven commodities, embracing all the chief products of labor, with the single exception of gold, have fallen about fifty per cent in price. Is this all chargeable to overproduction?"

"I suppose so. Improved machinery has made it possible to cultivate a larger acreage and improved mining machinery to increase the output."

"One more question and I am done."

"Out with it."

"As there has been an overproduction of everything else, why not have an overproduction of money also, to equalize things so that we farmers can pay our taxes and debts with the same amount of produce we could ten or twenty years ago and have a little money left over to buy the necessaries and comforts of life instead of going half clad in the midst of this greatly overproduced abundance as we are now compelled to do? This plan of equalizing things would also furnish work for the employes of mills and factories who, also, in spite of the cheapened abundance of food products you describe are walking the streets and patronizing soup-houses, half starved and clad."

If our political orator had been the editor of the Chicago Tribune or some similar erratic goldbug organ, he would have at this juncture yelled "crank," "fiat," "dishonest fifty-cent dollars," "dishonest granger," and used similar weighty (?) arguments, but as it was, his patience was exhausted and he refused to answer any more questions.

WHY SILVER AND COMMODITIES FALL IN PRICE.

Referring again to Chart No. 5, please take notice how closely in their gradual downward trend the price of silver bullion and the average price of commodities keep pace together.

Notice, also, the effect silver legislation or administrative policy, favorable or otherwise, has had on the price of other commodities. The Bland act, for example, which was favorable to silver.

This act, entitled "An act to authorize the coinage of the standard silver dollar and restore its legal tender character," directed the Secretary of the Treasury to purchase silver bullion and coin not less than two nor more than four million dollars a month, and also provided for the issue of what is known as "silver certificates," which represent coined dollars deposited in the treasury.

The effect as soon as its influence could be felt was to advance the price of silver and with it all commodities, which remained steady until the election of Cleveland in 1884. Cleveland is an avowed enemy of silver and at once began a warfare on it. In his message he recommended the repeal of the Bland act.

Immediately, as you will see from the prices on the chart, the price of silver began to fall, and with it the prices of all commodities except gold.

In explanation of falling prices, a chart showing prices for silver and wheat in England, since silver was demonetized, was printed for private circulation by the Corn Trade News of Liverpool, in 1890. In explanation of recent low prices, the following was printed at the bottom of the chart, under 1885, "Suspension of the coinage of the Bland dollar recommended by the United States of America President."

The English, as we see, well knew the cause of falling prices.

During Cleveland's first term the value of silver in a silver dollar as compared with gold fell ten cents and in harmony with it the price of all other products fell in about the same ratio.

Harrison was in a measure friendly to silver. He was not an avowed enemy. He wanted its full restoration but thought it could only be accomplished through international agreement. As a consequence, under the working of the Bland act, which increased the circulating medium to correspond with the increase in population, the per capita circulation remaining about the same, the price of silver and commodities as measured by money remained steady.

Then in 1890 came the Sherman act. This was followed by a sharp rise in the price of silver and products. While it was only a compromise measure agreed to by the security-holding class to secure themselves from the consequences of a free coinage bill, and by the bimetallists as the best they could get, it was yet favorable to silver and had the effect of temporarily raising prices. Its beneficial effects were doomed to be short-lived, however. The security-holding class in both Europe and America began a formidable warfare against it in 1892, the details of which I have already alluded to. Largely through Wall street money, and the influence and money of corporate monopolies, Cleveland was again elected.

The effect of his election was immediately visible in the price of both silver and products. His first official act of importance was to call Congress together in extra session to repeal the purchasing clause of the Sherman act. This proclamation was issued June 30. As if in direct co-operation the English government about the same time closed the Indian mints to the free coinage of silver. If you will refer back to Chart No. 2 you will at once see the effect of this combined action in the great fall in price of the three leading staples, wheat, corn and mess pork. The price of silver fell in almost exact ratio.

The work of repeal was finally accomplished Oct. 30. Referring again to this chart we see these products took another great tumble in price. All the other products, including silver, also fell in price in like ratio, and the tendency is still downward.

CHAPTER III.

A LESSON FROM WHEAT.

As will be seen by again referring to Chart No. 6. there has been a greater fall in the price of wheat than in the average of forty-seven commodities or of other food products. Surely, then, if overproduction is the cause it should manifest itself in the case of wheat.

A careful analysis of the statistics of wheat production, as furnished by the Department of Agriculture and other reliable sources, does not show an increase in the world's per capita production, while in the United States there has been a great falling off.

CHART NO. 7.

The following Chart, No. 7, is an object-lesson in wheat production which will bear careful study. It is compiled from the reports of the Secretary of Agriculture and other official sources, showing the total product, acreage, price and amount exported, and the world's production for the years named. Has there been overproduction?

Year average.	Bushels.	Total value.	Price per bushel.	Acreage.	Bushels per acre.	Bus. per capita.	Price per acre.	Per capita consumption about 5½0 bushels.
1870 to 1879	312,152,728	$327,407,258	$1.05	25,187,414	12 4-10	10	$13.00	
1890	498,549,968	474,201,850	.95	37,986,717	13 1-10	......	12.48	
1891	611,780,000	513,472,711	.84	39,916,897	15 3-10	10	12.86	
1892	515,949,000	322,111,881	.62	38,554,891	13 4-10	......	8.35	
1893	396,131,725	213,171,381	.53	34,629,418	11 5-10	6	6.16	

EXPORTATION OF WHEAT AND FLOUR.

	Bushels wheat.	Value.
1881	121,892,389	$146,270,867.00
1890	106,181,316	84,945,052.80
1891	225,665,812	180,532,649.60
1892	233,264,198	144,623,802.76
1893	200,222,804	106,118,076.12

WHEAT PRODUCTION IN INDIA.

The following figures are derived from the "Final Memoranda on the Wheat Crop of India," issued by the "Revenue and Agricultural Department" of India:

Years.	Area.	Product.
	Acres	Bushels of 60 lbs
1881-'85	27,820,223	299,155,584
1885-'86	27,405,742	258,317,622
1886-'87	26,735,484	238,585,947
1887-'88	26,854,882	266,882,112
1888-'89	25,911,700	237,522,133
1889-'90	24,773,000	228,592,000
1890-'91	26,424,000	235,434,667
1892		203,168,000

THE WORLD'S PRODUCT FROM DORNBUSCH'S LIST.

Year	Quarters
1890	236,319,000
1891	246,699,000
1892	249,234,000
1893	235,500,000

It will be seen that in 1880, with a much larger crop than in 1893 and a much smaller foreign demand, the farmers received ninety-five cents a bushel for their wheat, or $12.48 per acre.

In 1891 we produced the largest amount of wheat ever known in the history of the country, nearly 612,000,000 bushels, and as large amount per capita (ten bushels) as we ever produced. The world's supply also was large, yet we got eighty-four cents a bushel on the average, or $12.86 per acre, a loss of eleven cents a bushel since 1880 but a larger price per acre on account of increased yield.

Contrast this with 1893 with over one-third less production. A yield of only six bushels per capita in the United States and a decreased world's supply and yet the price has fallen to fifty-three cents a bushel and the value per acre to $6.16, a fall of thirty-one cents per bushel and $6.70 per acre in two years. Surely the rule of overproduction as a cause of falling prices will not fit this case. Under the natural and untrammeled law of supply and demand as a regulator of prices the price of wheat in 1893 should have been much higher than in 1891.

The theory of crowding out our wheat by foreign competition is equally a misfit. Until 1893 our exports
of wheat show a marked increase. There is a falling off
in 1893, due probably to the short crop and the underconsumption in Europe on account of the hard times which
prevail there also. Yet our exportation in 1893 reached
the no mean figure of 200,000,000 bushels, which is nearly
twice that of 1890.

It is the common opinion that there has been an enormous increase in the wheat production of India as accounting for a reduction in prices, and that India is now supplying the English market to the exclusion of American
wheat. Doubtless you hold such opinions. They have been
industriously circulated by the monometallist organs and
campaign orators. A glance at the tables showing the
wheat production of India will dispel this illusion. India
is producing less wheat to-day than she did ten years ago
when wheat was worth nearly a dollar a bushel.

A GLUTTED MARKET.

"But the markets are glutted," you say, "and farmers
are compelled to feed their wheat to stock because there
is no demand for it. How do you account for that?"

On the same principle that we account for the closing
of the mills and factories. If the mills and factories
could sell their products they would not shut down.

It is because there is no market that the wheels of industry have ceased to move.

There is no market, not because there is no demand for
products, not because we do not need clothing, etc., and
are not anxious to buy. The farmer's wife and children do
not go half-clad from choice. It is not from choice that
the farmer fails to surround himself with home comforts and educate his children in the same schools and
colleges as does the banker and security-holder, but from
sheer necessity.

On the same rule it is not from choice that the working-men patronize soup-houses, and go half-starved. They would be only too glad to buy and consume more of the products of the farm. In both cases the lack of money with which to buy the products of the other compels both to underconsume.

It is not overproduction which has made trade stagnant but

UNDERCONSUMPTION.

The per capita consumption of wheat in this country, according to the treasury statistics, was 5.91 bushels in 1892, and 4.85 bushels in 1893. Here is a decrease of 1.06 bushels in one year; multiply the per capita decrease by population, 67,500,000, and we have 71,550,000 less bushels of wheat consumed by our own people. As the hard times also prevail in all countries which have adopted the gold standard, it is natural to suppose the same ratio of underconsumption will prevail abroad..

The per capita consumption of corn in 1892 was 30.33 bushels, and in 1893, 23 66 bushels. The decrease is 6.67 bushels per capita, or 450,225,000 for the whole people. If we put a value of fifty cents a bushel on the wheat, and forty-five cents a bushel on the corn, we have $35,775,000 worth of wheat and $202,601,250 worth of corn taken from the home maket of American farmers by the lowering of wages and shutting down of mills.

The farmers of America have lost more than $237,000,-000 from their home market by underconsumption. Add to this the great fall in prices, and is it any wonder times are hard?

The same effect has been felt in the two great staples imported into this country. The treasury statistics show that the per capita consumption of sugar was 63.5 pounds in 1892 and 63.4 in 1893. The reduction was one-tenth pound per capita, or 6,750,000 pounds, valued at $337,500.

The per capita consumption of coffee was 9.63 pounds in 1892 and 8.25 pounds in 1893. The reduction was 1.38 pounds per capita, or 93,150,000 for the American people, and this was valued at $23,287,500. Taking the two great domestic staples and the two great imported staples of America and $262,001,250 worth of food product was taken from our American consumption in one year. The statistics for 1894, when compiled, will no doubt make as bad, if not worse, showing when compared with 1892. There has been less work and greater reduction in wages, and necessarily more economy in living.

The whole of this mischief is directly chargeable to gold monometallism, which compels the producer to pay his debts and support the Government on a gold basis, while selling his products on a silver basis.

It is only countries which have adopted the gold basis which are thus suffering, except as their markets may be shut off by the inability of the people in gold standard countries to buy their products.

Countries on a silver basis, like Mexico, India (until the recent action of Britain in closing her mints to free coinage), China and other Asiatic and the South American countries, get just as much for their products measured by the silver standard as they did twenty years ago.

Silver also will buy just as much of the products of labor in the markets of the world. It has not depreciated in purchasing power, but in debt-paying power only, in countries which have made gold the unit of value, or measure of price. It is not silver which has depreciated but gold which has appreciated. The purchasing power of gold and all money, debts and securities based on it has doubled.

WHY WHEAT IS CHEAP.

The following table from the Mark Lane Express, Lon,. don, showing the fall in the price of the three staple farm

products in England from 1874 to 1894 inclusive, to which
. is appended the price of an ounce of silver for the same
period in round numbers, will further illustrate how
the prices of silver and farm products have fallen in like
ratio.

CHART NO. 8.

Per quarter	Wheat. s.	d.	Barley. s.	d.	Oats. s.	-d.	Silver. d.
1874	55	9	44	11	28	10	58
1875	45	1	38	5	28	8	56
1876	46	2	35	2	26	3	52
1877	56	9	39	8	25	11	54
1878	46	5	40	2	24	4	52
1879	43	10	34	0	21	9	51
1880	44	4	33	1	23	1	52
1881	45	4	31	11	21	6	51
1882	45	1	31	2	21	10	51
1883	41	7	31	10	21	5	50
1884	35	8	30	8	20	3	50
1885	32	10	30	1	20	7	48
1886	31	0	26	7	19	0	45
1887	32	6	25	4	16	3	44
1888	31	10	27	10	16	9	42
1889	29	9	25	10	17	9	41
1890	31	11	28	8	18	7	47
1891	37	0	28	2	20	0	45
1892	30	3	26	2	19	10	39
1893	26	4	25	7	18	9	33
1894	19	8	23	5	15	2	28

Present price of wheat in London, per quarter, 19s 8d,
the lowest known in 104 years.

England produces only a small proportion of the products she consumes. She imports the larger part of her
food products, all the raw materials for her textile fabric mills and much of the other raw materials for her mills
and factories. Her population is dense, and compared
with her other industries her agricultural interests are
small. Her sources of wealth are her manufactures and
commerce. She has also accumulated vast wealth, which
is loaned out all over the world. For these reasons it is
to the interests of her people to buy food and raw materials as cheap as possible in the marts of the world. Or in
other words, to get as much of food products and raw ma-

terials for her mills as possible in exchange for the interest
money on her foreign investments.

It is estimated by Gladstone that the English people
have $10,000,000,000 invested abroad, a large part of
which is in this country.

The interests of the Dutch provinces and Germany in
this respect are largely identical with those of England.
They all have large investments in this country.

The motives of English diplomacy, therefore, in securing the demonetization of silver are easily understood.
On the specie basis system of finance adopted by England
in 1694, and since by all commercial nations, the purchasing power of paper money and all other evidences of indebtedness is fixed by its base, or the metal in which it
is redeemable. If that base is broad and abundant, as it
would be now if both gold and silver were used as standard money, both being abundant, money would be cheap
and products would command good prices. The United
States being a debtor nation such a condition would be
to our advantage. We could pay our interest and divi-
dend debts on foreign capital with a less amount of our
products, and for the surplus which the foreign nations
are compelled to buy of us we would receive gold or a
greater quantity of their products in exchange, so that
our own people would be the richer by the transaction.

It is manifest that if Tom Jones, a farmer, owed John
Smith, a banker, $1,000, other things being equal, it
would be easier for Mr. Jones to pay the debt or the interest on it with wheat at $1 a bushel than with wheat at
fifty cents.

On the other hand, by demonetizing silver, which
was accomplished in England in 1816, and which
has been done by all the great commercial nations since
1873, following England's example, the quantity of
standard money or coin of ultimate redemption has been

reduced one-half. Naturally this has made a great demand for gold which under the law of supply and demand has advanced in value as compared with commodities. The purchasing power of all evidences of indebtedness being measured by it and redeemable in it have advanced with gold so that now it takes two bushels of wheat on the Chicago market and twenty pounds of cotton on the New Orleans market to buy a dollar, when one bushel or ten pounds of cotton a few years ago would have sufficed.

This as will be seen is greatly to the advantage of England and other creditor nations. It now takes double the quantity of our products to pay our interest obligations abroad than it would have done had we remained on a gold and silver basis, instead of adopting the English policy of a single gold standard.

As an illustration:

Our total exports for 1892 netted...............$1,015,732,011
For 1893.. 830,876,908
                                                 ───────────
    Loss......................................$ 184,855,103

Statistics show the bulk of our exports were just as large in 1893 as in 1892. The loss is in price only. By the united action of England and our short-sighted, or shall we say unpatriotic, President and Congress, the former in closing the mints of India to free coinage, and the latter through their unwise policy in repealing the Sherman act without adopting an adequate substitute recognizing silver, has cost the producers of the country in direct loss on our foreign exports, about $185,000,000 in one year's time. For 1894 the loss will be even greater.

As the amount of interest we have to pay in dollars and cents is not one whit less, the loss is net to us and clear gain to England and the other countries which hold our stocks and bonds. They have received $185,000,000 worth of our products as a clear bonus given them by our foolish financial policy without any adequate return.

What is to the advantage of the foreign security-holder is equally to the advantage of our own parasites. They get in the same ratio more of the products of the labor of the producer without rendering an adequate return.*

The English financiers well know what they are about. An editorial published in the London Economist in 1883 said:

England being the chief creditor nation of the world, it is to her interest to keep the volume of money as small as possible in countries from which debts are due in order to get more of their products in payment of interest due to her citizens.

England has more money invested in this country than any other nation.

In 1888, I think it was, the Queen appointed a commission to investigate the question of bimetallism. The following is an extract from their report:

It must be remembered, too, that this country is largely a creditor country of debts payable in gold, and any change which entails a rise in the price of commodities generally— that is to say, a diminution of the purchasing power of gold —would be to our disadvantage.

That great statesman and acute observer, Benj. Disraeli, in forecasting the consequences of the demonetization of silver in 1873, said:

It is quite evident we must prepare ourselves for great convulsions in the money market, not occasioned by speculation or any old cause which has been alleged, but by a new cause with which we are not sufficiently acquainted.

Six years later in another speech:

Gold is every day appreciating in value, and as it appreciates in value the lower become prices.

In January, 1876, the Westminster Review, speaking of the effect of demonetization, said:

One of the things involved we hold to be the probable appreciation of gold; in other words, an increase of its purchasing power, and that consequently, unless fresh discoveries are made, prices have seen their highest for many a long day, and that debts contracted in gold will, by reason of this movement, tend to press more heavily on the borrowers, and that it will be well if this pressure does not become so intolerable as to suggest by way of solution something like universal repudiation.

How well these predictions are being fulfilled. Even the bankers are becoming in a measure frightened at their own work and some of them are recommending a species of bimetallism with a string to it, something they can control; otherwise there is great danger of repudiation through sheer inability to pay, or the other alternative which is fast being accomplished, as will be seen by referring again to Chart No. 3, that of all the wealth of the country passing into the hands of the few.

With most remarkable foresight Ernest Seyd, the well known French economic writer, speaking of the effects of the demonetization of silver, with words which to us seem prophetic, said:

It is a great mistake to suppose that the adoption of the gold standard of value by other States besides England will be beneficial. It will only lead to the destruction of the monetary equilibium hitherto existing, and cause a fall in the value of silver from which England's trade and the Indian silver valuations will suffer more than all other interests, grievous as the general decline of prosperity all over the world will be.

Again with keen foresight the same writer, on the same subject, said:

The economic authorities of the country will refuse to listen to the cause here foreshadowed; every possible attempt will be made to prove that the decline of commerce is due to all sorts of causes and irreconcilable matters; the workman and his strikes will be the first convenient target; then "speculating" and "overtrading" will have their turn; many other allegations will be made, totally irrelevant to the real issue, but satisfactory to the moralizing tendency of financial writers.

The fulfilment of this prediction may be read every day in the public press. "Overproduction," "the tariff issue," "overspeculating," and various other causes are given for agricultural depression and the present terrible condition of the country, in which, in a land of plenty, millions able and willing to work are suffering for the necessaries of life.

The real underlying cause is found in the fine work and insatiable greed of the money class. The means used to accomplish this end was the demonetization of silver, and the way to undo their work and restore prosperity is to restore silver.

Speaking of the results of a fall in prices, Prof. Marshall, of Cambridge University, says:

A fall in prices lowers profit and impoverishes the manufacturer, while it increases the purchasing power of those who have fixed incomes. So, again, it enriches creditors at the expense of debtors; for if the money that is owing to them is repaid, this money gives them a greater purchasing power, and if they have lent it at a fixed rate of interest, each payment is worth more to them than it would be if prices were high.

But for the same reason that it enriches creditors and those who receive fixed incomes, it impoverishes those men of business who have borrowed capital, and it impoverishes those who have to make, as most business men have, considerable fixed money payments for rent, salaries and other matters.

The effects, as we have abundantly shown, are even greater on producers than on business men and manufacturers. The producers and working people are the worst sufferers. In relation to the effects of the falling prices on the artisans, Senator Jones in his speech at the International Monetary Conference held at Brussels in November and December, 1892, with almost prophetic foresight said:

Manufacturers decline to increase their plants to correspond with the growth of population. But, worse than either of these, the time arrives when even the plants in existence cannot be maintained in full running order without great sacrifices of capital. The manufacturers, many of whom operate in some degree upon borrowed money, endeavor by resorting to various small economies to avert or postpone the blow. But while prices continue falling, their efforts must be unavailing. Where possible, at such times, men endeavor to withdraw their capital altogether from industrial enterprises in order to invest in bonds, but failing to accomplish this, they endeavor to escape loss by running on short time or, in extreme cases, by discharging a portion of their working force.

How remarkably this has been fulfilled in 1893 and 1894. The other reason why mills close and all business languishes is the great underconsumption of products through sheer inability of the producing classes to buy.

The bond and mortgage holders and fixed incomes of government employes, etc., absorb all the surplus earnings of the producers so they have nothing left with which to buy the products of the mills.

Said the lamented French writer, Prof. Emile de Laveleye:

In the Greek democracies, the legislators, notably Solon, reduced sometimes all debts by law, in order that the people might not be brought to misery by usurers. After the discovery of America and that of the placers of California and Australia, nature, not law, reduced the weight of debts by increasing the quantity of money. To-day an arbitrary law has favored creditors in a most unjust manner inasmuch as everywhere - as in England in 1816—the people had previously a right to pay their debts with either metal, whereas they are now compelled to pay exclusively with gold. * * * What could be more odious? * * * Let us hope that the future leaders of the English democracy will see that the iniquitous monopoly accorded to gold sacrifices the most active part of the nation to the idle part and that they will restore to the two precious metals the role which science, history, commerce and the free consent of the people had guaranteed them throughout the past.

How about the American people who claim to have founded a democratic government? Shall we sacrifice the "active part," the wealth producers, to the "idle class?" That is the object of the demonetization of silver, and is what it is surely accomplishing. To accomplish this end is why money has been made dear and products cheap. With the same object in view and to counteract nature's bounty when the placers of Australia and California were increasing the volume of the world's money Germany and Austria and some other countries demonetized gold.

The most Rev. Dr. Walsh, Archbishop of Dublin, in an interview in the Freeman's Journal in behalf of the Irish land tenants said:

The adoption of bimetallism, or of some equivalent remedy, is, I am convinced, a matter of imperative necessity; that is, if the agricultural tenants of Ireland—and I do not at all limit this to Ireland—are to be saved from otherwise inevitable ruin. This is transparently obvious to every one who has mastered even the elementary facts and principles of the case.

In reference to who would resist the re-establishment of bimetallism for selfish reasons he further says:

But then account has to be taken of the dogged resistance that undoubtedly will be offered to any such measure of reform, by the capitalists, the money owners and the money lenders of the world. It is to their interest to prop up the present system of currency. That system, no doubt, in countless ways, grinds the faces of the poor. But what matter? It is all to the profit of the owners and holders of gold. So the owners and holders of gold will hold on by it to the death.

If the agricultural peoples of this country, and we do not by any means confine it to the agricultural classes, are to be "saved from inevitable ruin," with the venerable archbishop I say and repeat it emphatically, either bimetallism must be re-established or some equivalent adopted.

OTHER BRITISH INTERESTS.

From the foregoing it will be seen that there was a motive for the demonetization of silver. It was not accomplished because it was really wise national policy, but was a deliberate conspiracy on the part of the capitalist class to get more of the products of labor for their holdings, rents, interest and fixed incomes. As a result of this successful conspiracy and not through overproduction the prices of wheat and all other products are low.

England has another motive. It is to her interest to buy as much as possible from her colonies, members of her own family, so to say; a truly wise policy on her part, but one which is against our interests.

It is strange, therefore, that our own government and
legislators should become the cat's-paw to help her to
bring it about.

She is now largely dependent upon us for her supplies
of food and cotton.

On a fair basis India can not compete with us in wheat
and cotton. With our improved methods, machinery and
the superior intelligence of our farmers we can and do
grow a larger quantity per acre and produce it at a cheaper
price per bushel. If both countries, therefore, were on a
basis of bimetallism our wheat, both on account of its
superior quality and the cheaper cost of production, would
drive the Indian wheat out of the English market.

As it is now we are placed at a great disadvantage in
that the price of our wheat and cotton is measured by
gold and that of India by silver.

At a meeting of the British and Colonial Chambers of
Commerce, held in London in 1886, Sir Robert N. Fowler.
a member of Parliament, a banker, and an ex-Mayor of
London, said:

The effect of the depreciation of silver must finally
be the ruin of the wheat and cotton industries of America
and be the development of India as the chief wheat and cotton exporter of the world.

To the same board J. C. Fielden testified that "Wheat
—all wheat—would be worth $2.00 to $2.50 per quarter
more than it is were silver at par with gold."

The English Royal Commission, appointed to consider
the silver question, announced that cheap silver was stim-
ulating the industries of India and freeing the English
"from dependence upon the United States for wheat and
cotton." Before silver was demonetized very little wheat
and cotton came from India. Now not the American
product but the Indian fixes the price in the Liverpool
market, and that by the purchasing price of silver.

How this price is fixed and fluctuates with silver is

explained by an eminent English writer, Sir Moreton
Frewen, in his address before the silver convention at
Washington. He said:

An ounce of silver bullion will always buy a bushel of
wheat in India and pay the transportation on it to Liverpool.
Hence, the American farmer must always lay down his bushel
of wheat at Liverpool for an ounce of silver bullion. If this
ounce is worth but eighty-five cents in gold, then all the
farmer can get in gold is eighty-five cents less the cost of
transporting the wheat to Liverpool. Therefore, if the
farmer will deduct the cost of transporting a bushel of wheat
from Chicago to Liverpool from the price of an ounce of silver
he will have very nearly the price of a bushel of wheat in
Chicago.

This was written some years ago. How well the rule
applies can be seen at a glance. The average price of
silver for 1893 was about seventy-five cents per ounce in
London. It costs about fifteen cents to transport a bushel
of wheat from Chicago to Liverpool; deduct this from
seventy-five cents and we have sixty cents, which is about
the average Chicago price for wheat for the same period.

As measured by the other commodities of labor, the
Indian farmer is getting just as much for his wheat as
formerly; he is prospering at our expense.

English diplomacy and the stupidity of our own legislators has accomplished what England is seeking, cheap
raw materials and food products, and the development of
her dependencies at our expense.

We have the remedy in our own hands. Shall we apply
it? Shall we make another declaration of independence?

CHAPTER IV.

A LESSON FROM SILVER.

From the earliest ages of the world silver was used as money. It was the one universal currency. The first historical mention of it we find in the Bible (Gen. xiii: 2) which says Abraham was rich in cattle, in silver and gold. We find in those early times, in fact, throughout Bible history, that silver was mostly used for commercial exchanges, while gold was more largely used in the arts. Both were used as money, but the principal money was silver.

Abraham bought the cave of Machpelah for four hundred shekels of silver; Joseph was sold to the Egyptians for twenty pieces of silver. It was the money of ancient Egypt; Joseph gave Benjamin "three hundred pieces of silver." It was the money of the Philistines; the bribe offered Delilah to betray Sampson was eleven hundred pieces of silver. It was the money which the great and wise Solomon used in his commercial transactions. The record says: "And the king (Solomon) made silver to be in Jerusalem as stones." (I Kings, x: 27.)

Again, "And all the king's drinking vessels were of gold, and all the vessels of the house of the forests of Lebanon were of pure gold, none were of silver; it was nothing accounted of in the days of Solomon." (I Kings, x: 21.)

Commenting on this the Economist says that history is repeating itself in our own time, that silver has again become so abundant as to be "nothing accounted of" and for this reason it ought not to be used as money. In the latter conclusion it and our own government are not so wise as Solomon.

He had sense enough to use this abundant silver as "standard" money. He "had horses brought up out of Egypt and linen yarn. The king's merchants received the linen yarn at a price, and a chariot came up and went out of Egypt for six hundred shekels of silver and a horse for one hundred and fifty."

He also traded by the same means with the nations of the Hittites and with Syria. By making silver abundant and making money of it the wise king had abundance of money which was exchanged by his merchants for the wealth of other nations.

He bought good carriages of Egyptian make for about $400 in our money while a good horse was worth $100. His merchants also bought linen yarn at a price. All industries and commerce flourished because there was abundance of money.

Everybody got good prices for the products of their labor, and were happy. The days of Solomon and his glory and wisdom are looked back to by the Israelites as the halcyon period of their history, while the great wisdom of Solomon at that time was known throughout the commercial world. It attracted even the distant queen of Sheba who, overcome with a woman's curiosity, could not rest until she had made the perilous journey to see if the things she had heard were true, only to find "the half had not been told."

How different the action of our own administrators and legislators! With the richest gold and silver mines in the world and the largest output of the precious metals, which should make us rich with abundance of money, we foolishly demonetize one so as to make money scarce and dear, and then proceed to borrow foreign capital and pay a tribute to foreign bankers for the use of it, with which to de-

BIMETALLISM.

MONOMETALLISM.

velop our own natural resources, build our railroads,
manufactories, etc.

Was there ever such a piece of egregious folly?
To add to it, when we begin to talk about restoring silver
as standard money and opening the mints to it, thus to
make use of our own treasure-house of capital, the
bankers cry out in alarm, "Don't! You will scare foreign
capital. You will frighten away foreign investors. They
will take alarm and send our bonds home." Solomon believed in making capital of his own resources, and using
this abundant capital with which to buy things abroad
which could not be produced at home, and so to add to
the prosperity and happiness of his people.

If we had the good judgment to follow his example by
making money of our abundant silver resources and using
it abroad with silver nations, we could command the
trade of Egypt and Asia, as did Solomon, with the addition of Mexico and all other nations which recognize silver as standard money.

Silver has ever been the money of Asiatic countries.
It was also with gold the money of Rome. The Christ
was sold for thirty pieces of silver. It was also the
money of modern nations until 1873. It has always been
the money of the people. Gold, being the scarcer metal,
is more subject to fluctuations; consequently silver, on account of its greater stability, has always been the safer
and more reliable money metal. For this reason it was
made the unit of value by our forefathers and gold measured by it.

The following chart (No. 9) will be of great use in
studying this all important subject. It is taken from the
report of the director of the mint for 1893.

IS SILVER OVERPRODUCED?

It is claimed also that the fall in the price of silver as
measured by gold is due to overproduction. So thor-

oughly has this idea been driven into the minds of the average reader by the goldite papers that they look upon a person who has the audacity to deny it as a semi-lunatic.

CHART NO. 9.

	Gold— Annual av'r'ge of period.	Silver— Annual av'r'ge of period.	Per cent of producti'n.		
	Value.	Coining value.	Gold.	Silv.	Ratio.
1493-1520..	$3,855,000	$1,954,000	66.4	33.6	15 to 1
1521-1544..	4,759,000	3,749,000	55.9	44.1	15 to 1
1545-1560..	5,656,000	12,952,000	30.4	69.6	15 to 1
1561-1580..	4,546,000	12,450,000	26.7	73.3	15 to 1
1581-1600..	4,905,000	17,413,000	22.0	78.0	15 to 1
1601-1620..	5,662,000	17,579,000	24.4	75.6	15 to 1
1621-1640..	5,516,000	16,361,000	25.2	74.8	15 to 1
1641-1660..	5,928,000	15,226,000	27.7	72.3	15 to 1
1661-1680..	6,154,000	14,008,000	30.5	69.5	15 to 1
1681-1700..	7,154,000	14,212,000	33.5	66.5	15½ to 1
1701-1720..	8,520,000	14,781,000	36.6	63.4	15½ to 1
1721-1740..	12,681,000	17,924,000	41.4	58.6	15½ to 1
1741-1760..	16,356,000	22,162,000	42 5	57.5	15½ to 1
1761-1780..	13,761,000	27,133,000	33.7	66.3	15½ to 1
1781-1800..	11,823,000	36,540,000	24.4	75.6	15½ to 1
1701-1810..	11,815,000	37,163,000	24.1	75.9	15½ to 1
1811-1820..	7,606,000	22,479,000	25.3	74.7	15½ to 1
1821-1830..	9,448,000	19,144,000	33 0	67.0	15½ to 1
1831-1840..	13,484,000	24,798,000	35.2	64.8	15½ to 1
1841-1850..	36,393,000	32,440,000	52 9	47.1	15½ to 1
1851-1855..	132,573,000	36,824,000	78.3	21.7	15½ to 1
1856-1860..	134,083,000	37,618,000	78.1	21.9	15½ to 1
1861-1865..	122,989,000	45,772,000	72.9	27.1	15½ to 1
1866-1870..	129,614,000	55,663,000	70.0	30.0	15½ to 1
1871-1875..	115,577,000	81,864,000	58.6	41.4	15½ to 1
1876-1880..	114,586,000	101,851,000	53.0	47.0	16½ to 1
1881-1885..	99,116,000	118,955,000	45.5	54.5	19 to 1
1886......	106,000,000	120,600,000	46.8	53.2	20 to 1
1887......	105,802,000	124,866,000	45.9	54.1	21 to 1
1888......	109,900,000	142,107,000	43.6	56.4	22 to 1
1889......	118,800,000	162,690,000	42.2	57.8	22 to 1
1890......	115,150,000	172,235,000	39.7	60.3	19 to 1
1891......	120,510,000	186,733,000	39.2	60.8	20 to 1
1892......	130,817,000	196,605,000	40.0	60.0	24 to 1
1893......	155,522,000	208,371,100	31.1	41.6	28 to 1
1894.....	169,000,000	....	......	.....	....

Statement of the production of gold and silver in the world since the discovery of America. From 1493 to 1885 is from table of averages for certain periods compiled by Dr. Adolph Soetbeer. For the years 1886-1894 (brought down to date) the production is the annual estimate of the Bureau of the Mint.

I showed this chart to-day to a well-known citizen of this town, an ex-college professor, and pointed out some of the facts which it teaches, at the same time informing him that the table was taken bodily from the report of the director of the mint. Much to my surprise he replied that he did not care who the authority was or where the data came from, any statistics which did not show that silver had been enormously overproduced in excess of gold were false.

I had nothing more to say. I have lived too long to waste my breath on people who deny plain facts because they do not conform to their accepted theories or partisan political prejudices.

As will be seen by this table, the per cent of production of silver during twenty years from 1581 to 1600 was as seventy-eight per cent of silver to twenty-two of gold. Yet the ratio or bullion price of the two metals was not affected. Again, for a period in the beginning of this century the per cent of production was as seventy-five to twenty-four, yet the ratio was maintained at fifteen and one-half to one.

In 1857 to 1860 the proportion of production was reversed, being seventy-eight of gold to twenty-one of silver. Yet the ratio of fifteen and one-half to one remained unchanged.

The goldbugs were all silver-bugs at that time. Germany, Austria and some other countries actually did demonetize gold. This was done in the interest of security-holders for the same reasons that silver is now demonetized.

This great increase in the yellow metal filled the security-holders with alarm. As gold increased in quantity they feared it would decrease in its exchange value for the

products of labor. For thousands of years they had enjoyed the advantage of its scarcity, but now the products
of labor began to demand one-fifth more of the precious
metal as their price. Interest would not buy as much.
There was danger money would become so abundant as to
get beyond their control. The half-fed, half-clad people
who for thousands of years had suffered from the slavery
of Shylock's oppression were beginning to find clothes
and food, to surround themselves with home comforts and
walk and talk like free men.

This would never do, so "Down with gold" was the cry·
"It is too abundant and cheap to use as money."

The same arguments now used against silver were then
used against gold. The pens of journalists and economic
writers were then kept busy denouncing fifty-cent gold, so
to say.

De Quincey wrote his fears that gold would soon have
no value at all. The Frenchman Chevalier, in his paper
called "The Fall of Gold," translated into English by Cob-
den, affirmed that gold was becoming so plenty that its
value must decline, and that Europe must guard against
it without delay. There was great danger that debtors
would be able to pay their debts. That the world might
get onto a cash-paying basis, in which event Mr. Shylock
and his brood would be compelled to obey the Scriptural
injunction to "Work with his hands the thing ·that
is good," and thus be compelled to earn an honest living.
The bribed hosts of money bags were therefore mustered
and war declared on gold. First Holland, then Belgium,
followed by Austria and Germany, all went to the silver
basis.

England in 1816 had committed herself the other way,
and was more cautious. She sent her agents to California and Australia, who reported that the "gold beds"
were more limited than the "silver beds." Before the sil-

ver beds were developed, the continental money-lenders, taking their cue from England, faced about, retraced their steps and followed England's lead.

The same writers who had been industriously crying "down gold" now attacked silver. The hired hosts of Shylock were turned against that metal, and it in turn was demonetized by the creditor nations of Europe.

European governments are largely relics of the old feudal system. They are governments of aristocrats, by aristocrats and for aristocrats. There the classes make laws for the masses. It is not strange, therefore, that the work of demonetizing silver should be easily accomplished in those countries. It was in the interest of the classes. In America, however, the case is different. This Government is at least supposed to be a government of the people in which the interests of the masses of the people should be first considered. Being also a debtor nation there was not the slightest excuse for the demonetization of silver. On the contrary the interests of the people and of our nation as a whole would be best served by an abundance of money. It is unnecessary to say had the people known what was going on when this the greatest crime of the age was wrought it never would have been accomplished. The scheme was undoubtedly concocted in England at as early a date as 1867.

Silver must be controlled in America as well as in Europe, otherwise this vigorous young giant would upset all of Shylock's well matured plans. The well laid plot carried. By the aid of John Sherman and a few more in the secret, the law making gold the sole measure of value and relegating silver to the commodities was sneaked through both houses. There were not a half dozen Congressmen, let alone the outside public, who knew what was being done. It is said $500,000 was judiciously expended by English financiers to get this work done for them. In

this subtile way, as I have before said, England has reduced the price of American products which she has to
buy one-half since 1873, while retaining the same face
value of her interests, moneys and investments which she
has spread all over the world.

By controlling the price of our silver through our laws
passed in her interests, she first makes enormous profits
on our silver in India and the East, and then buys Indian
products with the same silver, the product of our mines,so
low as to shut American products out of the European
markets. The share our un-American Shylocks get out
of the deal is the increasing value of every dollar or every
security for the parasite or rich man which the producer
owes him. The creditor is made doubly rich at the expense of the debtor.

In speaking upon this subject in the Senate in 1878,
Senate Voorhees, who in 1893 became the cuckoo of President Cleveland and the right bower of John Sherman in
furthering Shylock's interests, said:

It was in the interest of this powerful class [the money-
lenders] that silver was demonetized in 1873, not because it
was not less valuable as money than gold, but simply because
retired capital desired to diminish the amount of money of
every kind circulating in the hands of the people. The managers of the great money centers in this country and in
Europe saw with avaricious alarm the bright streams of silver beginning to increase in volume and in value * * *
and now we hear from their angry throats and from an apparently still angrier newspaper press which they control, a
cry without ceasing against silver-inflation arising from an
overproduction of the metal. They have heretofore filled
the world with their hostile clamor mainly against a paper
currency not immediately convertible into coin of intrinsic
value; but it now appears that there can be, in their own
amiable language, an insane inflation of a currency which
has this very intrinsic value in itself. We now perceive that
even these precious metals may become more abundant than
is agreeable to those who want the purchasing power of
money increased by lessening the quantity in circulation, un-
till $50 will buy in a farm worth a thousand, under the foreclosure of a mortgage. * * * When the revelation of gold

took place in California and on the other side of the world in
Australia about the same time, an impulse was given to the
progress of mankind greater than had been produced by any
other event since Columbus discovered America. The whole
world rejoiced, with one exception. The creditor class in
every clime beneath the sun looked on in sullen distrust and
dread. * * * In 1856 * * this class broke forth in different countries in favor of demonetizing gold, because the supply was making money too plentiful. * * * Germany and
Austria, and some other European governments, in 1857,
actually demonetized gold, in order to maintain the scarcity
of money. The reason why this question did not seriously
agitate the financial circles of the United States is to be
found in the fact that at that time we had no great creditor
class in this country; we had no stupendous national debt
held as an investment for fixed incomes; no such State, mu-
nicipal and corporation debts as have since filled all the
stock-markets with interest-bearing bonds, and which are
now a draining tax on all the labor and production of the
country.—Congressional Record, January 15, 1878, page 334.

If Senator Voorhees had talked that way in 1893 and
voted and worked in line with this opinion the Sherman
act would never have been repealed without the passage
of a substitute recognizing silver.

Referring again to Chart No. 9 it will be seen that in
1893 the per cent of production is as forty-one of silver
to thirty-one of gold. Yet the ratio is twenty-eight to
one, or as it now stands over thirty to one. From the
discovery of America until 1873 the ratio was established
by law, and certain mints were open to the free coinage
of both metals on the established ratio. This fixed the
price of bullion so that no matter how production might
fluctuate the ratio or relative price of the two metals remained the same.

It is their use as money which gives value to both gold
and silver. If both were to be suddenly and everywhere
disused as money one would be of no more value than the
other and both would be a drug on the market. The demand for either of them would not be at all equal to the
supply. The fact that for all historic time both have been

used as money and that the greater part of the output of
the mines is now used for coinage is what gives them
value. Neither has any fixed intrinsic value. Consequently when one is disused as money and the mints closed
against it, its relative price as compared with the other is
immediately changed. The one having double duty to perform under the law of supply and demand advances in
value, while the demand for the other being less it falls in
price by the same rule.

It is not overproduction but demonetization which has
caused the change in the relative value of the two metals.

If silver had remained standard money and the mints
open to free coinage the ratio of price would have remained the same and there would have been no such advance in the value of gold and consequent fall in the price
of the products of labor as that from which we are now
suffering.

All authorities, even John Sherman himself, the goldite
of the goldites, admit that the restoration of the free coinage of silver will restore the prices of products.

It will be seen from this table of the world's production
that on the same basis of reasoning gold has also been
largely overproduced. If overproduction is the cause of
cheap silver, by the same line of reasoning gold should be
cheap also; but instead, in the face of largely increased
production, it has doubled in value.

In the past history of the world, abundance of gold and
silver was always accompanied with prosperity, while its
scarcity meant "hard times." The only reason we are not
now enjoying the greatest prosperity is because the parasites, in order to get more of the real wealth of the
country for securities they hold, have demonetized one of
the precious metals. The other, therefore, has been made
to do double duty, and consequently under the law of supply and demand it has doubled in price.

A QUESTION OF MORALITY.

"Give me neither poverty nor riches," said a wise man in the good Book. Also says the apostle Paul: "The love of money is the root of all evil," and "They that will be rich fall into temptation and a snare and into many foolish and hurtful lusts, which drown men in destruction and perdition." It would be easy, in view of the present condition of our country and the world, to preach a powerful sermon from either of these texts. In fact, to thinking men they are complete sermons in themselves, whose truthfulness finds every day exemplification. With the admixture of extreme poverty and extreme wealth, such as we find prevailing in this country at the present time, is found unrest, discontent and the greatest degree of unhappiness, leading to crime and national decay, while a better distribution of wealth with the condition of neither of the extremes of poverty or riches leads to national prosperity and individual contentment. No truer words were uttered than those of the poet:

"As wealth increases men decay."

The decay is at both extremes. Excessive wealth leads to licentiousness, while those who are deprived of their share of this world's goods, on account of the excessive accumulations of the other, decay through lack of opportunity, and through discontentment and poverty are led to crime.

It is not my purpose to preach a sermon, however, but to give some statistics showing that national decay has kept pace with the rapid accumulation of wealth which has been so materially accelerated by the financial policy pursued since 1865.

This decay is best shown by the increase in the inmates of jails and penitentiaries, murders and suicides. The following table, taken from the census reports for 1880

and 1890, will show the increase in crime and suicides in
ten years. These are years in which there was no panic,
only the tightening of the reins due to the gradual increase in the purchasing power of money:

Number of inmates in penitentiaries, 1880..............35,538
Number of inmates in penitentiaries, 1890..............45,233
Prisoners in county jai s, 1880........................12,691
Prisoners in county jails. 1890........................19,538
Number of insane in institutions, 1880 41,177
Number of insane in institutions, 1890 74,028
Number of suicides reported, 1880...................... 2,511
Number of suicides reported, 1890...................... 3,932

These figures are simply the number of convicts in penitentiaries, and do not include the prisoners found in various other places, and for the insane the figures are those
in institutions, not the total number reported insane June
1, 1890.

The Chicago Tribune brings the number of suicides
down to date. It says editorially: "The lamentable occurrence suggests a look at the statistics of suicide and a
question as to the cause of its greater frequency now as
compared with a few years ago. The following totals for
the United States are of startling interest in this connection:

Year.	Suicides.	Year.	Suicides.
1889	2,224	1892	3,360
1890	2,640	1893	4,436
1891	3,331		

It will be seen that, with a slight increase in population, the number of suicides has doubled during the last
four years. The tremendous increase in the crime of
murder during this same period is even more startling
than the number of suicides.

This table is taken from the American Statistical Association publications, page 359; it gives the number of
homicides in the whole United States in the decade from
1882 to 1891, as compiled by the Chicago Tribune, and re-

ceiving the indorsement of this statistical association publication:

Years.	Murders.	Years.	Murders.
1882	1,467	1887	2,335
1883	1,697	1888	2,184
1884	1,465	1889	3,567
1885	1,808	1890	4,290
1886	1,499	1891	5,906

This table of Mr. Cook's cannot be explained by an increase of immigration; nor the increase in crimes, insanity and suicides be attributed to immigration, as will be seen by the following table of immigrants coming to this country during the same number of years:

Years.	Immigrants.	Years.	Immigrants.
1882	788,992	1889	444,427
1883	603,322	1890	455,302
1884	518,592	1891	560,319
1885	395,346	1892	623,084
1886	334,203	1893	502,927
1887	490,109	1894	314,467
1888	546,889		

While it is true there are other causes leading to crime and suicide, so that all these cannot be credited to this great underlying cause, yet it is remarkable how the ratio has kept pace with falling prices and business failures.

Any cause which leads to poverty, with its accompaniment of discouragement and discontent, leads to crime and suicide. Excessive wealth, with its arrogance, voluptuousness and display, not only leads to the mental and physical decay of those who possess it, but breeds the greater discontent among the poor who witness it. It also fosters dishonesty and corruption. There is another saying of the good old Book which fits the case right here: "He that maketh haste to be rich shall not be innocent."

Very few of the great fortunes of the day have been accumulated by honest means; too many, indeed, have been built in corruption. Nevertheless they are built, and, while we believe those who have them would be much happier with less money and a clean conscience in the sight of God, yet these men are held up or set themselves before the young as successful business men—object-lessons, so to say, whose corrupt paths the young man is led to believe lead to success.

While the restoration of an adequate supply of primary money by the restoration of bimetallism will not cure all these evils, it will be a big stride in the right direction. It will turn the scale of falling prices which has been accompanied, as the statistics show, with a loss of wealth among the producing classes to the rich; it will restore prosperity to the humbler classes, work and wages to the workless, good prices to the producers, increased trade to the merchants and manufacturers, more commerce to the carriers, and thus bring increased prosperity all around.

Is it not reasonable, my friends, to suppose that such increased prosperity would check crime and suicide by re moving its most prevalent cause, poverty, with its re· sultant discontent and discouragement? What is our duty, then, as lovers of humanity or as patriotic citizens of our common country, or, shall I say it, as Christians? Shall we favor the rich by voting to perpetuate falling prices so they can get a larger slice of the labor of the worker for their interest and loans by favoring the gold standard, or shall we favor the great army of wealth producers by casting a vote for the restoration of bi. metallism?

CHAPTER V.

In the foregoing chapter I trust I have made·it clear why the security holder wants the quantity of primary money limited. In addition to the advantages to be derived from the enhanced exchange value of money the bankers have still another reason. The profit of banks is largely derived from the modern system of doing business on credit. When the quantity of the circulating medium is limited its place must be supplied with bank credits. For this reason we not only find the banks working to establish the single gold standard in order to limit the quantity of primary money, but also to limit the quantity of credit money issued by the Government as well. They want to monopolize all credits and thus increase their profits.

While there are plenty of men in the world whose lives are actuated by pure, unselfish motives, at the same time, in discussing a question of this kind, it would be folly to ignore facts. A fact which we cannot ignore is that the average business man, in dealing with his fellows, is selfish. This is especially true of the moneyed class. The position they occupy in the world and the means used in acquiring wealth have in most cases either found or made them so, while perhaps scorning to do anything lawfully dishonest. The law being in the business world the landmark of honesty, he will not hesitate to take every advantage within the limits of the law, or even to use influence to shape legislation to extend its limits to his own advantage and to the disadvantage of his neighbors.

Bankers are no more patriotic or philanthropic than other people, and are none the less actuated by this selfish principle which unfortunately governs the business world.   In fact, the nature of their calling requires them to do many things, such, for example, as foreclosing loans where the subject has been unfortunate, the tendency of which is to harden the heart and dull the conscience. Also many opportunities are thrown in their way to grasp property often worth many times the face of the loan, which few would resist. This being the case, there is nothing strange that the aggregation of bankers known as the Bankers' Association should be found working with other security holders to restrict the quantity of primary money so as to create a greater demand for bank credits; also working to have the Treasury note and silver eliminated from the currency of the nation.

As will be seen by a reference to page 14 there is now in circulation in round numbers $800.000,000 of paper credit money issued by the Government directly to the people. The Bankers' Association made a vigorous effort during the last Congress to have this large amount of credit money refunded into gold bonds, this money to be replaced by bank notes.

The Baltimore plan, indorsed by the Bankers' Association, in its session at Baltimore, also the Cleveland plan, recommended by the President in his message. and the Carlisle-Springer plan, drawn up by Secretary of the Treasury Carlisle and introduced into the House by Representative Springer, of Illinois, chairman of the House Committee on banks, are all of this nature. The people easily discern the motive. There was nothing patriotic in those bills. Their authors were not inspired by love of country or a desire to promote the welfare of the country, but by bankers' greed. As it now stands this money is practically a Government loan without interest. The people are willing to accept the Government's promise to pay, without interest, and use it as money. If the banker's program is carried out, these non-interest-bearing notes would be converted into, say, three per cent gold bonds. This would impose a burden of $24,000,000 a year on the wealth producers of the country, on that which now costs them nothing. The bankers' friends, the bondholders, would receive this handsome sum. This $800,000,000 would then be replaced by bank notes. Unlike the people's Government and ordinary people, the banks demand interest on their promises to pay. Unfortunately, should they succeed in getting such a law passed they would be in a position also to enforce their demands.

The people must have money, and as the total stock of gold in the United States is only from four to six hundred million dollars they would be compelled to go to the banks and pay them from six to eight per cent, or even more, to get bank notes. This would at least cost the people $50,-000,000 a year more, making a total of $74,000,000 a year which the banks and bondholders would gain and the people lose should the bankers' shameless plans be crystallized into law.

The shameless part which the administration took in aiding and abetting the bankers in their efforts to carry out their plans goes further to prove that it is owned by Wall street. It is to the credit of the last Congress that it refused to pass the bills. It is an old fight, and is in line with the efforts of the moneyed class to enslave the producing classes to serve their greed.

The above estimate of cost of such a financial policy is not all. The issue and sale of such an enormous quantity of gold bonds would further enhance the value of gold and, to a corresponding degree, depress prices, to the further enriching of the security holding classes.

THE USE OF BANK CREDITS.

It is the boast of the worshipers at the shrine of the golden calf that the commercial world does not now need as much money as formerly—that bank credits and the check system supply the place of money, and, therefore, with these supplemental aids, they argue, the gold supply will be sufficient and silver not needed.

It is unfortunately too true that bank credits are now to a large extent supplying the place of money. That is our misfortune. Uncle Sam lends us his credit for nothing, also the use of money in business transactions costs nothing, but the use of bank credit is expensive.

This can best be illustrated by a comparative table made up from the Treasury reports and the balance sheets of banks.

In 1865 the total money in circulation, exclusive of coin, all issued by the U. S. Government, was $1,996,678,770. Under the refunding act of 1873 $1,230,999,085 was withdrawn and converted into bonds, leaving only $765,679,685 in circulation, or with $25,000,000 in coin in circulation on the Pacific coast, a total of $799,679,685. This severe contraction resulted in the panic of 1873. What effect this had on bank credits may be seen from the following exhibit from the books of national banks:

Private loans and discounts.	1865.	1872.
National banks	$ 487,170,000	$ 877,198,000
Loans to banks and brokers	107,372,000	128,181,000
Bank circulation	171,322,000	333,495,000
Bank capital paid in	393,157,000	679,929,000
Total	$1,159,021,000	$2,018,803,000
Total increase in national bank credits		$859,782,000

This does not include private and State banks, loan and trust companies, loans made by insurance companies and other loan agencies. As the private and State banks at this time were more numerous than national banks, it is reasonable to suppose that the increase in loans and discounts of the other institutions increased in the same ratio with those of the national banks.

In 1865 there was about $50 per capita of money in circulation. The people were practically out of debt and business was done largely on a cash basis, thereby making loans and discounts unnecessary.

When the currency was contracted perforce, commercial paper, on which banks profit, took the place of money. As a consequence the people kept getting deeper and deeper into debt, with an ever increasing toll to pay to the bankers and bondholders.

A continuation of this table to 1892, the year before the last panic, will show how enormously bank credit has increased, as shown in the enormous increase in loans and discounts.

```
Loans and discounts, national banks, 1892......$2,153,498,829
Private and State banks, 1892...................  2,209,130,392
                                                ───────────────
   Total...............................  ...........$4,362,629,221
```

The goldites say that this enormous increase may be accounted for in the increase in population and consequent business transactions. The following table, compiled from the above, will show that while population has not quite doubled bank credits have trebled:

	1865.	1872.	1892.
Population	35,000,000	40.000,000	65,000,000
Borrowed from national banks,			
per capita, round numbers...	$14	$22	$33
Other banks, trust comp'nies, etc	14	22	34
Total.....................	$28	$44	$67

To illustrate in another way how bank credits replace currency to the profit of the banks, we find, by consulting the statistics published by the United States Government, hat in 1893 the total deposits in banks on a certain day

were $4,848,862,680.   This amount exceeds the total
money in circulation by about $3,300,000,000.   Making a
fair allowance for money not in the banks at that date,
the amount of the deposits in excess of actual money
would amount to $4,000,000,000 in round numbers.

The balance is furnished by bank credit in this way:
Suppose A deposits $10,000 in real money, it is placed to
his credit on his bank book and he checks against it from
time to time.   The bank now has $10,000 in its vaults.
B wants to borrow $10,000.   He gives security for it,
agreeing to pay seven per cent interest.   The interest is
deducted in advance and $9,825 placed to his credit.   B
does not want the cash, but checks against the loan.   C
also wants to borrow $10,000, which is loaned in like
manner, also D is accommodated, so that A's $10,000 is
stretched by bank credit into $40,000, on which the
banker draws interest.   In this way $1,000,000,000
actual cash deposited is stretched to $4,848,862,680.

The $1,000,000,000 actual cash costs the people no in-
terest, while on the other $4,000,000,000 in round num-
bers they are compelled to pay $280,000,000 in interest
for the privilege of allowing the banks to supply the place
of money with bank credits.

As we have already shown by the above tables, with a
larger per capita circulation there is less need for bank
credits, and, with a smaller circulating medium, bank
credits must take the place of money.   Also by eliminat-
ing Treasury notes and supplying their place with bank
notes, with silver demonetized, the business of the country would have to be of necessity transacted entirely on
bank credit.   The motive, therefore, of the banks is apparent.   It is easy to see why they are ranged on the gold
side in this controversy.   The question is a grave one for
the producing classes, who have to carry all these burdens.

PROFITS IN BANKING.

The following extract from the testimony of G. G. Williams, president of the Chemical National Bank of New York, given before the Banking and Currency Committee of the House, December 14, 1894, shows from their own testimony the enormous profits there is in banking:

Mr. Williams, when questioned as to the condition of his own bank, said its capital was $300,000. It had a surplus of $6,000,000. The undivided profits were more than $1,000,000. The deposits reached $30,000,000. probably the largest in the United States. The dividends were 150 per cent annually. The bank stock sold for $4,300 per share of $100.

It would naturally be supposed that an institution paying 150 per cent annually and undivided profits on hand of over three times its capital stock ought to be satisfied. Yet much wants more. Like the horse leech's daughter, banks of the school of the Chemical National are continually crying, "Give! give!" Mr. Williams was before the committee to urge the funding of all paper money issued by the Government into three per cent bonds and the substitution therefor of national bank notes. He urged that "these notes should be funded $50,000,000 at a time until they were eliminated from the fiscal system. Bonds of three per cent should be received as security of national bank notes on a basis of par for the bonds, the Government to have a first lien on the assets of the bank. These notes should be redeemable in New York City, and when issued in sufficient volume, and being readily convertible, would furnish adequate elesticity to the currency. The tax on the circulation of national banks should at once be removed."

We find from the coinage laws of the United States, 1884 edition. page 462. that in 1891 the net profits of the banks in the United States were $75,763,514 on a capital of $760,108,201, or an average of about ten per cent for all banks, small and large. This does not include the fat salaries paid officials and the many other luxuries which go into the expense account.

We venture to say that productive industries for the same period, with proportionate salaries to those engaged in them, did not pay one per cent, whereas during the last few years they have been run at a loss.

This same table shows that during panic years the banks, on the average, make the most money. In 1873, for example, on a capital of $488,100,951 the profits were $65,048,578, or about fifteen per cent.

No wonder the bankers are a sleek, well-fed class of citizens, and on any subject that does not threaten their system they are patriotic, intelligent people. They cannot see why they should not loan the same money over and over again until they work the quantity in existence up to the quantity required. To have what money there is play through the banks like a shuttle-cock, weaving their fortunes, is a system they consider worth defending. The Shylocks of old loaned their own money; the Shylocks of to-day have a system by which they loan other people's money. They are defending that system and will bear watching.

They are organized. Page 1,026 of volume 7, part 2, Congressional Record of February 14, 1878, says: "The capital of the country is organized at last, and we shall see whether Congress will dare to fly in its face." This was read in the United States Congress from the files of the New York Tribune, the corporation which the honorable gentleman is with. What say you, the people? Will you dare?

IS IT SAFE?

The question arises, Is it safe to trust the banks with the power they are seeking, or even with what they already have? We have nothing to say against banks as

such.   In their proper field they are a very useful institution.   Like railroads and other public corporations they
are useful public servants, but when they take upon themselves the role of masters they become greedy and tyrannical in the extreme.   We need no better example of this
truth than that best of teachers, experience. This teacher
is the only safe guide.   Its text-book is an open one.   It
is the pages of history.   We are satisfied from reading its
text that before this or any other country can enjoy
complete and permanent prosperity the privileges which
the banks now enjoy must be curtailed.

Before the emancipation of the producing classes from
the bondage of money power can be completely accomplished, it will be necessary to devise and put into operation some plan to take from the bankers the control they
now exercise over the finances of the country, and also to
lessen interest charges to a living, minimum rate.

As long as the finances of the country are controlled by
the banks we shall have frequently recurring panics, with
periods of inflation and depression.   History repeats
itself.   The same causes are invariably followed by the
same effects.

The financial history of Great Britain and this country
is punctured through and through with disasters caused
by the failure of rotten banks, while periodical panics
have swept both countries, leaving trails of ruin and
misery behind them far more serious in effect than that
wrought by devastating armies.

England is the father of the present banking system.
Looking back over her financial history for 100 years and
the record is appalling.   In 1792 and 1793 no less than

three hundred out of three hundred and fifty banks in the United Kingdom suspended payment. It is true that was a trying period on account of the breaking out of the French Revolution, but it is the storm which tries the sea-worthiness of a vessel. A staunch vessel should weather the storm. So a sound financial system is that which will stand the test of adverse circumstances.

In this case the nation was saved from bankruptcy, and the wars against that great smasher of rotten institutions, Napoleon, conducted by the issue of what our goldbug friends would call "fiat" paper money.

This was followed by another severe panic in 1813-14, when 240 banks suspended. Other panics occurred in 1825, 1837, 1847, 1857 and 1866, each of which may be traced directly to the instability of banks, and of the financial system of which they are the integral part.

PANICS IN THE UNITED STATES.

To more fully illustrate this fact and make it plain, I will refer to the causes of some of the more important panics in this country, beginning with that of 1837. The roots of this panic are found in the United States Bank.

This institution was chartered by Act of Congress April 10, 1816, the charter extending for twenty years. Its capital stock was $35,000,000, the United States being one of the stockholders to the extent of seven millions.

It was made a bank of issue and was also the sole depository of United States funds. It was supposed, in fact, to act for the United States in the same capacity that the Bank of England does for England.

The Act delegating the powers of the United States Treasury to this bank was bitterly opposed by Jefferson and Madison, who claimed that the United States Government alone had the power to issue money. In 1832 the bank, whose power was now very great, applied for a re-

newal of its charter. The act granting it another twenty
years lease of life passed Congress, but was vetoed by President Jackson. The reasons for the veto were the same as
those given by Jefferson and Madison: the unconstitution-
ality of the act—delegating the powers of the Government to a private corporation. The bank then entered
politics, and as is usual with the money power, used
money freely in buying the influence of the press and cor-
rupting politicians to advocate its interests. Three million
dollars was spent in this way. Jackson proved the greater
tactician, however. Noting the corrupt use which was
being made of the public funds, he had the treasury deposits, to the amount of $40,000,000 in specie, withdrawn
from the bank. This act destroyed its power and eventually proved its ruin.

After the United States Bank ceased to exist, some 800,
more or less, banks of issue sprang into existence in the different states. On June 23, 1836, Congress made a mistake
in ordering that the funds of the United States should be
divided among these banks, they, on their part, agreeing
to perform for the Treasury all that the United States
Bank had done. These banks which received the treasury
funds obligated themselves to repay the same at any time
in coin.

These banks also issued a large amount of bank notes
also supposed to be redeemable in coin. There was no
check to this issue, so that the country was flooded with
this wildcat paper called money, but possessing no legal
tender functions.

In 1837, a political change took place, Martin Van
Buren having been elected President. No sooner had he
taken his chair than, as one of his first acts, he called in
all the treasury deposits in the custody of the banks
which were to be paid in coin.

The famous specie circular was also issued, which stated

that coin only would henceforth be received in payment
for public lands.

This discrediting of the banks by the Administration
alarmed the public and caused a run on the banks to exchange notes or credits for specie. Instead of getting
down to a specie basis by the slow, tortuous process put
into operation at the instigation of the banks and bondholders by Secretary McCulloch in 1865, resulting in the
panic of 1873, by this act of the Administration and the
raid on the banks, the nation was reduced to a specie
basis at one fell jump.

May 10, the New York banks suspended and all others
immediately followed. Over 250 business failures occurred
in two months, and 20,000 people were thrown out of employment in three weeks time. The population was comparatively small at that time and the country in its in-
fancy so that, in comparison with the great panic of 1893
followed by some 3,000,000 out of employment, this may
seem insignificant, but it was a terrible calamity for the
time. Tens of thousands were hopelessly ruined financially and misery and poverty in the midst of plenty
prevailed.

The Government lost all its available funds in this
crash, and as all bank issues were discredited and there
was not specie enough to transact the business of the
country, recourse was had to that patient burden-bearer,
the treasury note, to rescue the financial ship of state from
its awkward predicament.

No sooner had it performed its good offices, however,
than, as has ever been the case, it was attacked and discredited by the banks and its withdrawal and cancellation insisted upon.

PANICS OF 1847 AND 1857.

In 1847 another panic occurred, a result of the same
cause, rotten banks, a scramble on the part of the people

to get their bank notes and credits into specie, followed
by a withdrawal of all credits, resulting in inability to
pay debts and consequent general disaster.

In 1856 the Government again found it necessary to discredit banks. By act of Congress the Government was
divorced from all banks and all bank notes were excluded
from the treasury. The receipts of customs and other
treasury receipts were confined to gold, silver and treasury
notes.

This act had been preceded in 1853 by an act depriving
fractional silver coins of their legal tender and was followed
by the act of February 21, 1857, demonetizing foreign
coins which hitherto had been legal tender in this country. These coins and fractional currency had been largely held by banks as redemption money, but being deprived
of their legal tender they could no longer be used for this
purpose.

These successive acts tended to weaken the confidence
in the banks, so the raid began and the large amount of
paper money issued by the banks became worthless.
Again ruin and poverty stalked abroad in the midst of
plenty. As a further example of the rottenness of the system then in vogue, a system which the banks through the
Baltimore plan and Carlisle-Springer plan, or some other
similar system, are trying to again foist upon the country, I will say that out of 1,409 banks of issue at that time,
there were only 463 whose notes were not counterfeited.

There were also 1,462 imitations, 1,119 alterations and
224 spurious, that is, 224 species of notes in circulation
without any bank at all behind them.

PANIC OF 1860.

In 1860, on account of the beginning of the war, gold and
silver quickly disappeared from circulation, proving a very
poor staff to lean upon in the hour of the country's greatest need. The banks proved rotten also and their notes

worthless.   When called upon to redeem them they had
nothing to redeem with, or refused to give up what they
had.   Out of 1,500 banks of issue at the beginning of the
war the notes of only 253 were uncounterfeited while there
were out 1,861 bogus imitations, 3,039 alterations and
1,685 spurious.

What a record!   What a farce! Imagine the insecurity,
uncertainty, and losses, the latter mostly falling upon
the poorer classes, and yet there are alleged statesmen
to-day clamoring for a restoration of this wretched system or one akin to it wherein the banks shall again have
full control of the issue of paper money.   The following
table shows the

FLUCTUATIONS OF THE VOLUME OF BANK CURRENCY AND UNITED STATES
NOTES FROM 1836 TO 1873.

Bank currency in 1836	$ 141,000,000
Contraction in five years	83,000,000
Bank currency in 1843	58,000,000
Bank currency in 1854	204,000,000
Contraction 1854 to 1858	49,000,000
Bank currency in 1858	155,000,000
Bank currency in 1860	207,000,000
Contraction 1860 to 1862	23,000,000
Bank currency 1862	184,000,000
Bank currency 1863	202,000,000
Total currency exclusive of coin, 1865	1,996,678,770
Contraction to 1873	1,230,999,085
Money in circulation 1873, exclusive of coin	765,679,685
Coin in circulation 1873	25,000,000
Total circulation 1873	790,679,685

The currency thus withdrawn from circulation by the refunding
act of 1866 was placed into bonds bearing six per cent interest.

This table will serve as an excellent object-lesson in the
study of the cause of panics.

THE TREASURY NOTE AGAIN.

Again the patient cureall of panics and restorer of
prosperity, the bank-abused treasury note, was trotted
out.   The banks clung to the hoarded gold in their vaults
and refused Lincoln's appeals for aid to save the life of
the nation.   Disheartened at the greed and unpatriotic
conduct of the banks that greatest of statesmen turned

to the people.   His greenbacks were received by the people with open arms and every manifestation of joy.

I remember well, although but a small boy at the time, the relief that was felt when these treasury notes first came into circulation.   When my father brought home the first batch received in exchange for farm products, they were examined with great interest.   "Now," he said to my mother, "we have got some money we can depend upon."

Lincoln's greenbacks carried to a successful conclusion the greatest and most expensive war in history, and left the nation, especially the producing classes, in a condition of the greatest prosperity they have ever attained.   In 1865 the producing classes were practically out of debt. This was brought about by a financial system conducted largely independent of and in defiance of the banks.

Every step of this financial independence was sharply contested by the banks.   No stone was left unturned then, or since, to get or resume their former control of the finances of the country.   Through their influence in Congress the wings of the greenbacks were clipped by the mutilation of its legal tender.   Had it not been for this act the greenbacks would have remained throughout the war on a par with gold.   Everything in the power of the banks was done to discredit the greenback, and the warfare still continues.   In the vain hope of pacifying them another point was conceded.

They were given the needless right to issue national bank notes, a concession which has yielded the banks many millions of profit and placed a great power in their hands, a power which they have not hesitated to use to the disadvantage of the producing classes of the nation.

After Lincoln's death and the close of the war, during the sway of their willing tool, Secretary McCulloch, at the instigation of the banks and bondholders, the iniquitous refunding act was passed. This severe contraction of the currency, shown in the above table, resulted in the panic of 1873.

These repeated disasters, directly traceable either to the insecurity or influence of the banks, prove conclusively that the power to control the finances of the country must be taken out of the hands of individuals or corporations.

THE PANIC OF 1893,

From the dire effects of which we are still suffering and will continue to suffer until the great underlying cause, the contraction of primary money to a gold basis, is removed, is still another forcible example of the imperative necessity for a change.

How and through what influence this great industrial depression was brought about has been fully explained in other parts of this book, so that it is not necessary to repeat it here.

The Hazard circular; the declaration of the intention of the New York banks to curtail credits in the West and South to compel the people of the West and South to stop the agitation of the silver question, made just before the panic; the Cleveland "object-lesson," the panic and subsequent depression, together with the subsequent great effort on the part of the banks to strengthen their power by the destruction of the greenback and silver certificates and the substitution therefor of bank notes—all go to show the danger of allowing greedy corporations to control the finances of the country.

Whatever agency controls the finances of the country controls the country and has it in its power to practically enslave the people. This being the case no further argument is needed to prove the necessity that the people as a whole should control their own finances, and especially make and issue their own money and regulate its quantity.

Experience teaches that this reliance on one-fourth currency and three-fourths wind, alias bank credit, is a poor reliance. It is enormously expensive in fair weather, but when the storm comes the whole fabric quickly collapses.

WHAT OF THE REMEDY?

The first step to curb the power of the banks and bondholders must of necessity be the restoration of bimetallism. Then, as outlined in another part of this book, let the Government issue a paper treasury note for every coined dollar and let both go into circulation, reserving twenty-five per cent of the coin in the treasury vaults for an emergency fund. This would lighten the burden of this enormous load of debt very materially and bring a great measure of prosperity to the producing classes.

TO PREVENT PANICS,

further curb the power of banks and give stability to our finances, it will be necessary for the people themselves through their Government to enter into competition with the banks. This can best be done by establishing postal savings banks at every money order office on the plan outlined below or some equally good one.

Panics are caused by the fear of the insecurity of banks. The depositors from some cause become alarmed and raid the bank for the money. In a general panic there is a general raid on all the banks.

One of two things then happens, either the bank fails and the depositors are large losers, or the depositor gets his money, withdraws it from circulation and hides it away for safe keeping. During the late panic the enormous sum of $500,000,000 was thus taken out of circulation and hid away in safety vaults during a very brief period of time.

This enormous and sudden contraction of the currency could have but one result. The banks dare not if they could, extend credit to their customers, while the business world, unable to get money from the usual sources, or, in fact, from any source, was unable to pay its debts, and must, in many cases, go into bankruptcy, while the wheels of industry were either clogged or entirely at a standstill.

In the case of Government banks, the absolute security which the Government offers would allay this fear. There would be no run on Government banks. But in case of a run on a private bank in all probability the funds withdrawn, instead of being hid away would be deposited in the Government banks and through this agency would again go into circulation and the public disaster due to sudden contraction be averted.

THE REGULATION OF INTEREST CHARGES

would also be accomplished in the same way. through competition. In fact, this is the only way.

It is next to useless to pass usury laws. The sharp money-lenders always find ways to avoid them, while the necessities of the borrower compel him to accept any terms offered.

An example which will serve as an illustration was recently brought to my attention. A friend of mine who owned a 200 acre farm, worth about fifty dollars an acre, had the misfortune to lose his crops, and consequently was compelled to borrow money to live. To a Mr. Isaacs he went and offered his farm as security for the loan of $500 for one year. "Certainly, I vil let you hafe it," said the money-lender. "You vil gif me your note for $500 at ten per cent. I vil scharge you fifty dollar commishuns vich I vil take oud."

He went to Mr. Abrahams and to Mr. Jacobs, but could make no better terms, so he had to be content to take

$450, give his note for $500 and pay interest on that amount. Doubtless many readers of this book are cognizant of similar cases.

On the loan plan outlined below the competition which would be therein established would effectually fix the interest rate as no law could. If this plan had been in operation my friend would not have been compelled to patronize the fleecing sharps like Mr Isaacs, but unless Mr. Isaacs would make equally good terms he would get the money at the postal savings bank at three per cent with no commission. He would also have the satisfaction of knowing that instead of contributing his interest money to the support of some idle money-lender to, in all probability, be squandered in Europe, he was helping some other thrifty producer to get a home or farm.

Thus competition would surely lessen the rate of interest on all farm and home mortgages to three per cent, while the interest on all other forms of loans and indebtedness would be lowered in sympathy.

I submit this plan to the public, especially to the producing and mercantile classes, feeling sure it will meet with hearty approval.

POSTAL SAVINGS BANKS AND LOAN PLAN

SECTION 1. That each postal money order office shall, in connection with its other duties, be constituted a postal savings bank, to receive savings deposits and repay the same to the depositors or their heirs or legal representatives, and to loan the same with such additional amounts as may be required on approved real estate security.

SEC. 2. That bonds of the denomination of $5, $10, $15, $25, $50 and $100, to be known as postal savings bonds, bearing interest at the rate of two per cent per annum, shall be prepared and put on sale at said postal savings banks under the direction of the Secretary of the Treasury; said interest to be payable semi-annually at the office where the bonds are registered, beginning with the first day of the calendar month immediately following the date of sale. All interest payments as made from time to time, together with the date of sale, shall be endorsed in blank spaces provided for this purpose on the back of said bonds. Said bonds shall be non-transferable.

SEC. 3. On application of the owner of the postal savings bond or his lawful heirs at the office where the bond is registered, the postmaster shall redeem the same with such interest as shall be due thereon, in lawful money of the United States, or in a postoffice money order, or postal savings draft as hereinafter provided, at the option of the owner, provided that no interest shall be paid for a period of less than thirty days, and further provided that should the postmaster be short of ready money when the bonds are presented for payment, he may require ten days' notice. Before redeeming a bond the postmaster shall require the owner to endorse the same in his presence and shall compare the signature with the one in the book of record. If the signatures correspond payment shall be made. When a bond has been paid the postmaster shall cancel the same with a cancellation stamp bearing the date of payment, provided for this purpose, and shall carefully preserve the same as a voucher, until turned over to an inspector appointed by the Secretary of Treasury who shall receive and receipt for the same.

SEC. 4. That each postal savings bank shall be provided with a suitable blank book in which it shall be the duty of the postmaster to register each postal savings bond sold at his office with the number, date of sale, and amount thereof, and the signature and address of the purchaser, also the amount of interest paid thereon from time to time; and when the bond is redeemed the date of such payment, also the date of the filing of the cancelled bond with the inspector, and his signature which shall be his receipt therefor.

SEC. 5. That for convenience in transmitting credits from one postal savings bank to another or for transferring credits from one individual to another, each postal savings bank shall be provided with postal savings drafts prepared under the direction of the Secretary of the Treasury. On the application of the owner and surrender of his postal savings bond or bonds, as provided in section 3, he may, at his option, receive in exchange therefor, either in full or in part, either a postoffice money order, on payment of the required fee, or a postal savings bank draft. The said draft to be transferable on endorsement—and payable after the proper identification of the person presenting the same at any postal savings bank. The fee for said draft, which the postmaster shall collect, shall be one cent for each twenty-five dollars or fraction thereof.

SEC. 6. That accumulations of postal savings moneys in excess of the ordinary daily requirements, together with a full detailed report of the transactions of this department of his office for the time prescribed, shall be forwarded by the post-

master at stated intervals, not less frequently than once a
month, to such central offices or Subtreasuries as may be
designated by the Secretary of the Treasury as depositories
of postal savings funds. That the inspectors of the Postoffice
Department, acting jointly with the Treasury Department,
shall inspect the funds and accounts of the postmaster at
each postal savings bank, and make a report thereon with
vouchers to the officers authorized to receive the same at said
depositories, not less frequently than once a month. And the
officer of the Treasury at such depositories shall, at certain
periods, not less frequent than once a month, make detailed
reports to the Secretary of the Treasury of all moneys received and disbursed by him for the preceding period, together with a summary of the transactions of the various
postal savings banks in his district.

SEC. 7. A good and sufficient bond shall be required of
each postmaster or other officer or agent of the Government,
handling postal savings funds, which shall be sufficient in
amount to protect the Government against loss through the
dishonesty or carelessness of the said postmasters, officers or
agents.

SEC. 8. That it shall be the duty of the Secretary of the
Treasury to loan to individual applicants, upon approved real
estate security and under such rules and regulations as he
may prescribe, such postal savings funds and other moneys
as hereinafter provided for.

SEC. 9. That any person who is a citizen of the United
States and who is the owner of unincumbered real estate to
the value of $500 or more, may file an application for a loan
with the postmaster at the postal savings bank nearest to said
property. Such application must describe the land and state
its cash value and the nature and value of the improvements,
if any, thereon; also its assessed valuation for taxation purposes for five years previous to the application; the amount of
the loan sought, which must not exceed half the average assessed valuation of the property, the object for which the
loan is sought, the time it is to run, which must not exceed
ten years, how it is to be repaid, whether in monthly or
yearly installments, and such other matters as the Secretary
may by regulations prescribe. No loans shall be made to
the same person of less than $250, or exceeding in the aggre-
gate $3,000, and no loans shall be made to corporations or
business firms.

SEC. 10. That upon the filing of such application with the
postmaster the applicant shall deposit the sum of ten dollars
to pay the costs of examining the title to the land, inspection
and appraisement thereof and the notary's and recorder's fees.

SEC. 11. That the Secretary of the Treasury shall appoint
in each county or district to be marked out by him, a person

who shall be known as United States Examiner of Titles, who, in conjunction with the postmaster with whom the application for a loan is filed, shall examine the title, inspect and appraise the property offered as security for the loan, and if in their judgment the title to the property is not perfect in the applicant or is not, at a fair cash valuation, worth double the amount of the loan sought, they shall so notify the applicant and, if he cannot remove the objections, shall reject the application. But if the postmaster and Examiner of Titles are satisfied that the title is perfect in the applicant and the property at a fair cash valuation is worth at least double the amount of the loan sought, they shall forward the application with their report to the officer of the Treasury designated by him for this purpose, who, after having reviewed and examined the application and report, if he is likewise satisfied, shall notify the applicant through the postmaster that his application is granted and shall instruct the postmaster to pay the amount to the applicant on delivery of the securities properly executed and as hereinafter provided.

SEC. 12. That the applicant for a loan, on receipt of a notice that his loan is granted, shall execute, sign and acknowledge according to the State in which he resides a trust deed to the United States for the property offered as security for the loan, also notes representing the full amount of the loan in equal monthly or yearly payments as the applicant may desire, with interest at three per centum per annum. It shall be the right of the maker thereof to pay his notes at any time before maturity if he so desires.

SEC. 13. That if upon the land described in the application there is an existing lien or incumbrance to secure the payment of money presently due and payable, and in an amount less than the loan sought and granted, then the land shall be deemed unincumbered, but instead of paying the amount loaned to the applicant it shall be the duty of the Postmaster, out of the sum loaned, to pay off the amount due, and to cause to be discharged the lien or incumbrance, deducting the amount of such payment from the amount due the applicant.

SEC. 14. That if the person applying for a loan wants it for the purpose of making a permanent improvement on his land he shall so state in his application, describing the improvement it is his intention to make thereon with an estimate of the cost thereof, which shall be considered a part of the realty and the loan granted accordingly, except that the money shall be paid the applicant only as the work of building progresses, and it shall be the duty of the postmaster, before making final payments, to ascertain that the building is as described in the estimate, and that the contractors and workmen are paid in full for material furnished and work done on such building, so that there shall be no mechanics' liens or other liabilities unsettled which would be an incumbrance on the property.

SEC. 15. That it shall be the duty of the postmaster to see that the property is insured in reliable companies in a sufficient sum to protect the interests of the United States against loss by fire, and the expense of such insurance shall be charged to the person making the loan.

SEC. 16. In case of non-payment of principal or interest or both as agreed and specified in the bond, the Secretary of the Treasury or the officer of the treasury designated by him for this purpose shall at his option take possession of the property in the name of the United States and sell the same at public auction, provided no bid shall be accepted of less amount than the amount of the loan and accrued interest, and after deducting the amount due on the loan with interest and expenses of the sale shall pay the balance if any to the person making the loan.

SEC. 17. That should the postal savings moneys be inadequate to supply the demand for loans provided for in this act, the treasurer of the United States is hereby authorized to supply such deficiency by causing to be printed, signed, and ready for use. circulating notes of the United States to be known as postal savings bank notes of the denomination of one dollar, two dollars, five dollars, ten dollars, twenty dollars, fifty dollars, one hundred dollars, five hundred dollars, and one thousand dollars, in amounts from time to time as shall be necessary to meet the requirements of this act, and said notes shall be legal tender in payment of public or private debts equally with gold and silver coins for like amounts. The security or basis of issue for said notes shall be the trust deeds and notes taken as security for loans.

SEC. 18. That the postmaster of a postal savings bank shall be an intelligent person qualified to fill the responsible position and shall be appointed only after careful examination by qualified persons appointed for this purpose by the President, by and with the consent of the Senate of the United States, and shall hold his office permanently, unless disqualified by age, disability, or misconduct.

SEC. 19. That the provisions of the several statutes relating to the larceny, embezzlement, or misappropriation of the postal funds, money order funds, postage stamps, stamped envelopes or postal cards, and to the forging or counterfeiting of postage stamps, and stamps printed upon stamped envelopes, or postal cards, bonds or notes of the United States, or the dies, plates, or engravings used in the manufacture of the same, be and they are hereby extended, including the punishment prescribed therefor, and made applicable to the commission of similar crimes in connection with the postal savings bank system hereby established.

SEC. 20. That it is hereby made the duty of the Postmaster-General and Secretary of the Treasury to designate such officers and subdivisions of their respective departments to take charge of all business in connection with postal savings funds as may be necessary, and are hereby authorized and directed to promulgate rules and regulations, not inconsistent with law, and provide all necessary blanks for carrying out the purposes of this act, and for conducting the business to which it relates.

SEC. 21. That the rule of the common law, that statutes in derogation thereof are to be strictly construed, shall have no application to this act. This act establishes the law respecting the subject to which it relates, and its provisions and all proceedings under it are to be liberally construed with a view to effect its object.

SEC. 22. That this act shall be in force from three months after its date.

I will say in this connection that the United States alone of all the leading nations, with one exception, has not adopted the postal savings bank system. In all countries where it is in use it has proved a great success. Frequent efforts have been made to establish the system in this country, but they have been invariably defeated through the influence of the bank lobby. The latest was the bill introduced in Congress by Postmaster General Wanamaker during the last administration. The difficulty hitherto has been how to dispose of the funds. I think the plan proposed will meet the approval of all classes except the bankers and money lenders.

The plan is suggested by the plan of the numerous building and loan associations which have proved a great although an expensive blessing to the thrifty.

This plan would give the thrifty a safe place of deposit for their money, and when enough had accumulated to buy a lot would assist him in securing a home at the nominal rate of three per cent on the money borrowed. If Shylock's finger can be kept off the pie this plan can be successfully carried out. It would also relieve one-half of the farmers of the United States from Shylock's grasp by enabling the one-third who have mortgages on their farms to refund them, while the numerous and ever increasing army of renters would be assisted to get farms of their own. In fact, it would be a vast co-operative system, or a building and loan plan on a national scale with the nation itself for its sponsor, under which the productive and working classes would help each other without contributing the products of their labor to the maintenance of an army of parasites.

PART TWO.

CHAPTER VI.

A GREAT CRIME.

HOW IT WAS ACCOMPLISHED.

In the foregoing lectures, which for the purposes of this book have been enlarged upon, we trust we have made it clear to the reader what ails the country and how it was brought into its present deplorable condition.

We have charged that it is directly due to a conspiracy on the part of the security and fund holders of the world to increase the purchasing power of their species of wealth at the expense of the producers. I am aware that such charges are easily made. and further that they ought not to be made without evidence of the most certain character. I am no more in sympathy with those who are over ready to attribute evil motives and cry fraud when no evidence of fraud exists than I am with those who call every one who differs with them or has progressive ideas which takes him out of the habitual ruts, cranks, lunatics or jackasses. Both show lack of honesty and intelligence.

At the same time I have no sympathy with those who whitewash corruption for fear it will hurt the party. When it does exist it should be exposed and punished even though it strikes the highest in the land.

Crime is rarely ever committed without a motive. In trying a supposed malefactor for an alleged crime it devolves upon the prosecution to show a motive. Witnesses are produced for this purpose. If a motive can be shown the prosecution has accomplished a large part of its work.

In charging this, the greatest crime of the age, upon the

moneyed class it devolves upon us to show a motive.   This
can be easily done, as the motive is plainly apparent.

The security-holders and money-owners of the world
wanted less money in the world, so that under the natural
law of supply and demand, or the rule of political economy,
which is another way of stating it, "A scarcity of money
makes cheap products," their own special kind of
property (money and securities) would command more than
its honest value in everything else.   They wanted one
metal, and that the scarcer of the two, as the only standard
money.   They wanted scarce and dear gold for the principal
and interest on their investments.   They wanted more of
the products of the labor of the producers for the principal
and interest on their investments.

Such is the motive which inspired the deed.   We have
but to look back over the pages of the history of man's
dealings with his kind to dispel the thought that no set
of men would be mean enough to be led by such motives.
It is the same motive which inspired the slaveholders of
the South, and is the same motive of greed which has
ever pervaded the financial world.

Let us give a notable example which will show both the
advantage a scarcity of money is to the security-holder
and how the Rothschilds, who are the principal security-holders of the world, profited immensely by the resumption of specie payments and the reduction of the
volume of money in the United States.

The year 1865 is noted as the most prosperous year for
the producers of this country.   In spite of the fact that
the country was just emerging from one of the greatest
wars of history, it had never seen greater prosperity.
Money was plentiful, work abundant.   There was a plentiful demand for products of both the farm and factory at
good prices.   The returning soldiers from the great dis-
banding armies readily found places where they could

again take up the duties of civil life where they had been dropped at the nation's call. Tramps in those days were unknown or unheard of.

The reason for this great prosperity is accounted for in the large volume of money in circulation as shown in the following table from the books of the Treasury department September 1, 1865, showing the currency in circulation at that date :

United States notes (greenbacks).....................	$433,160,569
Fractional currency...................................	26,344,742
National Bank notes..................................	185,000,000
Compound interest legal tender notes	217,024,160
Treasury five per cent legal tenders................	32,536,991
Temporary loan certificates..........................	107,148,713
Certificates of indebtedness.........................	85,093,000
Treasury notes, past due legal tenders, not presented...	1,503,020
State Bank notes.....................................	78,867,575
Three-year Treasury notes...........................	830,000,000
Total.....................................	$1,096,678,770

This, it will be noticed, is exclusive of coin, of which there was but little in circulation at that time. The business of the country was transacted wholly on a paper money basis.

As the population at that time did not exceed 35,000,-000 this would give a circulation of over $50 per capita. It must also be taken into consideration that but a small part of the currency at that time had penetrated the South. The bulk of it was, therefore, in circulation in the Northern States.

As a consequence of this abundant prosperity which was the direct result of plenty of money, business was done on a cash basis, and as Hugh McCulloch, the then Secretary of the Treasury, said, the people were individually out of debt.

At this time, while Hugh McCulloch was Secretary of the Treasury, Baron James Rothschild and an English syndicate of which he was the head owned United States bonds known as "five twenties" to the extent of $420,-

000,000, which had been bought at about forty-two per cent on the dollar as measured by gold. These bonds were payable in greenbacks. There was at that time no question about this. Even John Sherman himself together with every member of Congress so admitted.

On this subject Sherman in a letter dated November 30, 1868, to Dan Voorhees used these words:

I think the bondholder violates his promise when he refuses to take the same kind of money he paid for his bonds. * * * He is a repudiator and an extortioner to demand money more valuable than he gave.

For some inscrutable reason, which I leave it to the reader to surmise, in less than two months after this letter, Senator Sherman became an ardent advocate of coin redemption. Senator Voorhees, in commenting upon this sudden change of front, said:

John Sherman, then a Senator, advocated and procured the passage of the act of March, 1869, for the payment of the bonds in coin, which he had declared payable in currency, thereby establishing the open repudiation of a solemn and binding contract, and fastening an extortion of not less than five hundred millions of dollars on the staggering industries of the country as the speculative profits of the operation. In t e whole financial history of the civilized world no parallel can be found to this audacious deed of broken faith, deliberate treachery to the people, and national dishonesty. * * * It will bear the names of those who enacted it to distant generations amidst the groans, the curses and the lamentations of those who toil on the land and on the sea; and, more deeply engraved than any other name, will be found that of the Secretary of the Treasury [John Sherman] as the author of what he himself said constituted the twofold crime of repudiation and extortion.

John Sherman is not, however, the only "high authority" intrusted with honored office in the gift of the people who made a sudden "flop" in line with the interests and policy of the great London syndicate.

Hugh McCulloch, whom Lincoln elevated to the position of Secretary of the Treasury, is perhaps an even greater example of "perfidy and dishonor."

Of this noted Secretary, Gordon Clark says in "Shylock:"

In the distress of a heavily laden, trustful soul, our martyred Lincoln turned to McCulloch. Though of no public significance, there was one thing in favor of the Indiana banker: he had been far from Wall street, while yet he might oe supposed to know its ways, and how to cope with its chicanery.

McCulloch entered the President's Cabinet. But the pistol of an assassin soon took away from us our protector and friend, Abraham Lincoln. Then the man, McCulloch, disciosed himself. As Wilkes Booth murdered our beloved President, who was all fidelity to the masses, so Hugh McCulloch betrayed that fidelity, and wrung from his master's dead hand the blessings it held in store. The Western banker, brought East for a shield against the gold-thugs, handed himself over to the only foes of his country left within its borders, and became their cat's-paw of pillage and their besom of destruction.

Of him the Hon. Wm. D. Kelley, of Pennsylvania, said:

Hugh McCulloch hamstrung the whole nation. I affirm that his management of the finances, while it enriched him and made him a great London banker, has cost the American people more than the war did.

It is easy to follow the trail of the serpent. As Benedict Arnold yielded to the seductive influence of English gold, so this perfidious traitor to his country and humanity sold the influence of his high office to enrich himself, and then became the willing tool of the bondholders, and at the end of his term deserted his country and became a London banker.

Of Mr. McCulloch Henry C. Carey, that noble patriot, said in 1875:

At the close of the war Mr. McCulloch was seated in the Treasury chair by Mr. Lincoln, in the full belief that he was a decided protectionist and as decided an opponent of contraction. That he was so in May, a few weeks later, I know from personal intercourse with him. Nevertheless, but three months later—and without the slightest explanation of the cause of the change—he presented himself in correspondence with his agent, then in England, in a totally different character. That change was to be followed in October by his Fort Wayne decree as discreditable a paper, in my belief, as was ever issued from the Treasury of any civilized country

whatever. By it all who were so unfortunate as to be in debt
were cautioned that they must sell off and pay their debts;
all who could command the use of money being simultaneously cautioned not to purchase, the prices of labor, materials,
houses and lands being all too high, and it being the deter
mination of the Treasury to bring them down to "hardpan,"
thus restoring to us the admirable system which had existed
before the war, when each successive British crisis brought
ruin to half the households of the country, and so effectively
prevented the growth of public confidence that the prices paid
as interest ranged between six and 200 per cent when not so
high as 500 per cent.

Shortly, therefore, the controller of the currency made a
report by which it was clearly shown that the total amount
of bank-notes, greenbacks and interest-bearing legal tenders
in actual use, as money, among our people, was but $160,000,-
000, being but $80,000,000 more than the notes of and under
$20, now in use among the people of France; and less by above
$100,000,000 than the total notes in use among a people who,
more than almost any other, had been accustomed to regard
the precious metals as the only description of money on
which they could place reliance. Add to the notes the metallic money in actual use in the country, and it will be found
that the currency in actual use exceeds by fully fifty per
cent that which then here existed, whose extraordinary
abundance was denounced by a gentleman who, a few months
before, had accepted office as an anti-contractionist. * * *
The Treasury was converted into a great manufactory of
bonds for exportation; and to the end that a foreign market
might be created, Congress was repeatedly urged to put the
country on a par with Spain, Turkey, Egypt and other semi
civilized countries, by providing that the interest should be
made payable on the London Exchange; these extraordinary
and expensive operations being intended, as we were assured,
as a means of reaching that early resumption of specie pay
ments, with its attendant advantages to the already rich,
which Secretary McCulloch had so utterly revolted, through
out the first weeks of his administration.

Of this willing tool of the English syndicate Berkey says:

McCulloch not only entered into the designs of the money
power, but became its most subservient tool, and retired with
the reputation of being the first Secretary of the Treasury
who had ever prostituted his high office for the purpose of
enriching himself and his associates.

Indeed, the record of the acts of this man and the other
willing tools in Congress and the Senate, when traced in

their dire effects upon the country, are distressing and maddening pictures. From 1865 to 1873 is indeed a dark page in American history.

In October, 1865, McCulloch issued his famous Fort Wayne decree, announcing his intention to contract the currency. At that time, as shown above, there was upwards of $50 per capita in circulation. The contraction act was passed April 12, 1866. By July, 1868, $70,000,000 of greenbacks had been retired.

By June 3, 1875, only $195,800 of the $830,000,000 of three-year treasury notes were left outstanding.

The compound interest legal tenders to the amount of $217,024,160 had also been retired, also the treasury five per cent legal tenders, temporary loan certificates, certificates of indebtedness. These legal tenders and various evidences of indebtedness had circulated as money. By the contraction act which was inspired by the Secretary they were converted into six per cent bonds which were sold in Europe considerably below par. The Secretary would have continued the investment of the whole of the greenbacks in six per cent bonds had not Congress, owing to the solicitation of the people, called a halt and compelled him to desist. These contraction and refunding acts are a disgrace to both the Secretary who imposed them and the Congress by which they were enacted.

Under this act about $1,300,000,000 of actual currency was taken out of circulation and turned into six per cent bonds. According to the books of the Treasury department the money in circulation exclusive of coin, of which there was but little December 1, 1873, stood as follows:

U. S. notes (greenbacks)	$367,001,685
Fractional currency	48,000,000
Certificates of indebtedness	678,000
National Bank currency	350,000,000
Total	$765,679,685

As shown above, the amount in circulation in the

Northern States alone on September 1, 1865, before the
policy of contraction began, was $1,996,678,770, a total
deduction of $1,230,999,085, with an increased population,
including the restored Southern States, of nearly 20,000-
000. Is it any wonder there was a panic in 1873? The
security-holders and their willing organs have taught the
people to believe that panic was due to an inflated currency.
The facts show that it is due to the same cause as every
other period of financial distress and convulsion—to a
contracted and insufficient currency.

After this severe contraction of the paper currency
came, a few years later, the resumption of specie payments. By these several steps the bonds which were
clearly understood to be redeemable in greenbacks were
made payable in gold. The profits to the Rothschild syndicate who owned about $500,000,000 of the bonds may be
summarized as follows:

Amount of bonds...	$500,000,000
Coin-interest, semi-annually, for ten years.............	403,096,133
	$903,096,133
Bondholders' cost, at 42 cents on the dollar..............	210,000,000
Profit in ten years....................................	$693,096,133

Other bond and security holders also, whose holdings
bought on a greenback basis were now raised to a coin
basis, profited in like proportion.

Here is a sufficient motive for the conspiracy. The effects are also apparent in the severe contraction of the
currency and the panic of 1873, and in the subsequent
hard times. As there is no effect without a cause, by
tracing back the effect we shall find the cause and the
motive which inspired the acts.

It is well known that the Rothschilds have repeatedly
by indirection taken a hand in American politics. The
change of front of Hugh McCulloch, the dirty work which
he accomplished, his sudden acquisition of riches while in

office, his sudden departure from the country to establish
a bank in London, shows the work of the unseen hand
guided by the English bondholders.

The confidential agent of the Rothschilds was August
Belmont. (His firm, August Belmont & Co., of
New York, is still their American agent.) While
chairman of the Democratic committee he was instructed by his employer, Baron James Rothschild, as
early as March 13, 1868, that unless the Democratic party
declared for paying the 5-20 bonds in gold IT MUST BE DE-
FEATED. But Belmont and his satellities were unable to
control the convention. Instead of obeying the behests of
the Baron it declared the bonds were "payable in the lawful money of the United States." The Baron, however, got
back on the party. His agent, August Belmont, owned
the controlling interest in the New York World, the then
leading organ of Democracy. In a double-headed editorial
in its issue of October 15, 1868, it denounced the Democratic nominee, Horatio Seymour, as unavailable and un-
fit for President of the United States and advised his
withdrawal. The platform on which Seymour ran called
for quick payment of the debt and in greenbacks when
coin was not stipulated in the bond; taxation of Government bonds; one currency for the people, the bondholder, officeholder, etc. Such a platform did not please
the foreign bondholders, so Belmont was instructed to
use the "World" and Manton Marble, its publisher, to
play Benedict Arnold just on the eve of election to defeat
Seymour.

It is noticeable that Manton Marble, who hitherto had
been in continual financial difficulty, suddenly acquired a
brown stone mansion on Fifth avenue and all that implies.
He has since removed to Paris, where he still resides.

Up to this time Sherman and other leading Republican
Senators had opposed coin payment of bonds. But the

unseen hand got in its work and Sherman and some others changed the color of their coats.

That great commoner, Thaddeus Stevens, whose voice was ever with the people, scented the unseen hand. In a speech in the Senate he said:

I have a melancholy foreboding that we are about to consummate a cunningly devised scheme which will carry great injury and great loss to all classes of people throughout the Union.

Again on his deathbed he said (he died before the panic of 1873):

When a few years hence the people shall have been brought to general bankruptcy I shall have the satisfaction of knowing that I attempted to prevent it.

Again in another speech this far-sighted, honest statesman said:

If I knew that any party in this country would go for paying in coin that which is payable in money, thus enhancing it one-half—if I knew there was such a platform and such a determination on the part of any party, I would vote on the other side. I would vote for no such swindle upon the taxpayers of this country. I would vote for no such speculation in favor of the large bondholders—the millionaires who took advantage of our folly in granting them coin payment of interest.

Lincoln himself had forebodings of evil similar to those expressed by Mr. Stevens.

In the light of developments since his death, the foresight of this great man seems wonderful. See Barrett's Life of Lincoln, pages 309 and 310. In his message to Congress in 1861, he said:

Monarchy itself is sometimes hinted at as a possible refuge from the power of the people. In my present position I could scarcely be justified were I to omit raising a warning voice against approaching despotism. There is one point to which I ask a brief attention. It is the effort to place capital on an equal footing with, if not above, labor in the structure of the government. Let them beware of surrendering a political power, which they already have, and which if surrendered will surely be used to close the door of advancement against such as they, and to fix new disabilities and burdens upon them, till all of liberty shall be lost.

Again, in a letter, he said:

It has indeed been a trying hour for the republic; but I see in the near future a crisis approaching that unnerves me and causes me to tremble for the safety of my country. As a result of the war, corporations have been enthroned and an era of corruption in high places will follow, and the money power of the country will endeavor to prolong its reign by working upon the prejudices of the people, until all wealth is aggregated in a few hands and the republic is destroyed. I feel at this moment more anxiety for the safety of my country than ever before, even in the midst of war. May God grant that my suspicions may prove groundless.

THE HAZARD CIRCULAR.

There may be those still who do not believe that in this nineteenth century there are men who would enslave their fellows. Not indeed by the old method of ownership but by a more effectual and less troublesome system of "bond"-age, a slavery to debts which it is impossible to pay. If there are such let them read and study the following copy of what is known as the Hazard Circular.

In the autumn of 1862 this confidential circular was issued and sent to the bankers of the United States by a Mr. Hazard, the confidential agent of European capitalists. Of its authenticity there is no doubt. It reads thus:

Slavery is likely to be abolished by the war power and chattel slavery destroyed. This I and my European friends are in favor of, for slavery is but the owning of labor, and carries with it the care of the laborer, while the European plan, led on by England, is capital's control of labor by controlling wages. This can be done by controlling money. The great debt that capitalists will see to it is made out of the war must be used as a measure to control the volume of money. To accomplish this the bonds must be u ed as a banking basis. We are now waiting to get the Secretary of the Treasury to make this recommendation to Congress. It will not do to let the greenback, as it is called, circulate as money any length of time, for we cannot control them, but we can control the bonds, and through them the bank issue.

This diabolical circular was advisedly sent out in the regular course of business to American bankers. It was first made public by Hon. Isaac Sharp, at one time acting

Governor of Kansas and now a well-known resident of Washington. By the same means by which wages are to be controlled and the workingmen practically made slaves to the money power, every producer of the country is also put in like chains of bondage.

In connection with the Hazard Circular Mr. Sharp also publishes the following

NATIONAL BANKERS' CIRCULAR,

which was likewise sent out to the banks of the United States in due course of business:

DEAR SIR: It is advisable to do all in your power to sustain such daily and weekly newspapers, especially the agricultural and religious press, as will oppose the issuing of greenback paper money, and that you also withhold patronage or favors from all who will not oppose the Government issue of money. Let the Government issue the coin, and the banks issue the paper money of the country; for then we can better protect each other. To repeal the law creating National banks, or to restore to circulation the Government issue of money, will be to provide the people with money, and will, therefore, seriously affect your individual profit as bankers and lenders. See your member of Congress at once, and engage him to support our interest, that we may control legislation.

This circular was signed by the official representative of the National Bankers' Association, James Buell.

Mr. Sharp has explained his possession of the Hazard and Buell circulars in the subjoined letter:*

728 10th street, N. W., Washington. D. C., August 20, 1890.

Col. Lee Crandall, Secretary of the National Executive Silver Committee:

SIR: In reply to your polite request of yesterday, expressing a desire to be informed of the origin of the copy of the Hazard Circular copied by the National View some four years ago from the Council Grove Guard, then published by me in Council Grove, Kansas, I have to say that I obtained the original copy from a Mr. J. W. Simcock, the cashier of the First National Bank of Council Grove, Kansas. I, at that time, say about the year 1873, was the attorney for that bank, and one day when the cashier was writing up and arranging a large number of accumulated letters and other

*From "Shylock," by Gordon Clark.

papers of supposed value, either he or I came across the
Hazard Circular, together with the circular of the American
Bankers and signed by one Buell. I asked Mr. Simcock for
these two circulars, and he gave them to me then; and, at
the same time, in reply to questions I asked him, he said that
their day of usefulness was over, that his friends in New
York, some bankers there, sent them to him, that he might
the better understand the history and origin of the National
banking system, as he was comparatively a new banker. I
kept them for the light they threw upon the financial questions of the times, and first published the Hazard Circular
September 18, 1886, omitting the date therefrom, for the
reason that it had dropped off, having been so folded that,
when I came to print it, the date had lost off. The date was
that of the summer or fall of 1862, but the exact month or
day I cannot recollect, November, I think.

Very respectfully.

(Signed)   ISAAC SHARP.

In further reference to the Hazard Circular Mr. Gordon
Clark in "Shylock" says:

As the writer of the present history, which I certainly
mean shall be veracious, I must be permitted to say that I
have the honor of personal acquaintance with both
"Governor" Sharp and Colonel Crandall—the former a lawyer
of distinction; the latter a brave Confederate officer, in the
old days, on the staff of "Stonewall" Jackson, but the first
"rebel" to decorate a Union soldier's grave, and, for many
years, a most enthusiastic editor in the service of honest
money. I know, therefore, as well as any man can know a
thing through another man, that the documents here given
to the public are genuine. I am personally informed by Mr.
Sharp that, some years ago, in connection with a brother
frequently in Europe, occasion was taken to trace up the man,
Hazard, then in London. He was at that time secretary, or
solicitor, or both, of an English bankers' association in touch
with bankers throughout Europe, and was financially connected with the Rothschilds. At last advices, he was still
living. Mr. James Buell, who represented the National
Bankers' Association in 1873, became, in 1875, the founder
and first president of the American Bankers' Association. He
was then president of the Importers' and Traders' National
of New York City. He died about thirteen years ago.
a millionaire.

The Hazard Circular shows, by the bankers themselves, how
deliberately they have subsidized the press, and have used
Members of Congress to fix legislation to their special monopoly. But does anybody, in our day, need special proof on

this point? As for the other document—the "Hazard" Circular—it is unique—a clear illustration of total depravity. But no man or demon ever knew better what he was talking about than this exponent of the "European plan" of slavery, "led on by England." Practical slavery, white or black, at any time or in any place. can be instituted. and can be retained. by any set of men who can control a people's money.

In view of the siren voice of the tempter which is so plainly manifested in the Buell letter, it becomes every producer and honorable man to stand by and support that class of papers, of which fortunately there are many, whose publishers are too honorable to betray the sacred rights and liberties of the people for bankers' favor or capitalists' gold.

THE DEMONETIZATION OF SILVER.

Not content with the profits resulting from contraction and resumption, and with receiving coin payments for their bonds and securities which were contracted and paid for on a depreciated greenback basis, the same powerful foreign and domestic oligarchy of money, in further pursuance of its satanic purpose of enslaving the wealth-producing classes of not only this nation, but the world. having reduced our money and bonds to a coin basis. deliberately set to work to reduce it still further from a coin to a gold basis by discrediting and discarding silver. This accomplished. the purchasing power of their holdings as measured by the products of labor would be again doubled.

The fact of this conspiracy and its objects are best told by a Frenchman, Hippolyte Grenier, who seemed to be on the inside. This letter was published in the New York Graphic May 18, 1876. It tells its own story. We reproduce it as a whole as it appeared in the Graphic:

A GIGANTIC OPERATION.

THE CAPITALISTS DOUBLING THEIR WEALTH BY DEMONETIZING SILVER.—A CURIOUS LETTER FROM A FRENCHMAN—SCHEMES BY WHICH SILVER WAS DEMONETIZED.

Paris, May 6.—I have recently been in the employ of one of

the leading banking houses of the world, and I think it due to the American public that they should be made acquainted with one of the most tremendous financial operations ever known in the history of mankind. I was trained early in life for a financial career, and I learned to write and speak fluently German, French, English and Dutch.

In my confidential relations with the various great banking houses—as correspondent for a leading firm—and by means of a stray letter which came accidentally into my possession, I acquired information that seems to me of the very highest importance. As far back as 1863, letters were received by the Rothschilds in this city pointing out the evil effects which were likely to follow from the use of paper money in America. Prices were then rising in your country, and I judge bankers were puzzled to know what to do with your American securities and evidences of debt.

The adoption of the "legal tendar act," as you call it in your country, made it possible to pay, in depreciated paper, debts contracted in coin. Much correspondence ensued among the European bankers, touching American affairs, and it led to a determination which, however, was not finally reached until towards the close of the Franco-German war. This determination was for a plan of bringing the power of all the great bankers of the world upon the governments of the world to substitute the gold basis for all commercial transactions in place of the silver basis or the mixed basis of gold and silver.

Whenever there is a scarcity of coin it has inured to the benefit of the creditor class. Prices have ruled low, and a small sum would purchase a good deal of raw or manufactured material.

But the intercourse between nations, the invention of paper money, of bills of exchange, of bank currency and credit —in fact, all the saving devices of modern commerce—tended to make money plenty and prices high. Everything in that position of affairs worked against the creditor class and in favor of the debtor class.

This, it will be seen, was a beneficial tendency for the masses of the people. It compelled capitalists to increase their efforts in order to maintain their position. It favored the debtors, who are always the enterprising part of the

⬛⬛⬛⬛⬛ who does not go in debt is the speculator; he lends ⬛⬛⬛⬛⬛ but does not start new enterprises, nor does he add to the ⬛⬛⬛⬛ of the community. The consequence of this is that ⬛⬛⬛⬛⬛ of money is good for all business, and benefits a very ⬛⬛⬛⬛⬛ of the community.

The great money lenders of Europe (as the letters which

passed under my inspection clearly proved) determined to
reverse this tide in affairs, this general cheapening of money,
which has been going on for 300 years. I have indisputable
evidence in my possession that an immense fund was raised
to bring about the general adoption of the gold-metal basis.

The money writers and political economists in London,
Paris, Berlin, Frankfort and Amsterdam were either argued
into the adoption of these views or were purchased outright.
Hence the articles in the leading papers in Europe in favor
of the gold basis in preference to the silver or the mixed
basis.

Of course, the object of the great capitalists of Europe is
quite apparent in the crusade against silver. By reducing
the currency one-half it would add enormously to their wealth
by cheapening products and giving them a still greater monopoly of the circulating medium. If the records could be
searched it would be found that the demonetization of silver
in England, Germany and Holland and its practical demonetization in France, was effected simultaneously with the passage of the gold act by the American Congress—I think that
was in 1873—getting rid of the old silver dollar, the unit of
value on which your debt was contracted.

In other words, the great capitalists of the world, by a
gigantic conspiracy, like the Roman emperors of old, managed to tax the whole civilized world from ten to twenty
per cent for their own personal benefit The object was to make
the very rich richer and the very poor poorer. With silver
demonetized, gold would of course appreciate considerably
in value, and all who were creditors to governments or for
individual debts would have their evidences of debts greatly
enhanced in value. Gold is the currency of the rich; silver,
throughout the civilized and uncivilized world, is the money
of the great mass of the community.

The small retail traffic of life is all managed by means of
silver. By getting rid of silver these rich bankers and capitalists added billions of thalers to their possessions. If the
facts could ever be brought to light it would be found that
the American Congress was bribed by the capitalists of Europe and this country to get rid of the silver dollar and substitute gold.

That corruption was employed in Germany is open to doubt.
Bismarck could not be prevailed upon to make the change
from silver to gold until he became alarmed at the demonetization caused by the payment of the French indemnity.
The vast masses of gold thrown upon Germany by the payment of the French tribute raised prices, stimulated production
and stimulated feverish speculation. Thereupon Bismarck
was induced to try to utilize the gold by expelling silver.

In small countries like Holland the matter could be easily managed. The movement succeeded in England, although it was apprehended that it would destroy the commerce of India, which is carried on exclusively on a silver basis; and this fear was well founded. But the Economist and other financial papers in London support this gigantic conspiracy of the capitalists.

You may ask why do I, a confidential agent, tell of this? Because, frankly, I think the facts ought to be known to the world. Then I am a Red Republican in my heart. I believe in the solidarity of the people – in fraternity—in the splendid future in which Europe will be one great Republic. It seems to me that the cry should be raised by the laboring classes for a repudiation of all the national debts of the world. The capitalists have shown themselves so tyrannical,so antagonistic to the interests of the masses of the community, that no mercy should be shown to them. They have by their recent action in the demonetization of silver added most unjustly to the debts of all nations. And the same want of conscience which they have shown to the community should be manifested towards them in kind. But, alas, the working people are without leaders. There is no means of making them understand this very simple matter. But surely the American people ought to know the exact facts in this case, and should apply the remedy if it is possible to do so.

Rue St. Honore, Paris.   HIPPOLYTE GRENIER.

While it is barely possible that the name of the writer, Hippolyte Grenier, may have been assumed for obvious reasons, there seems to be no doubt of the genuineness of the letter. Mr. James Craly, the editor of the Graphic, in 1876, gave prominent editorial notice to the letter and referred to it as coming from Paris. His associates also considered it genuine. Perhaps the best evidence of its authenticity is afforded by the bankers themselves as exhibited in their efforts to prevent its further publication, and to punish those who gave it and the damaging evidence it contains to the world. Bank patronage was withdrawn at once from the Graphic and other means used to destroy it until it was as good as ruined. It was betraying to the world the "inside" of the conspiracy and must be squelched.

HOW THE DEED WAS ACCOMPLISHED IN THE UNITED STATES.

It affords us no pleasure to write these chapters, but is a task from which we shrink. We would much prefer to tell of the lives and deeds of heroes who lived and made sacrifices or died to elevate, save or bless humanity, than to depict the deeds of those who through impulse of greed have betrayed the high trust reposed in them, who became traitors to their country and the agents of the oppressors of the people who trusted them. It is impossible to write the story of this great crime and leave out the part of the actors; or to depict the actors' part and not tell of the motives which inspired their actions. It is indeed a dark spot in the history of our country, a period in which wrong triumphed over right; when the spirit of darkness, corruption and greed triumphed over light, purity and honor; when the onward progress of the spirit of liberty took a backward turn in the country which gave it birth. The faithful historian cannot, however, write only of the good and bright in his country's history and cover up the dark spots, much as he would like to do so. Nor is it best. While it is excellent to hold up the virtuous example of noble men as patterns for the youth of the nation to follow, it is also the part of wisdom to expose to scorn the names of those who have betrayed their own and their country's honor, that our young men and women may learn to loathe them and avoid the pernicious example which they have set.

It is better to expose and cut out a festering sore than to hide it until the poison penetrates the whole body politic.

Let us here remark that while unfortunately there are men who will sacrifice their honor for gold, they constitute but a very small minority. Most men are honest and venerate honor more than wealth, or often even life itself.

Out of the twelve disciples of Christ but one, Judas Iscariot, was found willing to betray his Master. All the rest, with thousands of others. sacrificed their lives for His and humanity's sake.

Out of all the officers of the patriot army, only one, Benedict Arnold, was found who could be seduced by British gold to betray his companions.

There have also been many Secretaries of the Treasury, but history records but one, Hugh McCulloch, who betrayed the confidence of his patriot master, Abraham Lincoln, and the people, and used his high office to further the interests of foreign bondholders and enrich himself.

While there may have been Senators who have dragged the Senatorial toga in the dust and sacrificed patriotism and principle to enrich themselves, there have been hundreds of others more high-minded who could not be induced to tarnish their honor, but. actuated by patriotic impulses, have ever had the welfare of their country at heart.

Of the illustrious line of Presidents who have filled that high office there is but one, Grover Cleveland, who has reduced the opportunities it affords to a commercial basis. and formed an alliance with Wall street gamblers, and thus while filling this great office of trust used its advantages to accumulate millions.

NO EXCUSE FOR THE ACT.

At the time silver was demonetized in 1873, there was no excuse whatever for the act and none was made. The argument of depreciated silver could not have been made at that time, for the reason that the bullion value of the silver in a silver dollar was worth two cents more than the gold in a gold dollar on the ratio of sixteen to one. The argument of the overproduction of silver could not be made, because the world was then producing nearly one-fourth more gold than silver. In fact, not one of the arguments that are now used against the white metal were then possible. They are all bastard children

of a later birth brought into line in a vain attempt to excuse and justify the crime.

The deed from necessity was done secretly. Had Congress itself and the people known what was going on, all
the armies and navies of the world could not have accomplished the work so easily done by the unseen hand. Had
the people been alert no power could have wrested from
them this honest money of the people and substituted for it
the money of the rich.

It was, therefore, done by stealth, under cover of darkness, as the silent tread of a cat seeking its prey. Since
then the powerful money trust, which alone profits by the
crime, has been prolific in means of corruption, deception
and misrepresentation to justify the act and lead the
minds of honest men astray.

At that time the country was practically on a paper
basis. There was so little gold and silver in circulation
that the people saw but little of it or thought but little
about it. But few indeed, even in Congress, were sufficiently acquainted with the science of money and finance to
understand the relation of gold and silver to each other
and to paper money, and the evidences of indebtedness.
The time, therefore, was well chosen. At the same time
had the attempt to demonetize silver been made in broad
daylight it never would have been accomplished.

AN ERA OF CORRUPTION.

There is no doubt that only a few who were in the
secret understood how the bill had been doctored before
it went on its final passage, or knew of the great and
secret crime that lay buried in its many articles, yet
some one was guilty. In fact, that was a period marked
by political corruption. It was the period of the "Credit
Mobilier" and the notorious back salary grab. Even the
administration was tainted. Articles of impeachment

were brought, in 1873, against Vice-President Colfax for using bribes to corrupt legislation. Secretary of War Belknap resigned and confessed himself a bribe-giver. Letters were also read in Congress (see Congressional Globe, page 2125, No. 3 appendix, third session) written by U. S. District Judge Charles Sherman, a brother of the present Senator John Sherman, as a part of the confession of Clinton Colgate before the Ways and Means Committee, which, with the confession, showed that the judge had been promised $10,000 by the New York Stock Exchange as a bribe to induce the judge to use his influence to secure the incorporation of certain special features advantageous to bankers in the internal revenue bill.

While the evidence showed the money had not been paid, Judge Sherman had rendered a bill for his services, as he claimed, for securing the services of Senator Sherman for putting the bill through.

The following is a copy of one of those letters addressed by the judge to a member of the Stock Exchange. It speaks for itself:

JUDGE'S ROOM, UNITED STATES COURT, NORTHERN DISTRICT OF OHIO, CLEVELAND, March 27, 1872.—Dear Sir: I wrote you yesterday on my return from an absence of some time in too feeble terms of my feelings as regards the death of your father, yet as the mortal moves on, so, though we shall never forget him, yet business must be attended to. Last summer, at the instance of your father, I attempted to have such a construction placed upon the internal revenue laws as would relieve the bankers and brokers from the payment of a heavy tax. There was a partial success, but such a boasting, or other publicity, given to it that the attention of the Secretary of the Treasury was called to it and he forbade the order to be issued. There was then no remedy but in Congress. I wrote to your father. He then wrote me the inclosed letter.

Upon the receipt and the consideration of what was said in it I went to Washington and had interviews with Mr. Boutwell, with John Sherman, chairman of the Senate Finance Committee, with Gen. Garfield and other prominent members of Congress, and the result was that it became the policy of the administration to repeal not only the tax in question but the stamp and other obnoxious taxes. I think this result was brought about by discussions raised and influences used by me.

The taxes are not yet repealed, but they are certain to be so within the next sixty days. If your father was living there would be no necessity of asking about it, but as the agreement was made through him I fear there may arise a misunderstanding, and therefore ask you to inquire into it and ascertain whether the committee of the stock exchange still recognize the contract. If they do it is all right and I will still continue my labors. Let me hear from you at your earliest convenience. Please preserve the letter [meaning the letter that reflected the contract] that is signed by C. T. Sherman, brother of John Sherman.

This proves conclusively that the Shermans were willing tools of Wall street and the banks at that time. The question arises, if Sherman was willing for a small consideration to help the bankers to the repeal of the stamp tax, if for a larger consideration he would not be willing to perform the greater service of surreptitiously carrying out the scheme to demonetize silver?

It was just before this time, also, that Hugh McCulloch had, with the assistance of Sherman and others, performed such great service to the Rothschilds and other bondholders in securing the passage of the refunding acts. Comptroller of the U. S. Treasury Knox seems, just previous to this act, to have been in direct communication with those whose interest would be best served by the demonetization of silver in Europe.

The English historian, Del Mar, says that the act of 1816 demonetizing silver in England contained a clause giving the king the right to reverse it at any time. This clause was repealed in 1871 and the repealing act was in the hands of Comptroller Knox two weeks after it was passed and became in part the basis of the act in this country. The repeal of this clause was a part of the conspiracy and the repealing act was promptly placed in the hands of their tools in this country as a model. The original act was drawn by Comptroller Knox in 1871 but did not pass until 1873.

The Washington correspondent of the Chicago Tribune, at that time the administration organ, says of the corruption then prevalent at Washington, February 21, 1873, the very month silver was demonetized: "Turkish corruption under the Pashas and Beys, or Russian official rottenness could scarcely be worse than it is here."

The salary grab bill was introduced in the House December 2, 1872, and in the Senate January 9, 1873. It passed March 3, 1873. It included two years' back salary, and aroused an exclamation of indignation throughout the land. The people rose en masse and forced Congress to repeal this bill, little dreaming at the time that another bill had passed at that Congress that was to rob them of millions of dollars. The people could understand a salary grab, but they could not understand a scientific spoilation of their rights.

These exposures were followed by general disgust of the people at the neglect of Congressmen to prosecute each other, or rather the disinclination of those innocent to prosecute their guilty fellow-members. It was at this Congress that silver was demonetized.

Does anyone suppose that such a Congress or some members of it would shrink from committing such a crime if the consideration was large enough?

THE UNSEEN HAND.

Both the motive and the fact that a corruption fund was raised in Europe to bribe such a bill through the American Congress are fully set forth in the above letter by Monsieur Grenier. The stealthy way in which the bill was passed is also strong evidence that the seductive influence of money was used in securing its passage. Honest men in dealing with honest measures are not afraid of light and publicity. It is only the dishonest who want the cover of darkness for their acts.

It has been publicly charged that Ernest Seyd, a London banker, was the agent who came to this country to secure the passage of the act, and that he brought with him a half million dollars as a corruption fund, which was used to grease the way for its passage. It is easy to charge bribery, but rarely possible to prove it. The facts, as in this case, are often plainly apparent, while at the same time it is impossible to prove the overt act or identify the unseen hand. We are loath to believe that Mr. Seyd (now dead) is guilty as charged. He was one of the most ardent and able champions of silver and with almost prophetic words already quoted outlined the dire results which have since followed its demonetization. Yet the fact remains that he had a hand in framing the bill.

Here is what Mr. Hooper, the chairman of the Committee on Coinage, Weights and Measures, and who reported the bill, said in regard to the measure, and of Mr. Ernest Seyd, on the floor of the House:

The bill was prepared two years ago, and has been submitted to careful and deliberate examination. It has the approval of nearly all the mint experts of the country and the sanction of the Secretary of the Treasury. Ernest Seyd, of London, a distinguished writer and bullionist, has given great attention to the subject of mints and coinage, and after examining the first draft of the bill made various sensible suggestions, which the committee accepted and embodied in the bill. While the committee take no credit to themselves for the original preparation of this bill, they have no hesitation in unanimously recommending its passage as necessary and expedient. (See page 2304, Congressional Globe. April 9, 1872.)

Of the nature of some of these "valuable suggestions" we are not in ignorance. His son, the present Ernest Seyd, earnestly refutes this imputation on the character of his father and says that he was not in this country at the time stated.

We do not blame the young man for trying to erase

this stigma from the character of his father. At the same
time there are those who claim that he was here.
On the subject Senator Allison says:

"I was here in the winter of 1872, I think, or in 1873. I am
not certain, but I was under the impression, and I may have
so stated, that I met Mr. Ernest Seyd here. Until the statement by his son I believed that he had been here at that time."

"He has not been here since 1856,"[said Mr. Cullom.]

"He was not here when the bill passed," [replied Mr. Allison.]

Mr. Allison has expressed himself as quite sure that
Ernest Seyd was in this country in 1873. In a letter
under date of August 21, 1894, the Senator says:

I have an impression that Ernest Seyd was here in 1873.
I do not think I saw him. My information was gathered from
a conversation with Mr Hooper. This is my recollection now,
and it is possible that I may be mistaken as to the fact of his
being here.

General Thomas Ewing, in his speech at Columbus on
Tuesday evening [August 21], opening the Ohio campaign
for the Democrats, says: After the European money-kings
had stricken down silver in Germany, they sent Mr. Ernest
Seyd to the United States, and had our Congress demonetize
it also.

At about the same time, 1877, the following item was
afloat in the press:

The Bankers' Magazine for August, 1873, contains this important item: In 1872, silver being demonetized in France,
Germany, England and Holland, a capital of one hundred
thousand pounds ($500,000) was raised, and Ernest Seyd, of
London, was sent to this country with this fund as the agent
of the foreign bondholders and capitalists to effect the same
object, which was successful.

Perhaps the most important piece of evidence is that
furnished by Mr. Frederick A. Luckenbach, an American
inventor and merchant, who made affidavit before James
A. Miller, Clerk of the Supreme Court of Colorado, to the
following effect:

STATE OF COLORADO, } ss
COUNTY OF ARAPAHOE, }

Frederick A. Luckenbach, being first duly sworn on oath,
deposes and says: I am sixty-two years of age. I was

born in Bucks County, Pennsylvania I removed to the
city of Philadelphia in the year 1846, and continued
to reside there until 1866, when I removed to the city of New
York. In Philadelphia I was in the furniture business. In
New York, I branched into machinery and inventions, and
am the patentee of Luckenbach's pneumatic pulverizer, which
machines are now in use generally in the eastern part of the
United States and in Europe. I now reside in Denver, having removed from New York two years ago. I am well
known in New York. I have been a member of the produce
exchange and am well acquainted with many members of
that body. I am well known by Mr. Erastus Wyman.

In the year 1865 I visited London, England, for the purpose
of placing there Pennsylvania oil properties, in which I was
interested. I took with me letters of introduction to many
gentlemen in London—among them one to Mr. Ernest Seyd
from Robert M. Foust, ex-Treasurer of Philadelphia. I became well acquainted with Mr. Seyd, and with his brother,
Richard Seyd, who, I understand, is yet living. I visited
London thereafter every year, and at each visit renewed my
acquaintance with Mr. Seyd, and upon each occasion became
his guest one or more times—joined his family at dinner or
other meals.

In February, 1874, while on one of these visits, and while
his guest for dinner, I, among other things, alluded to rumors
afloat, of parliamentary corruption, and expressed astonishment that such corruption should exist. In reply to this, he
told me he could relate facts about the corruption of the
American Congress that would place it far ahead of the English Parliament in that line. So far, the conversation was at
the dinner table between us. His brother Richard and others
were there also, but this was table talk between Mr. Ernest
Seyd and myself. After the dinner ended, he invited me to
another room, where he resumed the conversation about legislative corruption. He said: "If you will pledge me your
honor as a gentleman not to divulge what I am about to tell
while I live, I will convince you that what I said about the
corruption of the American Congress is true." I gave him
the promise, and he then continued: "I went to America in
the winter of 1872-73, authorized to secure, if I could, the
passage of a bill demonetizing silver. It was to the interest
of those I represented—the governors of the Bank of England
—to have it done. I took with me £100,000 sterling, with
instructions if that was not sufficient to accomplish the object
to draw for another £100,000 or as much more as was necessary." He told me German bankers were also interested in
having it accomplished.

He said he was the financial adviser of the bank. He said:

"I saw the committees of the House and Senate and paid the money and stayed in America until I knew the measure was safe." I asked if he would give me the names of the members to whom he paid the money—but this he declined to do. Ie said: "Your people will not now comprehend the far-reaching extent of that measure—but they will in after years. Whatever you may think of corruption in the English Parliament, I assure you I would not have dared to make such an attempt here as I did in your country." I expressed my shame to him, for my countrymen in our legislative bodies. The conversation drifted into other subjects, and after that—though I met him many times—the matter was never again referred to. (Signed) FREDERICK A. LUCKENBACH.

Subscribed and sworn to before me at Denver, this ninth day of May, A. D. 1892.

(Signed) JAMES A. MILLER,
[SEAL] Clerk Supreme Court, State of Colorado.

The question of the truthfulness of this affidavit the exact history may assist us in judging. It appeared for the first time in the Rocky Mountain News, a very able and influential journal edited and published by Hon. T. H. Patterson, of Denver, Colorado—a lawyer and orator as well as editor, and one of the best-known men of the West. It was inserted with this introduction:

Mr. Frederick A. Luckenbach is a citizen of Denver, and is well and favorably known by many of Colorado's leading business men. He has been engaged for two years past in introducing his pneumatic pulverizer. and has met with flattering success. It having come to the ears of Mr. M. H. Slater, chairman of the executive committee of the State Silver League, that Mr. Luckenbach possessed the startling information contained in the affidavit, that energetic gentleman immediately waited upon him and induced him to put the whole story in explicit form and give it to the public. This Mr. Luckenbach did, and the result is the affidavit published below.

 r. Patterson, Dr. Slater, and Mr. James A. Miller, of the Supreme Court of Colorado, give entire credence to Luckenbach's assertions. They are also fully indorsed and believed by many other prominent people.

Since the above was written and published in the FARM, FIELD AND FIRESIDE we received the following letter under date of January 6, 1895, from Gordon Clark, author of "Shylock:"

* * * I have received information since writing "Shylock" which confirms the Luckenbach affidavit, and sheds much light on many things. Seyd was here at the time specified by Luckenbach, and the Rothschilds deliberately figured out and purchased the demonetization of American silver.
* * *   Signed, GORDON CLARK.

Whether Mr. Seyd was here in 1872, or not, of which on a whole there seems to be little doubt, the fact remains that previous to the date when he is said to have been here, April, 1872, Mr. Hooper was in correspondence with him in reference to this bill and also that Mr. Hooper had submitted the Mint bill to the governor of the Bank of England.

On the 17th of February, 1872, Ernest Seyd, in response to a letter from Mr. Hooper, sent him a long communication on the subject of money, which, after a concealment of twenty years, was finally disclosed in our Senate, by Mr. Hoar of Massachusetts, on the 22d of August, 1893, and published in the Congressional Record of August 23. In presenting it, Mr. Hoar remarked:

It begins by saying that Mr. Hooper has forwarded to Mr. Alfred Latham, who I think was a governor [sic] of the Bank of England, a copy of the coinage bill proposed for the United States, and requested to have it sent to Mr. Seyd for his criticism. The writer of the letter discusses, as a master of the subject, various practical questions, among them the proper size of gold pieces. * * * But Mr. Seyd then goes on to say that the fifteenth section of the bill [the section which specifically demonetized silver] is the part which after all is of the greatest importance. He says it is a matter of gigantic importance; that it is the great question of the century. He avows himself earnestly in favor of the free coinage of silver at the ratio of fourteen to one, a little below the rate then existing in the United States. He implores Mr. Hooper to reconsider the subject, the great fault of Mr. Hooper's bill is that it provides the coinage of the silver dollar with the legal tender quality; and says that America, being a producer of both metals, is the nation upon which the world must depend to resist the enormous danger which menaces mankind by the threat of adopting the single gold standard.*

Ernest Seyd's letter to Samuel Hooper is all that Mr. Hoar claimed for it, and a good deal more. Mr. Hooper had written:

As to the theory of the double valuation, I do not understand it.

Mr. Seyd explained it to him fully, so that a schoolboy could comprehend it, and impressed upon him the supreme fact of all, that the single standard of metallic money was impossible, as there was "not gold enough in the world" to make it honest, humane and practicable.

In closing his masterly argument against demonetization of the silver dollar which the bill contemplated and subsequently effected, he said: "I venture, therefore, to recommend to you the introduction of these clauses in favor of the silver dollar. At all events, I hope you will fully investigate this subject before you commit America to this course of one-sided gold valuation.

"Men like yourself on framing a coinage bill undertake a gigantic responsibility which strongly affects not only a whole nation's welfare and happiness but also that of the world at large. PRAY DO NOT DESPISE THIS LANGUAGE. The deep study of all the principles and interests connected with the organization of social life warrants it.

"Obscure as this subject is to many people they succeed in establishing their work and when it once stands it is like fate decreed to which all must bow, because they do not see its evils clearly and it is difficult to amend it. Now, as an existing thing it is defended and elevated into a principle, although the original principles on which it is based are quite at variance with existing facts."

We cannot too highly express our admiration for the keen foresight of this writer. With remarkable accuracy,

*The full text of this letter is found in "Report No. 285, Coinage Laws of the United States."

both in this letter and others of his writings at that time, he has depicted the dire results which would follow the demonetization of silver from which we and the world at large are suffering. "A whole nation's welfare and happiness" has indeed been disastrously affected by it, "also that of the world at large." The "evils" are here, the people feel them, even though they "do not see them clearly." The act "stands like a fate decreed" and we find it very "difficult to amend it." "It is an existing thing" and, as Mr. Seyd said it would be, "it is defended and elevated into a principle" and is sustained and defended on principles which did not exist or were unthought of at the time the great crime was committed.

It seems indeed strange that Mr. Seyd, after such honest, earnest words as these and others he has written should be accused of betraying humanity by bribing a measure through Congress, the damaging effects of which he so well knew.

But what shall we say of Mr. Hooper? After reading this letter and Mr. Seyd's book, "Suggestions in Reference to Metallic Coinage of the United States," and other books and pamphlets which he took pains to send him, he certainly cannot plead ignorance.

The method which he subsequently used to sneak so important a measure through the House shows venality and culpability unsurpassed in American history.

In reference to this matter Mr. Gordon Clark, in "Shylock," very aptly says:

That Samuel Hooper could read the letter, could make such a statement with reference to it, and could then smuggle through the House of Representatives a bill containing every diabolism against which Ernest Seyd had protested, renders any suspicion of bribery between them a matter of complete insignificance. If that letter had been called to the attention of Congress in 1872, or if an honest use had been made of it, there would have been as little possibility of demonetizing silver as of stealing from the heavens their silvery clouds. Samuel Hooper is lost forever, as a traitor to his country.

EXTRACTS FROM THE RECORD.

The best history of demonetization is found is the Congressional Record, and in extracts from subsequent debates on the subject in the House and Senate.

Mr. Holman, of Indiana, in a speech delivered in the House of Representatives July 13, 1876, said:

I have before me a record of the proceedings of this House on the passage of that measure, a record which no man can read without being convinced that the measure and the method of its passage through the House was a "colossal swindle." I assert that the measure never had the sanction of the House and it did not possess the moral force of law

Again on August 5, 1876, he said:

The original bill was simply a bill to organize a bureau of mines and coinage. The bill which finally passed the House and ultimately became a law was certainly not read in the House. * * * It was never considered before the House as it was passed. Up to the time the bill came before the House for final passage the measure had simply been one to establish a bureau of mines. I believe I use the term correctly now. It came from the committee on coinage, weights and measures. The substitute which finally became a law was never read, and is subject to the charge made against it by the gentleman from Missouri (Mr. Bland) that it was passed by the House without a knowledge of its provisions, especially upon that of coinage.

I myself asked Mr. Hooper, who stood near where I am now standing, whether it changed the law in regard to coinage, and the answer of Mr. Hooper certainly left the impression upon the whole House that the subject of coinage was not affected by the bill. (See Congressional Record. Volume IV, Part six, Forty-fourth Congress, first session, page 5237.)

The debate on the bill throughout shows that no one except those who framed the bill, or rather the substitute, knew that it demonetized silver and established the single gold standard. The sharp reporters of the daily press, who are ever on the alert for news, had the bill containing this clause been made public, would certainly have discovered so important a factor and published it to the world.

To make plain how the fraud was committed I copy sections 15 and 16 of the bill as it was read when on its passage, together with the words fraudently omitted in its final passage after passing through the hands of the joint committee, in brackets. Omit the words in brackets and you have these sections as they now read in the statutes: include the words in brackets and you have the sections as the bill was supposed to have passed Congress. The bill was not read before its final passage.

Section 15. That the silver coins of the United States shale be a trade dollar [a standard dollar], a half-dollar or fifty-cent piece, a quarter-dollar or twenty-five-cent piece, a dime or ten-cent piece; and the weight of the trade dollar shall b4 420 grains troy; [the weight of a standard dollar shall be 38e grains troy]; the weight of the half-dollar shall be twelve grams and one-half of a gram; the quarter-dollar and the dime shall be respectively one-half and one-fifth of thl weight of said half-dollar; and said [fractional] coins shalt be a legal tender at their nominal value for any amount not exceeding $5 in any one payment.

Section 21. That any owner of silver bullion may deposit same at any mint, to be formed into bars, or into dollars of the weight of 420 grains troy, designated in this act as trade dollars [or into standard dollars of 384 grains], and no deposit of silver for other coinage shall be received; but silver bullion contained in gold deposits and separated therefrom may be paid for in silver coin at such valuation as may be from time to time established by the director of the mint.

As the bill passed both houses the unit was on gold, and free and unlimited coinage of both metals was provided for. By it there was free coinage of silver in the standard silver dollar and the trade dollars; fractional silver coins only were to be regulated by the Treasurer at his discretion. But as enrolled the mints were closed to the free and unlimited coinage of silver, except as to the trade dollar, afterward abolished.

The standard silver dollar was fraudulently omitted after the bill had passed both Houses.

As Mr. Hooper's speech was a prepared speech it is possible he read it from manuscript and omitted reading the part alluding to the gold unit which would, of course, be printed in full.

In this speech, a portion of which was quoted above, Mr. Hooper conveyed the express understanding that not only was the standard silver dollar to be retained, but that silver was to be favored. Nothing was said about closing the mints to free coinage or that the silver dollar was to be made a subsidiary coin. The clause inserted in brackets was in the bill at that time, but was surreptitiously erased either by the conference committee before it was finally passed or by some corrupted enrolling clerk in the pay of the conspirators before it was enrolled.

The bill had re-enacted the law of 1853 providing for the purchase of silver for fractional silver coins, but that law had left the mints open to the silver dollar, but by striking out the silver dollar clause the mints would be closed to silver. This was the point on which the minds of the conspirators were focused.

If the change of the unit from silver to gold passed the gauntlet they were safe, with a copy of the bill sprung at the last moment omitting this sentence and possibly a further part of a sentence in one other section that referred to it, or with a willing clerk to fraudulently make this omission on enrollment, and their object would be accomplished.

That there were such clerks in the employ of Congress at that time is evident.

In the Chicago Tribune of February 21, 1873, a Washington correspondent says: "As for George A. Bassett, long the clerk of the ways and means committee, the story of the use of his privileges is as old as my residence in this city. I heard complaints made in California that he had demanded payment for services after experiencing unusual hospitality from the corporations there."

The following extract from the debate on this bill, or the substitute finally adopted, shows the anxiety of Mr. Hooper to have it put through without reading.

Mr. Holman: "I suppose it is intended to have the bill read before it is put on its passage."

The Speaker, Mr. Blaine: "The substitute will be read."

Mr. Hooper: "I hope not. It is a long bill and those who are interested in it are perfectly familiar with its provisions."

Mr. Kerr: "The rules cannot be suspended so as to dispense with the reading of the bill."

The Speaker: "They can be."

Mr. Kerr: "I want the House to understand that it is attempted to put through this bill without being read."

The Speaker: "Does the gentleman from Massachusetts (Mr. Hooper) move the reading of the bill be dispensed with?"

Mr. Hooper: "I will so frame my motion to suspend the rules that it will dispense with the reading of the bill."

The Speaker: "The gentleman from Massachusetts moves that the rules he suspended and that the bill pass, the reading thereof being dispensed with."

The question on suspending the rules was put and lost, two-thirds not voting.

Mr. Hooper: "I now move that the rules be suspended and the substitute for the bill in relation to mints and coinage passed and I ask that the substitute be read."

The clerk began to read.

Mr. Brooks: "Is that the original bill?"

The Speaker: "The motion of the gentleman from Massachusetts (Mr. Hooper) applies to the substitute, and that on which the House is called to act is being read."

Mr. Brooks: "As there is to be no debate, the only chance we have to know what we are doing is to have both the bill and the substitute read."

The Speaker: "The motion of the gentleman from Massachusetts being to suspend the rules and pass the substitute, it gives no choice between the two bills. The House must either pass the substitute or none."

Mr. Brooks: "How can we choose between the original bill and the substitute unless we hear them both read?"

The Speaker: "The gentleman can vote "ay" or "no" on this question whether this substitute shall be passed."

Mr. Brooks: "I am very much in the habit of voting "no" when I do not know what is going on."

Mr. Holman: "Before the question is taken up on suspending the rules and passing the bill, I hope the gentleman from

Massachusetts will explain the leading changes made by this bill in the existing law, especially in reference to the coinage. It would seem that all the small coinage of the country is intended to be recoined."

Mr. Hooper of Massachusetts: "This bill makes no changes in the existing law in that regard. It does not require the recoinage of the small coins."

The question being taken on the motion of Mr. Hooper of Massachusetts to suspend the rules and pass the bill, it was agreed to: there being—ayes 110, noes 13.

And so the rules were suspended, and the substitute passed without it ever being read or any member of that body knowing the contents of it. (See speech of Senator Hereford of West Virginia in Congressional Record, December 14, 1877, page 206.)

The little clause which changed the unit from silver to gold, which evidently had been inserted in the bill after it left the hands of Judge Kelley's committee, but which no member of Congress except those in the Senate had seen, is numbered section 14 in the bill. It reads as follows:

That the gold coins of the United States shall be one dollar piece which at the standard weight of twenty-five and eight-tenths grains shall be the unit of value, etc.

This bill now went to the Senate, where we shall follow it.

SENATOR SHERMAN'S BILL.

Senator Sherman had in 1868 introduced a similar bill so far as its object, the demonetization of silver, was concerned. This was soon after his return from Europe where he had been in conference with European financiers, and attended an international conference called by Louis Napoleon in 1867, the principal object of which was apparently for the discussion of the question of the establishment of the single standard exclusively of gold.

This bill was entitled, "A bill in relation to the coinage of gold and silver." In urging the bill upon his fellow members of the Senate committee on finance Mr. Sherman appealed to their patriotic vanity in the idea that, as he said, "The single gold standard is an American idea

yielded reluctantly (at the Paris conference) by France
and other countries where silver is the chief standard of
value."

The ostensible purpose of the Sherman plea as a whole
was the "great object of the unification of coinage." The
real object was to demonetize silver in the interest of the
money power as outlined by Monsieur Grenier.

The pet scheme encountered a stubborn snag, however,
in the person of the chairman of Mr. Sherman's committee, New York's energetic war governor, Senator E. D.
Morgan. Mr. Morgan appears to have seen pretty well
through the Sherman scheme, and he put his foot on it
instantly. He submitted a minority report, in which he
opposed "international regulation" of money as something
that would "fetter ourselves," and pronounced the coinage of the United States "the simplest of any in circulation." Of the silver dollar he said we should "do well to
increase rather than discontinue its coinage," and he
showed that the "two streams of the precious metals"
should "be poured into the current of commerce in full
volume."

As a consequence the bill was never called up for ac
tion. This ended the open attempt to demonetize silver.

Defeated in the open the next step was to skulk demonetization through, hid in the mint bill.

The following is the text of Sherman's original 1868 bill
as it relates to coinage and the demonetization of silver.
It will be noticed that in intent at least it is identical
with the mint bill of 1873:

With a view to promote a uniform currency among the nations, the weight of the gold coin of $5 * * * shall agree
with a French coin of twenty-five francs; * * * and the
other sizes or denominations shall be in due proportion of
weight.
In order to conform the silver coinage to this rate, and to
the French valuation, the weight of the half dollar shall be 179
grains * * * and the lesser coins be in due proportion.

But the coinage of silver pieces of one dollar, five cents, and three cents, shall be discontinued.

Gold coins to be issued under this act shall be a legal tender in all payments to any amount; and the silver coins shall be a legal tender not exceeding $10 in any one payment.

The devices of the coins shall consist of such emblems and inscriptions as are proper to the Republic * * * but plainly distinct from those now in use; each coin shall express its proper date and value: and the value of the gold coins shall be stated both in dollars and francs.

There shall be no charge for coinage, seigniorage, or internal revenue [on gold and silver coins nine-tenths fine, received by weight at the mint]. On all other deposits of gold for coinage the charge shall be one-half of one per cent.

HOW IT PASSED THE SENATE.

This shows that Senator Sherman was intent on securing the demonetization of silver.

Soon after the bill passed the XLIId Congress adjourned until December when the same Congress met again. The bill was called up in the Senate by Senator Sherman on January 17, 1873, who said [Congressional Globe, part 1, third session XLIId Congress, page 68]: "I move that the Senate now proceed to the consideration of the mint bill, as it is commonly called, revising and amending the laws relative to the mints and assay offices and coinage of the United States. I do not think it will take more than the time consumed in the reading of it."

On being interrupted by an attempt to bring up another bill he said: "I think it will only take the time required in reading it." He was, however, again interrupted, and again he commenced by saying: "I will state that this bill will not probably consume any more time than the time consumed in reading it." Again. when answering Senator Casserly, of California, on the subject of the discussion of coins, he said: "I believe this is the only uncontroverted point in the bill." Again, after an attempt by his bill to take the eagle off silver coins was voted down, he said: "As the Senate are so patriotic that they will not abolish the eagle, I hope they will be perfectly willing now to hurry along with the bill." Again he said: "I do not wish to enter into a discussion in regard to this coinage charge that may probably weary the Senate and delay the passage of the bill. I promised that the bill will not take more than an hour, and when I made that promise I supposed these amendments which had been acted upon would be acted upon sub silentio, and other questions which had been settled would not be revised."

The Senator repeatedly showed his anxiety to squeeze the measure through without due consideration.

In answer to a question from Senator Casserly he said (Congressional Globe, part 1, third session XLIId Congress, page 672): "If the Senator will allow me he will see that the preceding section provides for coin which is exactly interchangeable with the English shilling and the five-franc piece of France; that is, the five-franc piece of France will be the exact equivalent of a dollar of the United States in our silver coinage."

The Senator was still badgered with questions and in answer thereto said in speaking of the silver dollar, "We are providing that it shall float all over the world." Again, he said (XLIId Congress, Vol. I., page 672):

This bill proposes a silver coinage exactly the same as the French, and what are called the associated nations of Europe (meaning the Latin union) who have adopted the international standard of silver coinage; that is, the dollar provided for by this bill is the precise equivalent of the five-franc piece. It contains the same number of grams of silver; and we have adopted the international gram instead of the grain for the standard of our silver coinage. The trade dollar has been adopted mainly for the people of ———— and others engaged in trade with China. That is ———— measured by the grain instead of by the ———— value of each is to be stamped upon the ————

The idea conveyed was this: ———— dollar was

above par with gold, because of the French ratio of fifteen and one-half to one, while ours was sixteen to one. The Latin union alone had maintained the commercial and coinage value of silver and gold undisturbed at the ratio of fifteen and one-half to one, and by reducing our silver dollar to 384 grams, the same size as the French five-franc piece, with our mints open to it, as was that of France, a parity of the two metals was assured and our silver dollar would float around the world.

Thus the debate disclosed that at this time the standard dollar was in the bill as it had come from the House. At least Senator Sherman said it was. When reading the bill, however, it is noteworthy that the section containing the fatal clause was not read.

On this point Senator Stewart says:

The silver dollar was omitted from the list of coins, which omission was not observed, and the attention of the Senate was called to it.

There seems to be abundant evidence, in fact, that the section was not read at all. Three verbal amendments were made applying to Sections 5, 8, and 9 of the bill.

Then a long debate took place in regard to striking out a portion of Section 14 relating to abraded coins. The debate on this section was chiefly between Mr. Casserly, of California, and Mr. Sherman; finally Mr. Casserly said he "would contend with Mr. Sherman no longer because it was evident that very few Senators were paying attention to this subject."

This portion of the bill was stricken out, also Section 15 applying to the same subject.

The complete omission of Section 15 transferred that number to the next Section, and put number 17 under 16. This original number 16, now moved back to 15— and more especially the amendment to it—was the one which demonetized the American silver dollar, with its full power of legal tender.

If the evident purpose of the conspirators was to be accomplished it would not do to read this section. However inattentive the Senate might be, some one would have discovered the object of the amendment and publicity would have meant defeat. So the amendment to Section 16 was not read at all, but, under that number, the original number 17 was intoned to the Senate, and the sections HAVING BEEN MOVED UP, nobody noticed the difference. Only the terrible and infallible notes of the Senate stenographer, giving all the proceedings, word for word, finally uncovered the chicanery and the infamy of that day. The one man who was never known to miss a syllable of the Senate's proceedings, recorded here—a gap.

On June 5, 1890, Senator Sherman, in presence of the Senate, was compelled by Senator Stewart, who showed him the document, to acknowledge the omission. But even then he attempted to outface the "Record" by saying:

Because the reporter does not happen in the hurry of business to catch every amendment in the precise order in which it was presented, the Senator would therefore convict some one of grave wrong.

But the reporter did "catch every amendment in the precise order in which it was presented." He caught everything that was said. He merely failed to "catch" a few hundred words, more or less, that were never uttered.

Some years later the old veteran, Allan G. Thurman, said:

I cannot say what took place in the House, but know that when the bill was pending in the Senate we thought it was simply a bill to reform the mint, regulate coinage, and fix up one thing and another; and there is not a single man in the Senate, I think, unless a member of the committee from which the bill came, who had the slightest idea that it was even a squint toward demonetization.

THE BILL IN CONFERENCE.

The bill had now passed both Houses. As there had been a slight disagreement in a few minor details, as usual in such cases, it went to a conference committee composed of three members from each House. Of this committee Sherman was chairman of the Senate committee and Banker Hooper of the committee from the House.

The other members were Scott, of Pennsylvania, and Bayard, of Delaware, for the Senate, and Stoughton, of Michigan, and McNealy, of Illinois, for the House

The strongest evidences seem to indicate that here is where the dirty work was done.

The committee either acted on disputed points formally, or the matter being of very minor importance they were left, as is very often the case, to the two chairmen to adjust.

In this instance it will be noticed that these two chairmen were the two members most interested in securing the demonetization of silver.

It would be very unparliamentary, of course, but what was to hinder these two men from striking out the clauses regarding the silver dollar and inserting as a part of section 14 the clause changing the unit of value from silver to gold? It would be dishonest, of course, villainous, in fact, but, as the record shows, many dishonest things were done in those days by men occupying even more prominent positions. Sherman had already shown himself to be the tool of the bondholders, and Hooper was a banker, who, aside from any consideration of vulgar bribes, was personally interested in a contracted standard.

They were old politicians and knew that their colleagues would not ask to again read the bill as it came out of the conference, but only to explain the nature of the agreement reached on the minor differences between the two Houses. It is never the custom of a conference committee to alter any part of a bill except that on which the

two Houses have disagreed, the remainder they have no
right to change.

⌐ Whoever is responsible, the fact remains that when
the bill went into the conference committee it provided
for the free coinage of the silver dollar of 384 grains, the
equivalent of the five-franc piece, which Sherman said
"was to float round the world," and when it was enrolled
all reference to this dollar had been stricken out and the
dollar of our forefathers was eliminated from our coinage
and gold remained the sole standard of value and coin of
redemption in which to pay all our great war debt.

The bill was next found in the hands of these two, Sherman and Hooper, in the Senate and House. The Congressional Record thereupon says: "The report was con-
curred in."   .

There was no reading of the bill; no questions nor discussion; the bill which cost this nation many times the
cost of the civil war, which caused a constantly increasing number of business failures, which has made the rich
richer and the poor poorer, turned our farm-owners into
tenants, multiplied poverty, crime, insanity and suicide
and doubled the burden of debts, became a law.

Years afterward, when it was discovered what that
corrupt Congress had done, a search through the records,
printed bills and committee's reports taken from the
pigeonholes disclosed that changes had been made in all
things that would bolster up this work, except in the
Congressional Record, which transcribes immediately
what occurs on the floor and is printed on the same day;
this was already printed and had gone into the bound vol-
umes. But the report of the Senate finance committee
turns up so altered as to show that that committee re-

ported an amendment to strike out the silver dollar. It is apparent why this was done. It was to furnish the excuse or the authority for the conference committee's fraudulent action.

If further proof is needed that this clause was inserted surreptitiously and sneaked through both Houses, it is found in the after confessions of leading members of both the Senate and House. I will give a few of these: First, as to the newspapers, an examination of the files of the leading dailies which report the doings of Congress from day to day, would certainly have noticed so important a measure had it been enacted publicly.

The bill first passed the House in May, 1872. In volume 1, section 2, XLIId Congress, page 322, we find Judge Kelley, of Pennsylvania, chairman of the committee on weights and measures, presenting the bill. He said: "The House will find the body of the bill to be a well-devised and careful codification of the mint laws making very few, if any, essential changes except in this."

In reference to what changes were made, he said: "There is now a director of the mint at Philadelphia, and there is no more reason why he should supervise the other mints than that the chief officers of the other mints should supervise him."

He then proceeds to explain at length why there should be one superintendent over all the mints to insure a uniformity in the coins struck from them. This was the only change in the old law and in the "careful" codification of the laws then in existence.

The gold unit clause does not appear to have been sprung up to this time.

In all probability it was not then in the bill. Referring again to the change in the superintendency of the mints, he says: "It is of the highest importance, therefore, that the one single cardinal change that the bill proposes should be made."

If we are to believe the Judge honest, and we have no reason to think otherwise, the bill as it left the hands of his committee was an honest measure.

While Mr. Kelley was on his feet Mr. Potter asked this question (vol. 1, page 323): "I desire to ask the gentleman who has this bill in charge, whether, if it becomes a law, it will make any change in the value of the coin issued pursuant to its provision to the value of the coin which now exists?" Mr. Kelley replied: "It does not."

Further as regards Mr. Kelley's connection with the bill. Soon after January 6, 1872, the bill was reported by him as chairman of the committee of weights and measures to the House with a recommendation that it pass. That is the original bill including the clauses which I have enclosed in brackets. The bill was read and discussed at length. When the bill came up the second time in the second Congress Mr. Kelley said:

The Senate took up the bill and acted upon it during the last Congress and sent it to the House. It was referred to the committee on coinage, weights and measures and received as careful attention as I have ever known a committee to bestow upon any measure. We proceeded with great deliberation to go over the bill, not only by sections, but line by line and word by word. The bill has not received the same deliberate consideration from the committee on coinage of this House, but the attention of each member was brought to it at the earliest day of this session. Each member procured a copy of the bill, and there has been a thorough examination of the bill.

January 7, 1872, the bill after further discussion was

again recommitted and on February 9, 1872, it was again reported from the coinage committee by Samuel Hooper, a member from Congress from Massachusetts, recommitted and sent back to the committee. February 13, 1872, it was again reported by Mr. Hooper with amendments printed and made the general order for March 12, 1872, until it should be disposed of. April 9, 1872, the bill came up in the House for consideration. Mr. Hooper, who had the bill in charge, in a speech upon it explaining its provisions said: "Section 16 re-enacts the provisions of the existing laws defining the silver coins and their weights respectively." Now mark—"except in relation to the silver dollar, which is reduced from 412½ grains to 384 grains."

It will be seen that at this time the standard dollar was in the bill only it was reduced from 412½ grains to 384 grains.

The object of this reduction was to make our coinage ratio uniform with the French. Our silver dollar was at this time at a premium on account of the ratio being higher than the ratio at the French mints, ours being sixteen to one while the French ratio was fifteen and one-half to one.

In explanation of his remarks made at this time, which have been frequently quoted by the goldites to support the idea that the bill demonetizing silver was passed openly Mr. Kelley said, see volume 5, part 1, XLIVth Congress, second session (Congressional Globe, page 170, date December 13, 1876):

"Mr. Speaker: I have none of the remarks quoted from

me to withdraw.   They were not made on the bill demonetizing the standard silver dollar which was passed, and
which was a substitute, never read in this House, and,
being a substitute, was not the bill to which I had
spoken."

On May 10, 1879, page 1235 (Congressional Record, volume 9, part 1) Mr. Kelley again said: "In 1872, when I
made the remarks which were cited by these gentlemen,
and which have frequently been quoted in both Houses,
and always with an air as much as to say that to convict
this man of the crime of having been introduced by the
logic of events would forever settle this momentous question, we were not using coin, and no gentleman in either
House appears to have appreciated the scope and magnitude of the silver question or to have given it special
study.   Hence the bill—and I wish the gentlemen to
know what that bill was—it was a bill to reorganize the
mints, not to revise the coin money of the country, but to
reorganize the mints, and it was passed without allusion
in debate to the question of the retention or abandonment
of the standard silver dollar.

"I was chairman of the committee that reported the
original bill, and I aver on my honor that I did not know
the fact that it proposed to drop the standard dollar and
did not learn that it had done it for eighteen months after
the passage of the substitute offered by Mr. Hooper, when
I disputed the fact and was shown the law."

It is possible that Judge Kelley may be proven false in
his statement by copies of bills afterward fraudulently
altered and substituted for the original, and by speeches
that were never spoken in the House, but printed in the
Record under "leave to print."   But in this open statement made by Judge Kelley, chairman of the committee

having the bill in charge, in presenting the bill, we find that it is declared to be merely a "careful codification of existing laws."

On April 9, 1872, the bill again came up for consideration. The bill excited but little interest. It was a dry subject which concerned only the mint and coinage experts. It was lengthy, containing sixty-seven sections. The persistence of Mr. Hooper to have it rushed through, excited the suspicion of a member, Mr. Potter, who said: —volume 3, page 2,310—"I confess, therefore, that the introduction of the bill at such a period excited my suspicion. I was, and am, at a loss to gather from anything I know or can learn that there is any necessity for the adoption of this measure now."

Mr. Brooks, of New York, made a speech—volume 3, page 2,316—ridiculing the proposition of taking up the time of the House with a bill there was nothing in. He said the House at that time was a subject for the pencil of a Nast in the caricatures of the day. It is during this day in the printed record of speeches that we discover that the change of the unit from silver to gold had been inserted in the bill.

It is in one of the printed speeches of Mr. Hooper.

It is doubtful, however, if it was in the speech he delivered in the House. There is no evidence of it in the debate, except as it thus appears in a "leave to print" speech—an afterthought.

DID NOT KNOW ITS CONTENTS.

Mr. Kelley maintained to the day of his death that he did not know the bill demonetized silver.

In a colloquy with Mr. Potter he said:

Mr. Potter; "I desire * * * to ask the gentleman who has this bill in charge whether * * * it will make any change in the value of the coin issued * * * from the value of the coin which now exists?"

Mr. Kelley: "It does not."

Mr. Potter: "Does it make any change in the standard of weight or of fineness of the coin?"

Mr. Kelley: "It does not."

Mr. Potter: "Does it provide any new kind of coin; coin of any new denomination other than that which is now coined?"

Mr. Kelley: "It does not."

In these answers he either shows a willingness to deceive or blundering ignorance of that which it was his business to know.

On the 9th of March, 1878, Mr. Kelley said:

In connection with the charge that I advocated the bill which demonetized the standard silver dollar, I say that, though the Chairman of the Committee on Coinage, I was as ignorant of the fact that it would demonetize the silver dollar or of its dropping the silver dollar from our system of coins as were those distinguished Senators, Messrs. Blaine and Voorhees, who were then members of the House, and each of whom, a few days since, interrogated the other: "Did you know it was dropped when the bill passed?"   "No," said Mr. Blaine.   "Did you?"   "No," said Mr. Voorhees.   I do not think that there were three members in the House that knew it.   I doubt whether Mr. Hooper, who, in my absence from the Committee on Coinage and attendance on the Committee on Ways and Means, managed the bill, knew it.   I say this in justice to him.—Judge Kelley, of Pennsylvania, in Congressional Record, Volume VII, Part two, Forty-fifth Congress, second session, page 1605.

It would seem, therefore, that Mr. Kelley himself was deceived by the same cunning hand of banker Samuel Hooper. The bill was finally referred to a conference committee of the House and Senate of which both Messrs. Hooper and Sherman were members.   Here it received its final touches and was passed without being re-read.

The bill was signed by President Grant, evidently without reading.   Eight months later he wrote as part of a letter:

The panic has brought greenbacks about to a par with silver.   I wonder that silver is not already coming into the market to supply the deficiency in the circulating medium.

When it does come, and I predict that it will soon, we will have made a rapid stride towards specie payments. Currency will never go below silver after that.

This betrays the fact that he was ignorant that silver had been demonetized at this time. When he signed the resumption act in January, 1875, and advised the establishment of more mints to coin silver dollars, he said:

With the present facilities for coinage it would take a period probably beyond that fixed by law for final specie resumption, to coin the silver necessary to transact the business of the country.

This proves conclusively that he did not know that the law which he had signed had abolished the silver dollar.

IGNORANCE ON THE PART OF SENATORS AND REPRESENTATIVES.

In 1874 the distinguished Senator from New York, Mr. Conklin, asked in astonishment whether it was true that there was by law no American dollar. Blaine, who was Speaker of the House during 1873, was also ignorant of the offensive clause in the mint bill.

In a colloquy with Senator Voorhees on the subject he said:

Mr. Voorhees: "I want to ask my friend from Maine, whom I am glad to designate in that way, whether I may call him as one more witness to the fact that it was not generally known whether silver was demonetized. Did he know, as the Speaker of the House, presiding at that time, that the silver dollar was demonetized in the bill to which he alludes?"

Mr. Blaine: "I did not know anything that was in the bill at all. As I have said before, little was known or cared on the subject. [Laughter.] And now I should like to exchange questions with the Senator from Indiana, who was then on the floor and whose business, far more than mine, to know, because by the designation of the House I was to put the questions; the Senator from Indiana, then on the floor of the House, with his power as a debater, was to unfold them to the House. Did he know?"

Mr. Voorhees: "I frankly say that I did not."—Congressional Record, Feburary 15, 1878, page 1063.

Senator Allison, of Iowa, said:

But when the secret history of this bill of 1873 comes to

be told it will disclose the fact that the House of Representatives intended to coin both gold and silver, and intended to place both metals upon the French relation instead of our own, which was the true scientific position with reference to this subject in 1873, but that the bill afterwards was doctored, if I may use the term, and I use in no offensive sense, of course—

* * * * * * * * * * * *

I said I used the word in no offensive sense. It was changed after the discussion, and the dollar of 420 grains was substituted for it.—Congressional Record, Volume VII. Part two, Forty-fifth Congress, second session, page 1085.

Senator Morgan said:

Did the people demonetize silver? Never! It cannot even be fairly said that Congress did it. It was done in a corner, darkly. It was done at the instigation of the bondholders and other money kings, who now with upturned eyes deplore the wickedness we exhibit in asking the question even, who did the great wrong against the toiling millions of our people? * * * * * * *

How will Congress answer these people except to say that the silver dollar weighing 412½ grains was an honest dollar until the 12th of February, 1873, when we destroyed the money in your pockets and left a vast debt hanging over you, since when our bonds have been sold from hand to hand in the markets among stock gamblers. They knew that we had stricken down your rights and trusted to our honor that your rights should be restored. It would be dishonest in us to restore your money to its value and vitality. It is bullion now —mere pig metal—and is no longer money.—Senator Morgan, in Congressional Record, December 12, 1877, page 144.

Joseph Cannon, of Illinois, said:

This legislation was had in the Forty-second Congress, February 12, 1873, by a bill to regulate the mints of the United States, and practically abolished silver as money by failing to provide for the coinage of the silver dollar. It was not discussed, as shown by the record, and neither members of Congress nor the people understood the scope of the legislation.—Joseph Cannon, in Congressional Record, Volume IV., Part six, Forty-fourth Congress, first session, Appendix, page 193.

General Garfield in a speech made at Springfield, Ohio, in the fall of 1887, said:

Perhaps I ought to be ashamed to say so, but it is the truth to say that at that time, being Chairman of the Committee on Appropriation, and having my hands over full during all that time with work, I never read the bill. I took it upon the faith of a prominent Democrat and a prominent Republican, and I do not know that I voted at all. There was a call for yeas and nays and nobody opposed the bill that I know of. It was put through as dozens of bills are, as my friend and I know, in Congress on the faith of the report of the chairman of the committee. Therefore, I tell you, because it is the truth, that I had no knowledge of it.

Mr. Bright, of Tennessee, said:

It passed by fraud in the House, never having been printed in advance, being a substitute for the printed bill; never having been read at the clerk's desk, the reading having been dispensed with by an impression that the bill made no material alteration in the coinage laws; it was passed without discussion, debate being cut off by operation of the previous question. It was passed, to my certain information, under such circumstances that the fraud escaped the attention of some of the most watchful as well as the ablest statesmen in Congress at the time. * * * Aye, sir, it was a fraud that smells to heaven. It was a fraud that will stink in the nose of posterity, and for which some persons must give account in the day of retribution.

Senator Beck said:

It [the bill demonetizing silver] never was understood by either House of Congress. I say that with full knowledge of the facts. No newspaper reporter—and they are the most vigilant men I ever saw in obtaining information—discovered that it had been done.—Senator Beck, January 10, 1878.

I know that the bondholders and the monopolists of this country are seeking to destroy all the industries of this people, in their greed to enhance the value of their gold. I know that the act of 1873 did more than all else to accomplish that result, and the demonetization act of the Revised Statutes was an illegal and unconstitutional consummation of the fraud. I want to restore that money to where it was before, and thus aid in preventing the consummation of their designs.—Senator Beck again.

On examination of the files of the Chicago Tribune we find the only reference that appears in that paper is in a press telegram from Washington, which is this—I read it: "Mr. Sherman called up the bill to revise and amend the laws relating to the mints, assay offices and coinage of the United States, which was amended and passed." That is all—not another word.

The Chicago Tribune of February 23, 1878, when it was

an honest paper, said: "In 1873-4, as it was two years and more later discovered, the coinage of this silver dollar was forbidden, and silver dollars were demonetized by law. This act, which was done secretly and stealthily, to the profound ignorance of those who voted for it and of the President who approved of it, had, without the knowledge of the country, removed one of the landmarks of the government; had, under cover of darkness, abolished the constitutional dollar, and had arbitrarily and to the immense injury of the people, added heavily to every form of indebtedness public and private."

On January 19, 1878, this same paper said: "Harper's Weekly insists on the single gold standard, and has frequently denied that that the silver dollar was demonetized surreptitiously or unknown to Congress and the country. But it appears from Harper's own files that nobody about that concern had the faintest conception as late as January 9, 1875, that silver had been demonetized. In the issue of that date Nast illustrated the "Ark of State" floating toward a distant peak, just showing above the watery waste; on which is inscribed: "A Sound Specie Basis—Gold and Silver," while above gleams the bright rainbow of "Our Credit." This, recollect, was on the ninth of January, 1875, nearly two years after Dr. Linderman and his gold conspirators had sneaked the fraud through Congress, and up to that time neither Tom Nast nor George William Curtis nor Eugene Lawrence, the three editors of that publication, had yet an inkling of what the anti silver conspirators had accomplished."

This was before the Tribune got into the hands of the money power. It cannot now too strongly villify silver or the advocates of bimetallism. What influence has wrought this change?

But why multiply evidences? Enough have been produced to show that the dark deed was done under the cover of darkness, as all such deeds must be; that the unseen, stealthy hands of the bribe-givers and bribe-takers have stolen the liberties of the industrial classes, in behalf of the idlers. The syndicate of Jewish bondholders who control the finances of the world, through the secret

'DE SUN DO MOVE." SEE PAGE 240.

agencies which they know too well how to employ, and by
taking advantage of human weakness and cupidity which
they too well understand, have triumphed.

First, through their hired tool, Hugh McCulloch, and
others in high places in their employ, they succeeded in
passing the refunding act, which reduced the circulating
medium about $1,200,000,000 or from $2,000,000,000 to less
than $900,000,000 in a few years' time; or from upwards
of $50 per capita to less than $18. This caused the great
panic of 1873 and the resultant depression and suffering.
What does Shylock care how humanity suffers or what
afflictions he brings upon the race so long as he gets his
two pounds of flesh, or so long as his pile of gold over
which he gloats is increased? Then came the resumption
act. By these two, the refunding and resumption acts,
the purchasing power of Shylock's bonds was doubled.

By this transaction alone the Jewish syndicate headed
by the Rothschilds cleared over $600,000,000 on their
holdings of United States bonds. Not content with these
enormous profits, the great crime of 1893 was planned
and carried to completion to again double the purchasing power of bonds. This, too, has been accomplished. A
Government bond in 1894 will buy twice as much of labor's
products as it would have done in 1873 and four times as
much as it would in 1865. That is, dear reader, the industrial classes, to which you and I belong, will have to
expend four times as much labor to pay such bonds now
as we would have had to do if the currency in circulation
had remained at upward of $50 per capita, as in 1865, or
twice as much as we would, had the bimetallic standard
been maintained.

Measured by the average of labor's products, the only true
measure, the national debt of the United States has not
been diminished one iota, but on the contrary, on the present basis or relation between money and labor, as estab-

lished by the adoption of the single gold standard, it will take more of labor's commodities to pay the debt to-day than would have paid the much more voluminous amount as it stood at the close of the war.

The gloomy forebodings of the great commoner, Thad. Stevens, and of the immortal Lincoln, have come to pass. The influence of the great oppressor whom they feared now dominates this nation as well as those of the Old World.

The earnest warnings of Mr. Seyd have gone unheeded and his clear-sighted, prophetic predictions of what would follow the demonetization of silver are being fulfilled.

The "English plan" for enslaving the producing classes set forth in the Hazard Circular has gone into effect. The plans of the conspirators so plainly outlined and exposed by Hippolyte Grenier have been accomplished. As a result we are being driven into a slavery much more direful in its effects and much more blighting in its character than that which we spent so much blood and treasure to destroy.

I cannot do better in closing this chapter than to quote the words of another eminent American, who, perhaps, did more than any other man to abolish African slavery. Horace Greeley, with the clear foresight manifested by Lincoln, Seyd and others, saw what but comparatively few saw as clearly as he did, viz., that the establishment of the British system of finance meant slavery not only to the blacks but to the whites; and these were the words for which the bankers of New York drove him from the office of the Tribune with a broken heart to the grave. He said:

We boast of having liberated 4,000,000 of slaves. True, we have stricken the shackles from the former bondsmen and brought all laborers to a common level, but not so much by elevating the former slaves as by practically reducing the whole working population to a state of serfdom. While boasting of our noble deeds we are careful to conceal the ugly fact that by our iniquitous monetary system we have nationalized a system of oppression more refined, but none the less cruel, than the old system of chattel slavery.

If the old veteran could truthfully say this in 1882 what would he have said had he lived until the present day, when that slavery he foresaw is becoming an established fact?

The panic of 1893 and the great depression, the low prices of the products of the farm and mines, the reduction in the wages of the laborer, and the business stagnation that everywhere prevails are the direct results of the great crime of 1873 and the subsequent legislation by the different nations, including our own, in harmony with it.

To measure its weight in its fullness we must take into consideration not only the enhanced purchasing power of Government bonds but that of all forms of indebtedness, all of which have increased in value in like proportion, and that the weight of all indebtedness falls upon the producing classes.

These evidences of indebtedness in the United States are roughly estimated at $25,000,000,000, about $400 per capita, about ninety per cent of which is in the hands of the non-producing classes.

When we take into consideration the fact that the burden of this enormous debt has increased at least one-third by the demonetization of silver, we can realize the enormity of the offense aginst the industrial classes.

The question which confronts the American people is, What shall we do to relieve ourselves of the effects of this great crime? We wish the question of accomplishment was as easy as the answer how the work should be undone. First restore the silver dollar, make it a full legal tender for the payment of all debts whatsoever. Then enact a law making it compulsory for the Secretary of the Treasury to redeem paper money when presented or pay interest on bonds or the bonds themselves in whatever coined money he has the largest stock of in the vaults. If he has more silver than gold dollars let redemption be made in silver. If more gold, then in gold. In this way silver will be fully restored to its former power as money of ultimate redemption. Then forever tie the hands of the gold clique and reduce the purchasing power of gold and bonds to their former state by opening the mints to the free and unlimited coinage of silver on the ratio of sixteen to one. This policy put into effect would quickly reduce the purchasing power of money and advance the exchangeable value of commodities and restore prosperity.

The next step, in order to bring still greater prosperity to the producers and curb the power of the banks and fund-holding classes, should be to abolish the national bank circulation and issue a like amount of greenbacks redeemable in either silver or gold as aforesaid.

As the people prefer paper money to coined money, a paper dollar should be issued for each metal dollar coined. Sound financial policy permits the issue of a paper or credit dollar for each coined dollar, nor is it under such circumstances necessary that the coined money should all be kept as a redemption fund. Twenty-five per cent is all that is necessary. The balance can safely go into circulation. This plan adopted, the prolific mines of this country can be depended on to do the rest. Industrial prosperity such as this country has never known would surely follow such a sound financial policy.

As I have before intimated, it is easier to say what should be done than it will be to accomplish it. The same powerful agency which has brought us to the present crisis has lost none of its cunning, nor is it yet satisfied. Human greed is insatiable. It is still at work trying to aggrandize its power and strengthen its grip on the wealth of the world and further enslave the world's workers.

Its cunning hand is now seen in the persistent and continued efforts on the part of the banks to take from the people the right to issue any form of money except coined gold. These efforts are now directed towards securing the withdrawal of what remains of the greenback circulation and the silver certificates. These are offensive because they are issued by the National Government directly to the people. The banks want a complete monopoly of money and are determined to have it. The Baltimore plan, Carlisle-Springer plan and the Cleveland currency plan recommended in his message to Congress, December, 1894, are all in harmony with this purpose. Once in full control of the money of the country, their power is limitless. As the mainspring and inspiration of this power is insatiable greed, it is not difficult to measure the consequences.

It is in your power, friends and fellow Americans, to stop their further encroachments and undo the effects of this great crime. Will you do it? Do you love your liberties, your country, your wives and your children? If so, rouse yourselves, agitate, educate, distribute reading matter, let the light shine. Let every one who knows the truth become a miss'onary in this great cause of liberty. The people feel the unseen hand of the oppressor. Show them the hand at the screw. Unless all signs fail, in the campaign of 1896 all minor issues, such as the tariff, will be cast aside and we shall have a chance to measure swords direct with the money power. Hitherto they have blinded our eyes and kept us with divided partisan strength chasing will-o'-the-wisps. We must end this, stand together and see to it that every member of the great industrial army is arrayed on the right side with an intelligent vote for liberty, country and prosperity.

CHAPTER VII.

QUESTIONS ANSWERED.

The author has received many questions from members of Economic Circles and readers of the FARM, FIELD AND FIRESIDE relating to the various phases of the subject under discussion. These we shall arrange and answer in order.

QUESTIONS NOS. 1 AND 2.

The Constitution of the United States delegates to Congress the right "to coin money, regulate the value thereof and fix the standards of weights and measures." Art. 1, Sec. 8, paragraph 5.

It further says:

"No State shall * * * coin money, emit bills of credit, make anything but gold and silver legal tender in payment of debts."

Under these provisions which clearly imply that gold and silver should be a legal tender in payment of debts, has Congress the right to demonetize either gold or silver or to delegate to banks the right to issue legal tender money?

J. P. LELAND, Illinois.

This clause certainly imposes upon Congress the duty of providing for the coinage of silver and making it a full legal tender, because it especially provides that a State may make silver coin, as well as gold, a legal tender in payment of debts, and as it also prohibits the States from coining money it may be assumed as settled beyond question that the Constitution also imposed upon Congress the duty of making legal tender silver coin.

The Supreme Court decided some forty years ago in the celebrated Marigold case that whenever a statute gives power to a legislative body to perform that which is necessary for the public good such power is not optional but mandatory upon said body to perform said duty. The text of this decision reads (sec. 9 Howard, page 567 and 568):

We hold it a sound maxim that no power should be conceded to the Federal Government which cannot be regularly and legitimately found in the charter of its creation.

The court was composed of such men as Taney, Wayne, McLean, etc. This shows that they were strict constructionists. In the same decision they also used this language:

Whatever functions Congress is by the Constitution authorized to perform, it is, when the public good requires it, bound to perform.

DANIEL WEBSTER ON SILVER.

This question is further answered in the negative by the greatest constitutional lawyer America has produced, whose utterances are generally accepted as authority, Daniel Webster, who says on this subject:

I am certainly of the opinion that gold and silver at rates fixed by Congress constitute the legal standard of value in this country and that neither Congress nor any State has authority to establish any other standard or to displace this standard.

JAMES G. BLAINE FOR FREE COINAGE.

The greatest of Republicans, and perhaps we might say one of the greatest American statesmen, James G. Blaine, in a speech in the Senate, February 7, 1878 (see Congressional Record, page 820 and 822), said:

I believe gold and silver coin to be the money of the Constitution; indeed, the money of the American people anterior to the Constitution which that great organic law recognized as quite independent of its own existence. No power was conferred on Congress to declare that either metal should not be money. Congress has therefore, in my judgment, no power to demonetize silver any more than to demonetize gold; no power to demonetize either any more than to demonetize both.

In this statement I am but repeating the weighty dictum of the first of constitutional lawyers. "I am certainly of opinion," said Mr. Webster, "that gold and silver, at rates fixed by Congress, constitute the legal standard of value in this country, and that neither Congress nor any State has authority to establish any other standard or to displace this standard."

Few persons can be found, I apprehend, who will maintain that Congress possesses the power to demonetize both gold and silver, or that Congress should be justified in prohibiting the coinage of both; and yet, in logic and legal construction, it would be difficult to show where and why the power of Congress over silver is greater than over gold; greater over either than over the two. If, therefore, silver has been demonetized, I am in favor of remonetizing it. If its coinage has been prohibited, I am in favor of ordering it to be resumed. If it has been restricted, I am in favor of having it enlarged.

The opinions of such eminent men should have great weight. We believe they are entirely correct and effectually answer this important question. We further believe that if a test case could be brought to an impartial Supreme Court the law of 1873 and all subsequent acts limiting the legal tender of the silver dollar would be declared unconstitutional.

Republicans when they again come into power will do well to consider the words of their great leader, James G. Blaine.

In the same speech he further says (see page 821):

The responsibility of re-establishing silver in its ancient and honorable place as money in Europe and America devolves really on the Congress of the United States. If we act here with prudence, wisdom and firmness, we shall not only successfully remonetize silver and bring it into general use as money in our own country, but the influence of our example will be potential among all European nations, with the possible exception of England. Indeed, our annual indebtedness to Europe is so great that if we have the right to pay it in silver we necessarily coerce those nations by the strongest of all forces—self-interest—to aid us in upholding the value of silver as money.

Blaine did not belong to that white-livered crowd who are afraid to move in this matter unless England consents or leads, but truthfully says that if we lead we shall necessarily "coerce" other nations by the strongest of motives, "self-interest."

And further down on the same page, this distinguished man continues:

I believe the struggle now going on in this country and in other countries for a single gold standard would, if successful, produce widespread disaster in the end throughout the world.

The destruction of silver as money and establishing gold as the sole unit of value must have a ruinous effect on all forms of property except those investments which yield a fixed return in money. These would be enormously enhanced in value, and would gain a disproportionate and unfair advantage over every other species of property. If, as the most reliable statistics affirm, there are nearly $7,000,000,000 of coin or bullion in the world, not very unequally divided between gold and silver, it is impossible to strike silver out of existence as money without results which will prove distressing to millions and utterly disastrous to tens of thousands.

In this paragraph the great statesman shows eminent foresight, a certain result which should follow a known cause.

We are now actually suffering from the very condition he thus predicted would follow the policy against which he was so strongly and urgently protesting. Let the reader bear in mind that these words were uttered in 1878, sixteen years ago, before the effects of demonetization had begun to be felt in any perceptible degree. Now note the "ruinous effects on all forms of property" (the products of labor as manifested in the prices prevailing to-day), "except those investments which yield a fixed return in money" (bonds, mortgages, etc.). It seems strange indeed, that anyone can read such predictions and note their fulfillment, and then attribute the result to other causes than the demonetization of silver.

WHAT ALEXANDER HAMILTON SAID.

Mr. Blaine, in this same speech quotes from another eminent American statesman, Alexander Hamilton, to strengthen his position.

Alexander Hamilton, in his able and invaluable report in

1791 on the establishment of a mint, declared that "to annul the use of either gold or silver as money is to abridge the quantity of circulating medium, and is liable to all the objectiqns which arise from a comparison of the benefits of a full circulation with the evils of a scanty circulation." I take no risk in saying that the benefits of a full circulation and the evils of a scanty circulation are both immeasurably greater to-day than they were when Mr. Hamilton uttered these weighty words, always provided that the circulation is one of actual money and not of depreciate promises to pay.

And we take no risk in saying that the evils of a narrow scanty circulation of "actual money" are "immeasurably greater to-day" than they were when Mr. Blaine uttered the above weighty words.

Mr. Blaine then proceeds to discuss the reason why the United States above all other nations, should have unlimited coinage of silver, in these words:

I do not think that this country, holding so vast a proportion of the world's supply of silver in its mountains and its mines,can afford to reduce the metal to the "situation of mere merchandise." If silver ceases to be used as money in Europe and America, the great mines of the Pacific Slope will be closed and dead. Mining enterprises of the gigantic scale existing in this country can not be carried on to provide backs for looking-glasses and to manufacture cream pitchers and sugar bowls. A vast source of wealth to this entire country is destroyed the moment silver is permanently disused as money. It is for us to check that tendency and bring the continent of Europe back to the full recognition of the value of the metal as a medium of exchange.

GARFIELD FOR FREE COINAGE.

No truer words were ever uttered. If we would make real money of the resources of our own mines we would need no foreign capital and instead of being a debtor nation paying annually hundreds of millions in foreign tribute we would soon become a creditor nation. Restore silver as coin of ultimate redemption with full legal tender qualities and free coinage on the ratio of sixteen to one and we will "bring the continent of Europe back to the full recognition of the value of the metal as a medium of exchange," restore prices, compel England and Germany and other countries to pay a decent price for our products and restore prosperity—in fact, reverse the condition which Mr. Blaine so clearly foretold would come upon the country and which is now here, with all its direful effects. In the same debate in 1878 another eminent Republican and statesman, since President of the United States, James A. Garfield, said:

Every man who is opposed to the use of silver coin as part of the legal currency of the country I disagree with. Every man who is opposed to the actual legal use of both metals I disagree with.

I would endow the two dollars with equality and make the coinage free.

HOW CARLISLE STOOD BEFORE LED INTO TEMPTATION.

The present Secretary of the Treasury, Hon. John G. Carlisle, also took an active part in the aforesaid debate. Mr. Carlisle, before he was exalted to the high position he now holds and came under the influence of the siren voice of Wall street and the bankers' association, was an ardent and outspoken silver man. What influence has been brought to bear upon him to cause him to turn traitor to the interests of the people and serve Wall street we leave the public to surmise. His speech was not an expression of thought uttered in heat of debate, but was carefully prepared, and it was withheld from the Record for revision, and is printed on pages 41 to 44 of the Appendix. On page 42 Carlisle stated—"he was in favor of unlimited coinage of both metals upon terms of exact equality. No discrimination should be made in favor of one metal and against the other, nor should any discrimination be made in favor of the owners of gold and silver bullion and against the great body of people who own other coins or property." And on page 43 he said:

I know that the world's stock of the precious metals is none too large, and I see no reason to apprehend that it will ever become so. Mankind will be fortunate, indeed, if the annual production of gold and silver coin shall keep pace with the annual increase of population, commerce and industry.

Commenting on this speech of Carlisle's, the Hon. Joseph Wheeler, of Alabama, said, during the debate on the repeal of the Sherman act in the present Congress:

In 1878 the annual production of gold was $51,200,000 and the annual production of silver $45,200,000, the total being $96,400,000. The total amount of property in the United States in 1878 was $40,000,000,000; therefore the amount of property in the country was only 781 times the annual production of gold and 419 times the annual production of both gold and silver. The entire amount of property in the country to-day is at least $68,000,000,000. We produced only $33,-000,000 of gold last year and $74,989,900 of silver. Therefore the amount of property in the country is 2,060 times the annual production of gold and 627 times the annual production of both gold and silver. We therefore see that our relative production of gold in about one-third the relative production in 1878, when Mr. Carlisle made his speech, and yet there are men in this hall attempting to strike down silver and relegate this country to the gold standard.

As the function of money is to serve as a basis of exchange between commodities its quantity should be based on the volume of such exchanges, otherwise the facility of exchange is impaired and the demand for money caused by scarcity increases its purchasing power or exchange value. Mr. Wheeler shows that even if gold and silver were both actual money the volume would not have kept pace with the increase in the value of property and the volume of commercial transactions.

To further quote from this speech of Mr. Carlisle:

According to my views of the subject the conspiracy which seems to have been formed here and in Europe to destroy, by legislation and otherwise, from three-sevenths to one-half of the metallic money of the world is the most gigantic crime of this or any other age.

This language is very strong. The most gigantic crime of the age it is indeed. How shameful it is that a man who could talk thus in 1878 could be induced by political preferment to eat his words and sanction the crime in 1893. Mr. Carlisle proceeded in the following emphatic language:

The consummation of such a scheme would ultimately entail more misery upon the human race than all the wars, pestilences, and famines that ever occurred in the history of the world. The absolute and instantaneous destruction of half the entire movable property of the world, including houses, ships, railroads, and all other appliances for carrying on commerce, while it would be felt more sensibly at the moment, would not produce anything like the prolonged distress and disorganization of society that must inevitably result from the permanent annihilation of the metallic money in the world.

That misery thus clearly predicted is now here, and the Secretary's present course in yielding to Wall street and Cleveland's dictation is greatly intensifying it. His prophetic foresight was grand, his present position despicable. From Mr. Carlisle's speech, on page 44 of the Record, we learn that he even went so far as to want a constitutional amendment to unalterably fix the ratio between silver and gold.

I am in favor of every practicable and constitutional measure that will have a tendency to defeat or retard the perpetration of this great crime, and I am also in favor of every practicable and constitutional measure that will aid us in devising a just and permanent ratio of value between the two metals, so that they might circulate side by side, and not alternately drive each other into exile from one country to another. Our ratio, as recognized by the present bill, is 15.98 to one, while the ratio established by the states composing the Latin Union - France, Belgium, Switzerland, Italy, and I believe Greece also, is fifteen and one-half to one. We therefore undervalue silver, as compared with the valuation put upon it by those countries.

I have thus quoted at length from these eminent men both to show that the discarding of silver as a coin of ultimate redemption and impairing its legal tender qualities is unconstitutional and that the "public good" requires its restitution as the full money of the Constitution, and therefore under the decision of the Supreme Court before referred to, it is mandatory on the part of Congress to so restore it.

ANDREW JACKSON ON MONEY AND THE CONSTITUTION.

We can best answer the second part of the above question, Has Congress the power to delegate to banks the right to issue legal tender money, by quoting from the veto message of the eminent Democratic General, President and statesman, Andrew Jackson. In his message vetoing the bill to extend the charter of that vile octopus, the United States bank, he said:

It is maintained by some that the bank is a means of executing constitutional power "to coin money and regulate the value thereof." Congress has established a mint to coin money and passed laws to regulate the value thereof. The money so coined with its value so regulated and such foreign coins as Congress may adopt are the only currency known to the Constitution.

But if they have other power to regulate currency, it was conferred to be exercised by themselves and not to be transferred to a corporation. If the banks be established for that purpose with a charter unalterable without its consent, Congress has parted with this power for a term of years during which the Constitution is a dead letter. It is neither necessary nor proper to transfer its legislative powers to such a bank and therefore unconstitutional, * * * unauthorized by the Constitution, subversive of the rights of the States and dangerous to the liberties of the people. * * * When the laws undertake to grant gratuities and exclusive privileges to make the rich richer, the potent, more powerful members of society—the farmers, mechanics and laborers—who have neither the time nor means of securing like favors for themselves, have a right to complain of the injustice of government.

The act incorporating this bank was passed April 10, 1816. It had a capital of $35,000,000. It was bonded by the Government which held $7,000,000 of its stock. The notes of the bank were made full legal tender for the payment of all debts. It was an act to renew its charter for twenty years longer, passed through the means of the grossest bribery, which President Jackson vetoed. The bank attempted to continue in spite of the veto and without a charter, when the President finally destroyed it by withdrawing $40,000,000 Government deposits from its custody.

This was the last attempt on the part of Congress to delegate its constitutional power to make and regulate

legal tender money.   National bank and other bank notes
possess no legal tender qualities and therefore should be
abolished.

The great danger which threatens the American people
to-day, is that through the restless influence of the banks
all forms of legal tender paper money will be destroyed,
and the right to issue paper money delegated to the banks.
When this is accomplished to the satisfaction of the banks
and the bondholders, gold coin will be the only legal tender money, and the debtor will be completely at the
mercy of the creditor and the producer at the mercy of
the parasites.

QUESTION NO. 3.—WHAT IS BIMETALLISM?

What is meant by bimetallism or the bimetallic standard?
The professor of political economy at the college I attended
affirms that we might just as well have two yard-sticks of
different lengths with which to measure fabrics as to have a
double standard with which to measure values.

GEORGE MONTGOMERY, **Kansas.**

Your professor is either inexcusably ignorant of what
he is talking about or is wilfully misleading.   A bimetallic standard does not mean a double or two standards, but
one standard composed of two metals; both metals when
coined at a ratio fixed by law being full legal tender for
the payment of all debts either public or private.   Both
being coin of ultimate redemption into which credit money
(paper money) is convertible or redeemable, both having
equal rights of free coinage at the mints, both being
standard money, the unit (dollar) of either or both being
the measure of values by which to measure other commodities, they become one standard and unitedly serve to
maintain the equilibrium of prices and the relations between the price of commodities and debts.

The thought can best be illustrated by the pendulum
of a self-regulating clock or an adjusted watch balance,
which are so arranged that their expansion and contrac-

tion counteract each other. Thus through the agency of bimetallism the length of the pendulum or balance is maintained and the clock or watch does not vary with the changes of temperature. The bimetallic pendulum or balance thus serves to maintain correct time.

No one ever thinks of calling a bimetallic pendulum or balance wheel a double pendulum or two pendulums or balance wheels. A man would be thought crazy who would use the two yard-stick argument in discussing such a pendulum. Yet it is not more foolish than to use it as is so commonly done by those whose selfish greed or ignorance leads them to support the ruinous single gold standard policy. The bimetallic standard is just as necessary to maintain the equlibrium of fairness between debtor and creditor and between the producers and non-producers as the bimetallic pendulum is to maintain the uniform running of a clock.

That it is practicable has been demonstrated by the experience of the world for thousands of years—in fact, until 1873, when the United States and others of the great commercial nations unwisely departed from it.

That it is best is demonstrated by the experience of those nations, in particular our own, which have tried the disastrous experiment of the single gold standard. The prevailing hard times, depression of business, low prices for products and general unsatisfactory condition are a direct result of departing from the scientific, time-tried, God-given bimetallic standard.

WHY IT IS SCIENTIFIC

can be easily further explained on the principle that two metals united in one standard are much less liable to be subject to the varying changes in production than one metal alone.

For an illustration we refer the reader to the varying production and changes in the relative production of the precious metals during the past 400 years, as shown in the following condensed table. (For full table see Chart No. 9, page 111).

RELATIVE PRODUCTION OF GOLD AND SILVER IN THE WORLD FOR 400 YEARS.

Period.	Gold— Annual av'r'ge of period.	Silver— Annual av'r'ge of period.	Per cent of producti'n.		
	Value.	Coining value.	Gold.	Silv.	Ratio.
1493-1520..	$ 3,855,000	$ 1,954,000	66.4	33.6	15 to 1
1521-1700..	5,575,000	13,770,000	30.7	70.0	15 to 1
1701-1800..	12,429,000	23,708,000	35.7	64.3	15½ to 1
1801-1850..	15,749,000	23,205,000	34.1	65.9	15½ to 1
1851-1875..	127,567,000	51,548,000	71.6	28.5	15½ to 1
1876-1880..	114,586,000	101.851,000	53.0	47.0	16½ to 1
1881-1885..	99,116,000	118,955,000	45.5	54.5	19 to 1
1886.......	106,000,000	120,600.000	46.8	53.2	20 to 1
1887.......	105,302,000	124,366,000	45.9	54.1	21 to 1
1888.......	109,900,000	142.107,000	43.6	56.4	22 to 1
1889.......	118,800,000	162.690.000	42.2	57.8	22 to 1
1890.......	115,150,000	172,235,000	39.7	60.3	19 to 1
1891.......	120,519,000	186,733,000	39.2	60.8	20 to 1
1892.......	130,817,000	196.605,000	40.0	60.0	24 to 1
1893.......	155,522,000	208,371,100	31.1	41.6	28 to 1
1894.......	169,000,000	....	.....	.....	33 to 1

It will be seen that while the relative production varies enormously, the ratio fixed by law and maintained by free coinage remains the same.

The standard or yard-stick does not vary. Take, for example, the period from 1493 until 1700. It will be seen that during that period gold production fell off one-half, but its loss was supplied by the increase in the production of silver, so that the equilibrium was maintained. If the single gold standard had been in force during the period from 1493 until 1850, the progress of the world out of the dark ages into the progressive liberty of the nineteenth century would have been impossible.

I cannot, perhaps, better illustrate how intimately this money question is connected with the retarding or progress of civilization than by quoting from the report of the monetary commission.

This commission was appointed by act of Congress. It was composed of three Senators and three members of the House.

The report is dated March 2, 1877. On page 29 we read:

At the Christian era the metallic money of the Roman Empire amounted to $1,800,000,000. By the end of the fifteenth century it had sunk to less than $200,000,000. During this period a most extraordinary and baleful change took place in the condition of the world. Population dwindled, and commerce, arts, wealth and freedom all disappeared. The people were reduced by poverty and misery to the most degraded conditions of serfdom and slavery. The disintegration of society was almost complete. The conditions of life were so hard that individual selfishness was the only thing consistent with the instinct of self-preservation. All public spirit, all generous emotions, all the noble aspirations of man shriveled and disappeared as the volume of money shrunk and as prices fell.

There are, of course, other causes than the shrinkage of money for the fearful conditions of society during the dark ages, but there is no question but that it was due very largely to that cause. The report then proceeds in these words:

History records no such disastrous transition as that from the Roman Empire to the dark ages. Various explanations have been given of this entire breaking down of the framework of society, but it was certainly coincident with a shrinkage in the volume of money, which was also without historical parallel. The crumbling of institutions kept even step and pace with the shrinkage in the stock of money and the falling prices.

Bear in mind that this condition continued until after the discovery of America, and until the discovery of the rich silver mines of Potosi. During the ten years from 1546 to 1555 the production of silver averaged $17,000,000 a year, and this inflow of the precious metals to Europe was the beginning of a new dawn to civilization. The report of the monetary commission in alluding to the energizing influence caused by the shipping of silver from the mines of Potosi, says:

It needed the heroic treatment of rising prices to enable

society to reunite its shattered links, to shake off the shackles of feudalism, to relight and uplift the almost extinguished torch of civilization.

By now discarding silver and narrowing money to gold we are establishing another system of feudalism, that of the money kings and barons whose power promises to be even more despotic. The commission further discusses this subject in these words:

That the disasters of the dark ages were caused by decreasing money and failing prices, and that the recovery therefrom and the comparative prosperity which followed the discovery of America were due to an increasing supply, the precious metals and rising prices, will not seem surprising nor unreasonable when the noble functions of money are considered. Money is the great instrument of association, the very fiber of social organism, the vitalizing force of industry, the protoplasm of civilization, and as essential to its existence as oxygen is to animal life. Without money civilization could not have had a beginning; with a diminishing supply it must languish and, unless relieved, finally perish.

I now read from page 51:

It is in a volume of money keeping even pace with advancing population and commerce, and in the resulting steadiness of prices, that the wholesome nutriment of a healthy vitality is to be found.

I also read from page 53:

While the volume of money is decreasing, even although very slowly, the value of each unit of money is increasing in corresponding ratio, and property is falling in price. Those who have contracted to pay money find that it is constantly becoming more difficult to meet their engagements. The margins of securities melt rapidly away, and the confiscation by the creditor of the property on which they are based becomes only a question of time.

It will be readily understood that the falling prices from which we are now suffering are due to the increasing value of gold, now the sole money unit, and that in consequence debts are becoming more and more burdensome. This would not have happened had the bimetallic standard been maintained.

In the period from 1851 to 1875, we find that the relative production of the two metals was reversed, being 71.6 of

gold to 28.6 of silver. If but one metal had been the
standard at that time the relative values between money
and commodities and debtor and creditor would have
been very greatly disturbed. As it was, the bimetallic pendulum was unchanged. The ratio between the metals
stood this violent change in relative production, at fifteen
and one-half to one as established by law and maintained
by free coinage. The excess of production of the metals
which began at that time was necessary to keep pace with
the enormous increase in trade and the value of property
due to the introduction of steam and electricity.

CHART NO. 10.

RELATIVE PRODUCTION OF GOLD (IN VALUE)
MEASURED BY THE PRODUCTION OF SILVER.

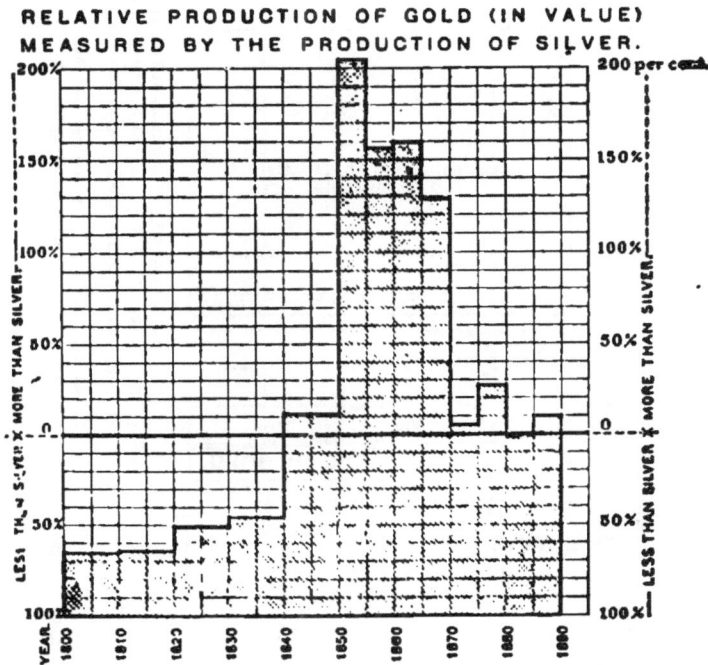

The above chart illustrates the relative production of

gold and silver during the present century until 1890 in another form.

CHART NO. 11.

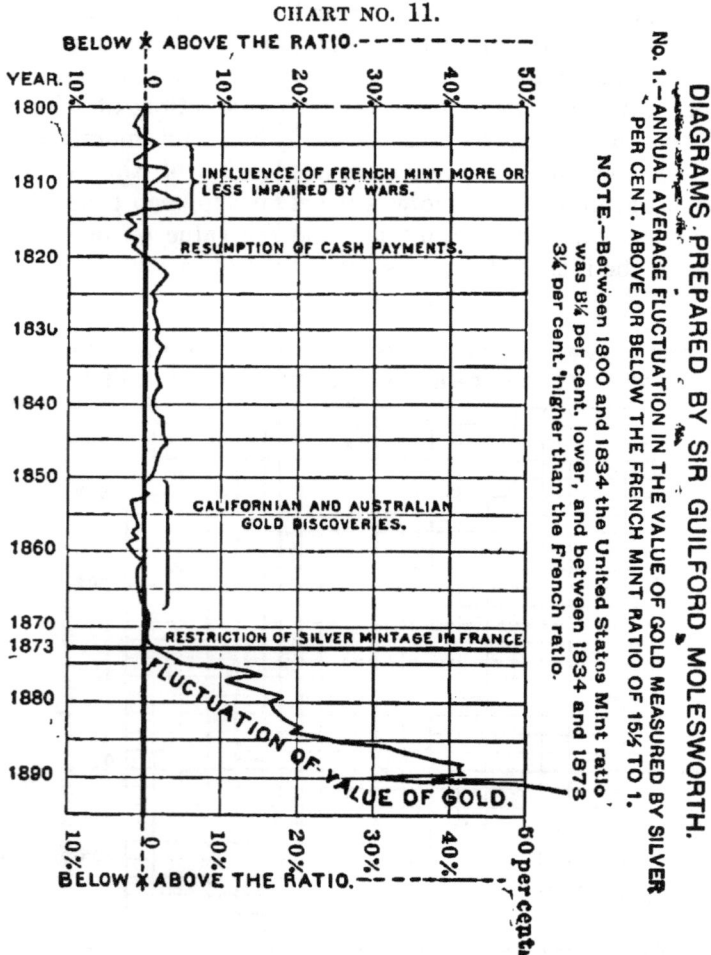

Chart No. 11 shows how the bimetallic standard maintained the relative prices of the two metals against violent changes in production during the present century

until silver was demonetized in 1873 and the French and
United States mints closed against its free coinage. Immediately, as we see, the value of gold as measured by silver began to rise and with it the purchasing power or
exchange value of all money, bonds and debts of all kinds.

CHART NO. 12.

No. 2.—FLUCTUATIONS IN THE PRICE OF COMMODITIES AND SILVER MEASURED BY GOLD.

Represents the Economist Index-Numbers for the Wholesale
Prices of 22 Principal Articles in the London Market.

Represents Dr. Soetbeer's Index-Numbers for the Prices of
100 Hamburg Articles, and 14 of British Export.

Represents Silver.

PRICES OF 1873 TAKEN AS ZERO.

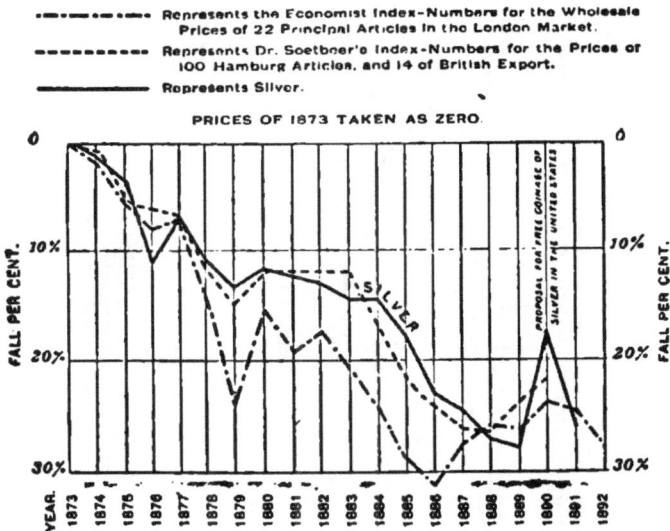

Chart No. 12 shows the fall in the price of silver
since 1873 as measured by gold and with it 100 articles,
the products of labor.

The fall in the price of both silver and commodities, as
everyone realizes, has been still greater, at least twenty-
five per cent, since these tables were prepared.

Chart No. 13 shows the variations in price of
twenty of America's chief productions between 1873 and
1892 as measured by the gold standard. The relative
fall in prices has been fully one-third greater since that

date. As between 1892 and 1893 we lost to Europe about $184,000,000 on account of falling prices.

CHART NO. 13.

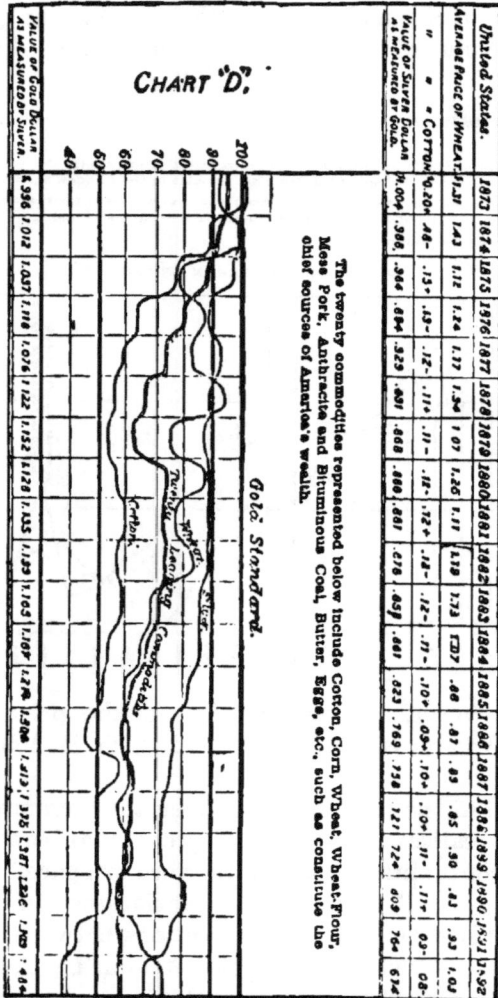

after silver was demonetized in 1873, and the self-regu-

lating bimetallic standard was destroyed, although there
is not such a wide difference in the relative production of
the metals as during the early part of the century the ratio
began immediatly to change and with the fall of silver as
measured by gold came the fall in like ratio of all the
products of labor, while debts, taxes, interest charges,
etc., remain on a parity with gold, thereby tremendously
increasing the burden of the wealth-producing classes,
who, as all wealth is produced by labor, must ultimately
pay all bonded indebtedness.

TOO EASILY CORNERED.

Another reason why it is best to maintain the bimetallic
standard is because one metal alone may be too easily
"cornered" by designing men, on the same principle
that "corners" are run on wheat or corn or other products on the board of trade. The great house of Rothschilds, with their own vast wealth and that of others
which they could at any time control for such a venture,
can effect a corner on gold, or, through the advantage which
the single gold standard plan gives them, control the
finances of the world at any time. In fact, it was to place
them in this position that they bribed or cajoled the
nations into adopting their plan. This plan is used now
as it was designed it should be, to increase the indebtedness
of the world. Our own Secretary of the Treasury and his
eminence Grover Cleveland are used as catspaws to
serve their ends. They are raking out the chestnuts (gold
bonds) for the Jewish bondholders and through their
agency our nation and people are being put more and more
under tribute. Does anyone for a moment suppose that all
this mischief would be now going on if we were under the
bimetallic standard? Instead of the slender thread of rapidly vanishing gold the Secretary would then have about
$500,000,000 in silver as redemption coin. It would also be
impossible for a combination of men to corner both metals.

The United States produced in 1893, $33,000,000 of gold and $75,000,000 of silver in round numbers. How short-

CHART NO. 14.

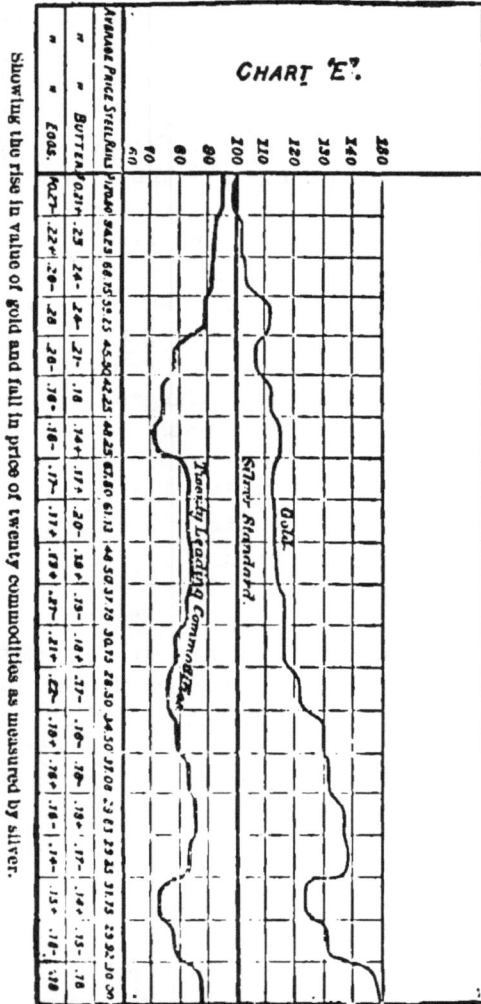

CHART 'E'.

Showing the rise in value of gold and fall in price of twenty commodities as measured by silver.

sighted in our legislators not to see what a great advanage it would be to have both these metals, especially silver, standard money on the ratio of sixteen to one.

We would have no need then for this costly "foreign capital" we hear so much about and which our bankers are so timid of frightening away, but would utilize our own vast storehouses of treasure concealed in the mountains to carry on our public enterprises, and save the enormous interest tribute we are now annually sending across the water.

If we must have but one metal for a standard, by all means let us have the most stable and that of which we have the greater supply.

Chart No. 14 will show that as a standard metal for use as a unit of value, silver is the more stable metal. It cannot be so readily hoarded as gold, and is less subject to fluctuations in value. It is a notable fact that at the present time silver standard nations are prosperous, while the reverse is the case in gold standard countries. The bimetallic standard is much the best, however.

We trust we have made the matter plain both as to what is meant by a bimetallic standard and why it is scientific and best. It is God-given because on account of the peculiar character of these metals they.and they alone are suitable for the purpose of money, and as they have been so used from the earliest times we believe this is the chief purpose of their creation by the all-wise God who does nothing in vain.

QUESTION NO. 4.—BIMETALLISM VS. MONOMETALLISM.

What is meant by the term bimetallism, or bimetallic standard, and monometallism or the single gold standard?
                                    HORACE JACOBS, Wisconsin.

By the term bimetallism or bimetallic standard, is meant that both gold and silver at a ratio fixed by law shall be standard or primary money; that is, money on which issues of paper or credit money are based and for which it is exchangeable at the treasury or sub-treasury of the United States at the option of the holder, the treasurer having the right to pay in either coin at his option. The unit of such primary money (the dollar) to be the unit of value or standard by which debts are contracted and paid and commodities exchanged. Such primary money and the money based on it to be legal tender for the payment of all dues and debts, including the bonds of the United States, custom dues., etc. In order that the bimetallic standard shall be maintained, it is necessary that both metals should have equal free coinage privileges at the mint, subject to such charge for seigniorage as the Government may exact to defray the expenses of coinage.

Monometallism substitutes the coins of one metal only for the two, making it alone primary money. Under our present system gold alone is primary money. In 1873 when Congress demonetized silver, by the same act it made the gold dollar the sole unit of value. In other words, it adopted the single gold standard. Since that time silver has been credit money, and like paper money under our system of finance, the silver dollar is maintained at par with the gold dollar, although there is a wide divergence in the price of the bullion of the two metals because it is exchangeable for gold at the option of the holder. If the bimetallic standard as it existed previous to 1873 was restored at the old ratio of sixteen to one and the mints opened to the free coinage of both metals the price of the bullion of the two metals would be quickly restored to the old ratio so that the metal bars of either could be used for redemption money for export instead of coin when the holder so desired.

MONOMETALLISM UNSOUND.

That under gold monometallism the finances of the country are in a very unsound condition can easily be demonstrated by figures as well as by the object-lesson shown in the present condition of this country and that of all gold standard countries. In fact, not only the finances of this country, but judged by the standard established by our present system of convertible credit money the finances of the world are in a very unsafe condition. This may be readily seen from the following chart compiled from the reports of the director of the mint.

CHART NO. 15.

PRIMARY MONEY VS. CREDIT MONEY UNDER THE PRESENT MONOMETALLISM.

Total money of all kinds, including bullion, in the United States, November 1, 1893.

Gold......................................$ 660,805,433
Silver.................................... 624,129,579
Paper..................................... 1,143,602,870

Total. $2,428,537,881

Sound financial policy dictates that credit money shall not exceed real money in amount. In the United States under our present system all money being redeemable in gold, it stands thus:
Credit money (silver and paper)...........$ 1,767,732,449
Real money (gold)......................... 660,605,433

Uncovered credit money....................$ 1,106,927,016

IN THE WORLD.

Gold......................................$ 3,700,000,000
Silver.................................... 3,800,000.000

Total.....................................$ 7,500,000,000
Paper.....................................$ 6,500,000,000
Credit money (silver and paper)...........$10,300,000,000
Real money (gold)......................... 3,700,000,000

Uncovered credit money....................$6,600,000,000

This accounts for the great scramble for gold at present going on among the gold standard nations. There is not redemption money enough to go around, an illustration of which is seen in the efforts of our own treasury to maintain its slender and entirely insufficient amount of redemption money by the frequent issue and sale of gold bonds. This cannot go on much longer and unless the bimetallic standard is adopted another crash will come and gold will go to a premium. Under a bimetallic standard, silver becoming also redemption money, it will be readily seen from the following chart that a better condition would prevail.

CHART NO. 16.

REAL MONEY VS. CREDIT MONEY UNDER BIMETALLISM.
IN THE UNITED STATES.

Real money (gold and silver).........................$1,284,935,012
Credit money (paper)................................. 1,143,602,870

Excess of real over credit money.....................$ 141,332,142

It is not necessary that the real money be retained in the treasury, but the greater part of it may safely be allowed to go into circulation.

IN THE WORLD.

Real money (gold and silver).........................$7,500,000,000
Credit money (paper)................................. 6,500,000,000

Excess of real over paper money.....................$1,000,000,000

The laws of the United States now practically provide that the treasurer shall redeem paper money in either coin at his option, but through the policies of this and the previous administrations this law has been made inopertive. When bimetallism is again adopted, as it must be before full prosperity can be restored, the recurrence of such a contingency should be provided against by making it mandatory upon the Secretary of the Treasury to redeem paper money when presented for redemption, and pay the principal or interest on bonds in whatever coin he has the largest amount of in the treasury at the time such notes or bonds are presented for redemption.

QUESTION NO. 5.—WHAT IS MEANT BY FREE COINAGE.?

What is meant by free coinage, and on what scientific hypothesis do you explain the fact that prior to 1873 the ratio of price between the two metals established by the laws of nations was maintained against varying production, and will again be maintained should bimetallism and free coinage be re-established?   P. G. GEORGESON, Kansas.

By free coinage is meant that holders of silver or gold bullion to the amount of $100 or more of standard weight and fineness shall have the right to have the same coined at the mints of the United States into coin of the weight and fineness provided by law, which at present is 412½ grains of standard silver in a dollar or 25.8 grains of gold. Said coins to be full legal tender for the payment of all dues, debts and demands, both public and private.

To this should be added a charge for seigniorage to cover the actual cost of minting which amounts to about one and one-half per cent. While this would not be in reality free coinage it would be so to all intents and purposes.

Under the old system of free coinage, under the laws of 1793 and 1837, the holder of bullion was given coined money in exchange therefor. When the system is again adopted the owner of the bullion should be allowed at his option to receive in exchange therefor either coined money or treasury notes.

It should also be made mandatory on the Secretary of the Treasury to issue the equivalent of all bullion received by him in treasury notes, said notes also to be full legal tender for the payment of all debts, dues or demands both public or private. Also as fast as possible to coin the bullion into money, putting it out also into circulation with the exception of twenty-five per cent, to be retained as a redemption fund against emergencies. In order to get both notes and coin into circulation outstanding bonds could be redeemed.

The people do not want coined money to any large extent for use. They prefer paper. The coined money would be useful for bank and treasury reserves.

HOW THE RATIO IS MAINTAINED.

It is not difficult to see how the ratio of price between the two metals when established by law is maintained under bimetallism when both have the privilege of free mintage without discrimination.

It is explained under the law of supply and demand, on the principle that the demand for money is unlimited and therefore the supply never equals the demand.

When the mints are thrown open to free coinage, the Government fixes the ratio, which at present is sixteen to one, and practically says we will take all the silver and gold that comes, an unlimited demand is established. Any one having gold or silver can bring it to the mint and have it made into money at this fixed ratio. This money being full legal tender he can pay his debts or taxes with it or exchange it for commodities. The demand, therefore, is only limited by the supply.

As this rule applies to either metal without discrimination, it is impossible for the relative value established by law to vary only a slight degree.

The reason of the present disparity between the price of the two metals is due to the fact that silver has been deprived of its former right of free coinage and consequent unlimited demand, and therefore, the demand being limited, the price has been regulated by the supply.

QUESTION NO. 6.—THE RATIO OF SIXTEEN TO ONE.

I have read your articles thus far, and I will confess they have given me new light on the cause of hard times. It is not quite clear to my mind what is meant by the ratio of sixteen to one; also, what reasons can you give for considering that such ratio is the best. Our Congressman in a recent speech advocated remonetizing silver at the ratio of twenty-eight to one.   J. L. WILSON.
Michigan.

Sixteen to one means that the bimetallic ratio shall be as sixteen parts of silver to one of gold. That is, as at present, a gold dollar shall contain 25.8 grains of standard gold to 412½ grains of standard silver in a silver dollar. This is not exactly sixteen to one, but is so near it that it is called so in round numbers.

IT IS BEST TO MAINTAIN THIS RATIO:

First, because all our present coinage is based on that ratio. That of France and other European states is based on a lower ratio of fifteen and a half to one.

Second, because it is desirable to restore the price of silver in its ratio with gold back to its former state. The reason is apparent. By consulting the foregoing charts it will be seen that the price of silver and other commodities has fallen as compared with gold in almost exactly the same ratio. It follows, therefore, that the restoration of the price of silver by the adoption of the bimetallic standard on the ratio of sixteen to one, will also with silver restore the price of commodities so that the farmer and other producers will be able to get a fair price for their products, and thus prosperity will be restored. To fix the ratio at twenty-eight to one or at the present ratio of about thirty-two to one, as some propose, will be to fix the price of silver as it now is and with it the prevailing unprofitable prices for all the products of labor except gold.

We must for the foregoing reasons accept no species of bimetallism that is based on a lower ratio than sixteen to one. The French standard of fifteen and one-half to one would be better, was it not for the fact that it would incur the necessity of the recoinage of all the silver dollars now extant.

QUESTION NO. 7.—FLEEING GOLD AND DUMPING SILVER.

I am willing to admit that it would have been better policy for the United States to have retained the bimetallic standard but now that we are under the gold standard I think it would be better to let things remain as they are. We will soon get used to it. Should an attempt now be made to change back again and restore silver the result would be to drive gold out of the country and make the United States the dumping ground for silver. In other words, in effect at least, we would only succeed in changing from gold monometallism to silver monometallism, with the accompanying disasters. I should like to ask Mr. Wilson if such would not be the case and why not.—Israel Isaacson, at the Austin Economic Circle.

So the goldite press and economic writers have repeatedly asserted. In fact, it is a part of their stock in trade.

So far as the loss of gold is concerned it could not be much worse than at present. In 1893 the excess of exports over imports of this precious metal was $87,206,463, which represents our loss of gold to Europe, and the stream is still rapidly flowing. At this rate it needs but little calculation to determine how long before it will dry up the fountain. I do not see any chance to stem the tide so long as the prices of products which we send abroad remain as at present. Fifty cent wheat and five cent cotton do not demand enough gold in return to offset our importations and the vast gold tribute which we are annually paying European bondholders. If we can devise some way of getting the fair price of a dollar a bushel for wheat and ten cents for cotton and a like advance on the meats, petroleum, etc., we annually export, the case would wear a different aspect. That is what we propose to accomplish by the restoration of bimetallism. We do not want things to remain as they are, nor do we want to get used to such a condition, but by a radical step to improve the condition under which the producers are now suffering.

While I am not prepared to admit that the oft-repeated assertion of the goldite writers would prove true, at the same time should it prove to be correct that the restoration of bimetallism would drive out gold and fill the country with silver, I can see no reason for apprehension on our part that such would result disastrously to the best interests of the nation as a whole. On the contrary I can see only good to follow.

The aforesaid economic writers uniformly assume some dire calamity would result from such a loss of gold and influx of silver, but having read them closely I fail to find any indication of the nature of such disaster. Let us for the sake of the argument adopt both these predictions, that such a policy would expel gold and cause an influx of silver as true, instead of being against the restoration of bimetallism in these assurances we find our safety in making the attempt.

Our further attempts to keep up our supply of gold in competition with the nations of Europe, striving as they are to retain the meager supply available for circulation and redemption money, must result in a further depreciation of the price of our export products. Every time we enter the market to buy gold with bonds we depreciate prices by advancing the exchange value of gold.

As we pursue a foreign market for gold, lower and lower must go those products on which our prosperity rests. Every drain of Europe's gold to us, wrung from her by the means now pursued, means lower prices for all commodities including those she must buy from us.

By the restoration of silver on a basis of honest bimetallism, on the contrary, we place ourselves in a position to part with our gold composedly. Instead of engaging in the arena in the great struggle for gold now going on to maintain our reserves, we would under such circumstances be able to loan it to Europe to our great advantage. To do so would be to loan Europe the vehicle with which to convey back our prosperity.

The director of the mint says there is over $600,000,000 of gold in the United States and that our annual product of gold available for money in excess of what is used in the arts is $20,000,000. Suppose the greater part of this gold is expelled from the country and goes to Europe as predicted what would the consequences be?

First, it would not go for nothing. Something would be sent us in exchange therefor. The same authority says that Europe would send our bonds home and take our gold. To, for the time being, individualize Uncle Sam, we can see no particular harm in a man paying his debts when he has the money to do so with. It stops interest and is greatly to his advantage. Such actions on the part of

Europeans would depreciate the price of bonds so that Uncle Sam could pay his debts with less money, and thus save more interest.

In other words, the bonds coming from abroad would be bought at a reduced price, which would be to the advantage of our people, and the annual tribute which we send abroad in gold to pay the interest on these bonds would remain in the country.

Count one, therefore, is in our favor. We should get our bonds back at a reduced price and save a large annual interest tribute now a drain on our gold resources.

Now for count two. The effect of this large influx of gold would largely increase Europe's aggregate of money, especially in England, where our bonds are most largely held, and where the prices of our products are fixed. According to the established rule of political economy, that an abundance of primary money raises prices of commodities, the effect of this plethoric of money would be to raise the normal prices of all commodities in Europe, including those for which they are dependent upon the United States to supply, viz., cotton, wheat, provisions, petroleum, etc.

The effect of abundance of money is also to increase consumption; therefore count two is in our favor in two ways, an increased demand and better prices for our products.

THE DUMPING THEORY.

Our goldite economic writers have also supplied us with the means of overcoming a difficulty which otherwise might prove serious, viz.: the contraction of the circulating medium which would otherwise result from the loss of gold, which it is claimed would ensue as a result of the remonetization of silver, is more than offset by the predicted influx of silver.

Senator Sherman, who is denominated the "Nestor of Finance," in his Akron, Ohio, speech, October 14, 1894, said:

The amount of silver in sight in the world is stated at 3,000,000,000 ounces, each ounce containing 480 grains. The annual production of the silver in the world is about 161,000,000 ounces. the commercial value of which is $125,000,000, but the coinage value at the present ratio is now about $225,000, 000.

This vast hoard of silver will be invited to the United States in the hope to obtain more for it than its market value.

In the same speech the Senator says:

Free coinage is by law to confer upon any holder of silver bullion the right to deposit it in the Treasury or mints of the United States and to demand and receive for it $1 for 371¼ grains of pure silver, 412½ grains of standard silver nine-tenths fine; or, in case the silver is not coined, the holder may demand a note of the United States for $1, and both the coin and the paper are money and a legal tender for all debts, public and private.

If such is the case, and we are assuming these goldite predictions, especially when made by so eminent an authority on finance, are true, when that 3,000,000,000,000 ounces of silver, which this accepted authority says will be attracted to this country, arrives we shall have abundance of "legal tender money" for all domestic purposes and to supply the place of the lost gold.

Where will the silver come from? Not certainly from Europe. What silver Europe has is coined on the ratio of fifteen and one-half to one. At our ratio of sixteen to one her coins would be at premium over gold. She is not, therefore, going to melt them up and send them here to be coined at the lower ratio and thus suffer a loss. Nor are they going to melt up their spoons and silver plate which has the added value of the labor expended upon it. Nor are the Hindoos, Chinese or other Asiatics going to melt their coin and works of art into bullion and send it to us to be coined into dollars at a less market value.

Not all the silver in the world, therefore, is coming to our shore. The Senator evidently stretched his eminent financial imagination in making his figures.

We shall undoubtedly get some silver, however, but it will come from the silver-producing countries in America. Mexico and other American states will send us silver, but they will not give it to us, neither will they take certificates therefor, but the products of our farms, spindles and workshops.

Another desirable end has thus been accomplished, a greater demand for our products from our American neighbors.

Also as we shall have abundance of silver recognized as full-fledged money, our trade with Asiatic silver standard countries would be materially increased. Count three, therefore, is also greatly in our favor.

Our domestic circulation has not been contracted, but rather increased, and our workshops and spindles set in motion.

MORE GOOD RESULTS.

Let us see if there are not still other benefits which would follow to further confirm these goldite predictions as our best assurances of the advisability of restoring bimetallism.

First. We are further assured that Europe would be afraid of our finances and would not loan us any more money. That would be to our advantage. We are big enough and rich enough to depend upon ourselves. If we will utilize our own abundant resources out of which to make capital we will find that to pay interest to Europe is folly.

Second. Under the same line of reasoning, for the time being at least, Europe would not take our silver in exchange for her products at the price we could get for it at our own mints, therefore importations would fall off. This would give a fresh impetus to our own mills and factories to supply our home markets, which would be another count in our favor.

Third. The price of silver would surely advance as a consequence of the action of the United States in admitting it to free coinage, so that the thimble-rig game England is now pursuing in buying silver in the United States on a gold basis, shipping it to India and coining it into rupees with which to buy wheat on a rupee basis would be ended. As a consequence wheat could no longer be profitably imported from India and the buyers would turn to the United States. Our wheat instead of Indian would then fix the price in the Liverpool market.

Fourth. Imports being lessened and the prices of our exports raised, Europe would be compelled to part with her gold to us in exchange for those essentials, wheat, cotton, meats, petroleum, etc., which she must buy of us. The only logical conclusion, therefore, assuming that these predictions of the expulsion of gold and the influx of silver are well founded, is that it would result in our having both the bonds and the gold, a largely increased trade and better prices for our products. We have nothing, therefore, to fear from such temporary silver monometallism.

One gap is left open. The interests of bondholders would be at the outset adversely affected by the depreciation of bonds, but we are not writing in the interest of bondholders. They have had things their own way for thirty years and as a consequence the country is found in the present deplorable condition. It is now high time for the producers to have a turn. On the welfare of the latter depends the prosperity and progress of the nation. If we as a nation would progress in wealth, education and the higher walks of civilization we shall do well to see that the interests of the great working classes have the first consideration in the acts of legislation and government.

QUESTION NO. 8.—INTERNATIONAL BALANCES PAID IN SILVER.

Franklin H. Head in the June '94 Forum says: "If any of

the great commercial nations should alone open its mints for
the free coinage of silver, the international balances would
be paid to that nation in silver while the other nations would
refuse to take it back when the balances were reversed."
Presuming this opinion to be a fact in practice, why would
not the law of reciprocity govern in silver as in meats?

Illinois.   D. W. STARKEY.

As applied to the United States as against European
countries they would first have to get this silver. None
of the commercial nations of Europe with whom we trade
are silver-producing countries. That is, they consume
more silver than they produce.

The only silver-producing countries of note are the
United States, Mexico, Australasia, and Bolivia. Of the
$200,000,000 coinage value in round numbers of silver pro-
duced in 1893 the United States produced $78,000,000,
Mexico $57,000,000, Bolivia $15,000,000, Australasia $27,-
000,000.

The silver exported from Australasia naturally finds a
market in India, so that European countries are dependent upon America and chiefly upon the United States for
their supply.

For reasons given in answer to question No. 6 it would
not pay them to melt up their coined money or silver
plate and spoons with which to pay their balances.

The silver produced in Bolivia is largely used in other
South American countries.

Mexico produced $57,000,000 of silver coinage value in
1893, of which amount she coined $28,000,000, leaving
$29,000,000 for consumption in the arts, of which the
Mexicans use large quantities, and for export.

The United States produced $78,000,000, of which we
coined about $9,000,000 and used in the arts about $11,-
000,000 coinage value, leaving about $58,000,000 for export.

In reality our exports amounted to $41,947,812.
It will therefore be seen that the United States is the
great silver fountain of supply.

The great silver-consuming nations are first, India which for the fiscal year ending in 1893 imported $60,934,726 more silver than she exported; Japan, which imported $17,638,748 more silver than she exported.

England, France, Belgium, Switzerland, Italy, Spain, Portugal, The Netherlands, Norway and Sweden and Russia on the average import quantities of silver largely in excess of their exports.

For these reasons it is improbable that balances will be paid in silver. Suppose such should be the case I cannot see that it would be to the detriment of the United States. If they send us silver it will be in exchange for our products.

With the ratio of sixteen to one established by law, and the mints open to free coinage without discrimination between the two metals, gold and silver, and the silver dollar made full legal tender for the payment of all debts and custom dues, such silver for domestic circulation and purposes would be worth as much as gold.

If the other commercial nations refuse to take it at the value we place upon it they would either have to stop selling us merchandise of their manufacture or exchange their products for ours, taking our other products in exchange for theirs, either of which, as shown in the answer to the previous question, would be to our advantage.

We have nothing to fear from being driven to a silver basis for the time being.

The immense resources of our mines as well as our other natural resources make the United States practically independent of foreign countries.

If we will only ourselves take decided action in favor of silver and stand by it, thus upholding one of our own chief products and sources of wealth, as Blaine well said we will coerce Europe into recognizing silver.

QUESTION NO. 9.—HAS GOLD RISEN IN VALUE?

We are asked to reply to an editorial in the Century

Magazine for December in which it is affirmed that "the fall in prices which has taken place in the last twenty years is not traceable to the appreciation of gold but to improvements in machinery, to cheaper transportation, and to the progress of invention and civilization." Also, "that there is no convincing evidence that there is not an ample supply of gold in the world to transact the world's business." Also, that arguments to the contrary "must melt away in the presence of the figures of the gold product in the last few years."

Whether gold has appreciated or not depends on the point of view. From our standpoint the sun appears to move around the earth and there are Reverend Jaspers who in the face of the exact teachings of astronomy still affirm "De sun do move." The earth also appears to recede from a man up in a balloon. Compared with itself the balloon has remained stationary but in its relation to the earth it has ascended. So with this question of gold.

By act of Congress, February 12, 1873, the gold dollar was made the sole unit of account or measure of price in place of the silver dollar which was then the unit. The privilege of free coinage which hitherto had been enjoyed by both metals alike, was then continued to gold and denied to silver. The gold dollar and the commodity gold must, therefore, remain of the same relative value. Likewise all forms of credit money redeemable in gold and all amply secured forms of indebtedness such as bonds and mortgages, which are either payable in gold or in credit money, redeemable in gold. All such must retain the same relative purchasing power as gold.

It is not strange, therefore, in view of the fact that it measures the price of all other commodities, that the Rev. Jaspers of finance should think that the commodity gold alone remains stationary while all other commodities "do move."

Measured by itself it is impossible for gold to either appreciate or depreciate in value but measured by other commodities it is plainly manifest that it not only has appreciated but has doubled in value.

An ounce of gold in 1894 will buy twice as much of other commodities as in 1873. Values are only relative. A pound of diamonds is worth many pounds of gold, because its exchangeable value for other products is many times greater. We say a thing is dear or cheap according as its exchangeable value with other things rises or falls. The same rule applies to gold. To settle the question whether it has appreciated in value or not it is manifestly unfair to measure it by itself or by credit money of which it fixes the price but it must be measured by its exchangeable value in other products of labor.

CHART NO. 17.—GOLD VS. COMMODITIES.

Showing fall of prices of labor products from 1872 to 1894 as compared with the exchangeable value of silver in a silver dollar and with gold.

Years.	Vegetable food products.	Animal food products.	Sugar, coffee and tea.	Minerals.	Textiles.	Sundry materials.	Grand average of 45 articles.	Silver in a coined dollar.	Gold in a gold dollar.
1873............	106	109	106	141	103	106	111	97.4	1.00
Ten years—1873 to 1882 inclusive.........	94	103	94	91	84	89	93	88.4	1.00
1883 to 1892 inclusive......	69	87	63	73	65	71	72	75.3	1.00
892...............	67	84	68	72	56	66	68½	65.4	1.00
1894 estimated.............	47	63	60	48	35	54	51	47	1.00

The full table may be found in a pamphlet prepared and published under the direction of the United States Senate Committee on Finance, entitled "The coinage laws of the United States."

These tables show that prices of forty-five of the leading commodities as measured by gold fell in price from $1.11 to sixty-eight and one-half cents during twenty years, from 1873 to 1892, or to about fifty-one cents at the present time.

In making such a comparison it would not be fair to

take any one or two commodities because relative values are
affected by local conditions of supply and demand.   Ease
of production through the application of new inventions
for lightening labor, cheaper transportation, the abundant supply or failure of crops,diseases of stock, etc., affect
from time to time the exchangeable value of the various
commodities affected.   It will be a fair test, however, to
take the average price of all the principal commodities of commerce year by year for the past twenty years
as a basis by which to measure the exchangeable
value of gold.   For the purpose of making such a test
these averages have been calculated by Mr. Augustus
Sauerbeck of London, England.   His lists and valuations
show the greatest care and are accepted generally as absolutely reliable.

Mr. Soetbeer,an eminent German statistician, who is an
accepted authority, has made a careful compilation of the
average prices of 100 Hamburg articles and fourteen
of British import as compared with gold.   These up to
1892 show a fall of thirty per cent.   If continued to date,
the fall as compared with gold would be fully fifty per cent.

The London Economist has prepared similar index numbers on twenty-two of the principal commodities,showing
the same results (See diagram Chart No. 17).   In other
words, according to the unmistakable evidences furnished
by these eminent authorities, the exchange value of an
ounce of gold in the markets of Europe is now double
what it was worth in 1873 as measured by 100 of the leading articles of commerce or the leading products of labor.
Has the earth or the sun moved?   Has the balloon as
cended or the earth receded?

It will be noticed by studying these charts that silver
and these 100 articles of labor's products have maintained
the same relative position, showing that silver is the more
stable metal.

Chart No. 18 will show the relative appreciation of gold during the same period, taking silver and 100 other commodities as the standard.

CHART NO. 18.

No. 3.—APPRECIATION OF GOLD MEASURED BY ITS PURCHASING POWER ON THE BASIS OF THE "ECONOMIST INDEX-NUMBERS."

PRICES OF 1873 TAKEN AS ZERO.

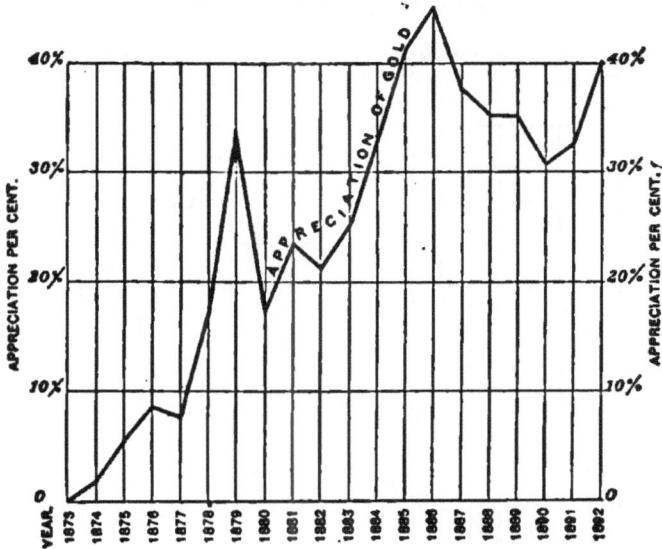

In studying these charts let the reader bear in mind that there has been a very great appreciation of gold since Cleveland's administration began and the Indian mints were closed to silver.

The "progress of invention" tends to lighten labor, shorten the hours of labor, diversify production and increase consumption, rather than to cheapen the product.

The ordinary working-man of to-day enjoys more luxuries than did the rich in the days of our forefathers. Pianos, cottage organs, sewing machines, railroads, telegraphs, street cars and a thousand and one other things which to us are every-day necessities, and the making of which occupies millions of hands, were to them unknown.

Chart No. 19 shows the relative position of gold and silver since 1873 to 1890.

CHART NO. 19.

No. 3A.—RELATIVE APPRECIATION OR DEPRECIATION OF GOLD AND SILVER MEASURED BY SOETBEER'S INDEX-NUMBERS* SINCE 1873.

Fluctuations in the value of Gold denoted thus. ————
"   "   "   " Silver "   "   ———————

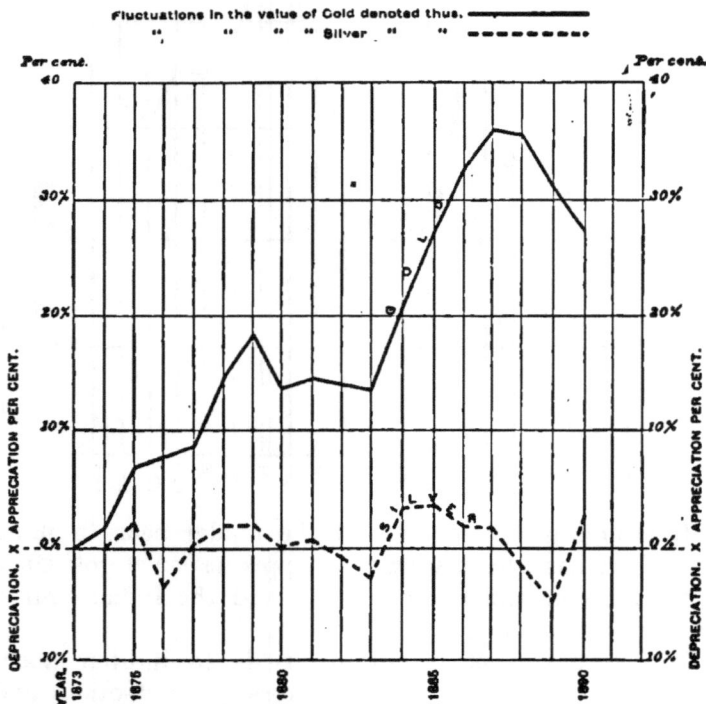

It must be borne in mind in studying this question that the greatest comparative fall in prices has taken place within the last three years, during which time there have been no noteworthy improvements in productive machinery, nor has the cost of transportation during that time been correspondingly lessened. Also that science and invention have been just as busy in developing methods and machinery for producing gold which is now produced in greater abundance than ever before and by the same rule should also have diminished in price.

CHART NO. 20.

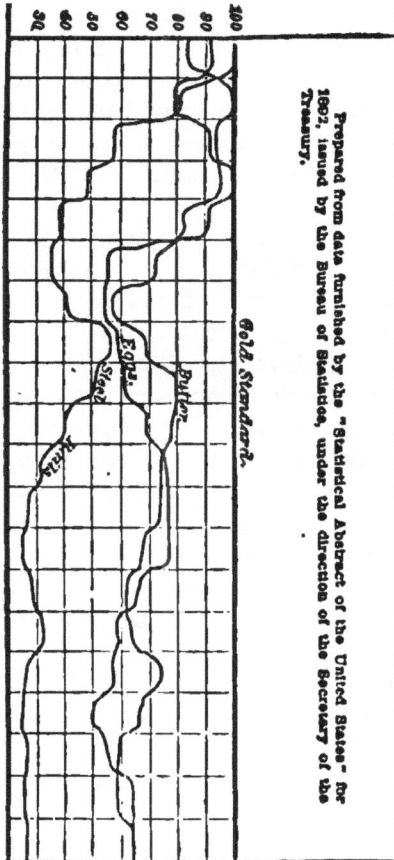

Chart No. 20 shows the relative fall in price of butter, eggs and steel rails as measured by the gold standard.

In one year's time, from January 1. 1894, to January 1, 1895, the aggregate value of live stock on the farms of the United States fell $340,000,000, or fifteen per cent, in value, not in numbers, but in the price such stock would bring in market.

Another evidence of the increased value of gold is found in the increased activity in gold mining. While mining other metals is at present unprofitable, the reverse is the case with gold, and on this account the energies of miners and prospectors have been directed to it. This also accounts for the increased production of gold, while the product of silver and other metals for the past year has diminished.

NOT GOLD ENOUGH.

The question of whether there is gold enough in the world to transact the world's business is one which is not difficult to answer. Its great appreciation in price as measured by other products of labor since silver was demonetized by the leading commercial nations is in itself sufficient evidence that there is not enough of it.

Under the present system of finance which the great commercial nations have uniformly·adopted, gold is the only real money. All other forms of money are credit money and are maintained at par with gold, because they are redeemable in it. Before demonetization silver was real money also, while paper and token money alone were credit money.

Both gold and silver were then basis money or money of ultimate payment, all other forms of money being redeemable in either at the option of the Government. Both metals having the right of free coinage, the ratio fixed by law was maintained.

Since the adoption of the single gold standard the silver dollar has become credit money also, and the exchange value of forty-seven cents' worth of silver is made equal to a gold dollar in the same way that a greenback dollar with no commodity value receives its value, because it is exchangeable for gold at the option of the holder.

Under this system of finance, also, the exchangeable value of credit money is not fixed by its quantity, but by the quantity of the real money in which it is redeemable. In other words, gold, by its own exchangeable value, fixes the exchangeable value of all other money.

The question, then, whether there is gold enough in the world to transact the business of the world resolves itself into whether its quantity is sufficient, in addition to what is used in circulation and in the arts, to serve as a basis of redemption for all other forms of money without the additional demand for it, which would naturally result from the increased burden placed upon it by the demonetization of its sister metal, so appreciating its value as to ruinously affect prices.

By the strict rule of sound finance credit money should not exceed redemption money in quantity. It is not necessary that all the redemption money should be held in the treasury, but there should be a sufficient quantity of it in the country, or, on a broader basis, in the world, to redeem all the paper money in the world. A few facts in this line will show the fallacy of the claims made by the editor of the Century.

According to statistics gathered and published by the director of the mint there is paper money in the world to the amount of about $6,500,000,000 in round numbers, and coined money to the amount of $7,500,000,000. Of this amount $3,700,000,000 is in gold and $3,800,000,000 in silver. As silver is now largely credit money, we add it to the paper money, making $10,300.000,000 credit money to $3,700,000,000 of real or redemption money, a condition manifestly unsound, and which has resulted in a scramble for gold among the nations in their efforts to hold their

redemption money, which has resulted in greatly enhancing the value of gold.

Chart No. 15 (page 185) will serve to show at a glance
the relation of credit to primary or real money of the
United States and in the world, showing an unsound
financial condition.

The effort of our own Government to hold its redemption money is a good object-lesson. Twice already we
have been compelled to sell bonds to buy gold to replace
the slender excuse for redemption money which it is
deemed necessary to hold in the treasury, and again it is
rapidly being depleted. The President, in his special message to Congress January 28, makes a frantic appeal for
power to issue more bonds. This time it is proposed to
issue $500,000,000. He is simply trying to work the im-
possible. It would be very different if the Secretary of
the Treasury would use the $500,000,000 of silver stored
in the treasury as redemption money.

The most ridiculous part of the thimble-rig system of
finance which the treasury and the Jews have got up between them, to the enriching of the latter at the expense
of the people, is the cure recommended by the President
and the bankers, viz., that credit money should be abolished. That is, the greenbacks and silver certificates be
withdrawn and refunded into interest-bearing bonds.
This would stop the present thimble-rig game—selling
bonds to buy gold to exchange for greenbacks to be used
again in buying more bonds—but it is much like cutting
off the patient's head to cure the disease. This whole
gold bond business is intended to irrevocably fasten the
single gold standard upon the nation and the collar of the
bondholders' slavery forever upon the necks of the people.

In view of these facts and figures the trifling increase
of production of gold amounting to $19,000,000 for 1894, a
large part of which will be consumed in the arts, cuts but

an insignificant figure. And the necessity for the restoration of silver as money of ultimate redemption, if the world's finances are to be put on a sound basis, is apparent.

Still another evidence that there is not gold enough to transact necessary business is the fact that we are now suffering the severest business depression during the last half century. Such depressions are due to a contracted or restricted currency.

The purpose of money is to serve as a basis of the exchange of commodities and pay debts. The volume should therefore keep pace with the volume of commodities. In other words, as the volume of business transactions increases the quantity of the medium of exchange should be increased in like ratio. This is a reasonable proposition which all will admit.

Instead of this being the case, while the volume of business during the past twenty years has increased enormously, through the discrediting of silver, the quantity of real money has been greatly diminished. As a consequence it has been necessary to do business on credit. When, in 1893, on account of falling prices and consequent inability to pay, credit got to the end of its tether the resultant panic and hard times followed. We can see no real hope for a return to prosperity until silver is restored to its former position of real money, which a suitably framed act of Congress could effect. Then, our credit money on a sound basis instead of as now hanging on a slender thread of gold, with free coinage on the ratio of sixteen to one, our prolific mines could be depended upon to do the rest.

QUESTION NO. 10.

The New York Voice, the leading champion of Temperance and Prohibition, sends us the following questions:

1. What serious objection, if any, do you see to a national currency made up exclusively of United States treasury notes, upon a bullion basis, as proposed by ex-Secretary of the Treasury Windom and outlined in the accompanying Voice editorial and article of Prof. Commons?

2. Would not such a currency be at once both safe and flexible, at the same time increasing immediately the per capita circulation, and the available assets in the hands of the United States Treasurer?

3. Are not both the "Baltimore plan," including the Carlisle and Springer substitutes, as well as free coinage of silver open to the serious objection of being class legislation, the former being an especially dangerous form of such legislation, in that it places the issue and control of our currency largely in the hands of private corporations and individuals for purposes of private profit?

If it is proposed to demonetize both gold and silver and make the treasury notes redeemable or convertible into bullion at the treasury or sub-treasuries of the United States at market price at the option of the holder, the objections would be:

First, to demonetize either gold or silver or limit the tender of either would be unconstitutional. It is true that Congress did demonetize silver in 1873 and that its legal tender is still limited, but in so doing, according to the opinion of so able a constitutional lawyer as Daniel Webster, and such eminent statesmen as Alexander Hamilton, James G. Blaine and others, it exceeded its authority. See Question No. 1. page 206.

Second, under such a system both metals would become simple commodities subject to the same conditions as other commodities. Not having the support of the law of legal tender and free coinage to fix the debt-paying power and maintain their relative value, the two basis metals would vary greatly in price. In other words it would be a double standard and subject to all the objections our goldite friends urge against such a standard under the mistaken notion that a bimetallic is a double standard.

The varying values of the two metals, manipulated, as they would be sure to be, by speculators, would afford an unstable basis, the fluctuations of which would afford a prolific field for gamblers who would profit at the expense of the treasury. Under any system of convertible paper money the financial world would be suspicious of a basis of issue which lacked the essential element of stability.

Third, there would be the same objection urged against the Bland and Sherman acts, viz., the uselessness of storing up vast hordes of the precious metals where it will do nobody any good.

Fourth. The serious objection of class legislation would be with good reason urged against the plan.

Under it the Government would specially favor the miners of gold and silver by affording them an unlimited market for their products while doing nothing for the miners of other metals or the producers of other imperishable commodities.

The producers of wheat and cotton and other similar farm products would have a right under such a system to ask that the Government should use their products as a basis of issue under the sub-treasury plan. Or the miners of iron, copper, lead, etc., that their products be bought by the Government and used as a basis of issue.

It would thus become a prolific cause of righteous complaint and dissatisfaction which would keep up the financial ferment and result in further uncertainty and instability.

In fact, all the charges of unfairness, discrimination in favor of the silver miners, etc., urged against the late Sherman act could be urged against such a plan with double reason.

IN ANSWER TO THE SECOND QUESTION.

There would be no doubt about the safety of such treasury notes, providing they were made full legal ten-

der for the payment of all dues and debts both public
and private. Any kind of paper money backed by the
Government possessing these requisites, even though it
does not possess the right of convertibility into gold or
silver at the option of the holder, providing it is not
over-issued, is safe so long as the Government stands. If
it is exchangeable for custom receipts, tax receipts, or
for accounts or debts owed, at its face value, it must ever
remain at par and be convertible at par value into other
commodities.

Second. It would be too flexible in that it would
afford wealthy manipulators the opportunity of contracting
and expanding the currency at will. This they would accomplish by alternately buying or selling bullion of or to
the treasury, which would result in the cancellation or
reissue of the treasury notes as best suited their speculative purposes. As to the right kind of flexibility, that
which increases the supply of money at times of the
greatest demand, in the fall of the year, for example,
when crops are to be moved, I do not see wherein this
system affords any advantage over the present one, or
any system of money issued by the Government.

Third. As the plan contemplates retiring all other
forms of money and issuing these treasury notes in the
place thereof, instead of expanding the currency, the result
would be a severe contraction.

According to the report of the director of the mint,
we have about $1,200,000,000 worth of the precious metals
in the country, coinage value. As half of this is silver,
there would be about $900,000,000 at market price, whereas
by the same authority we now have about $1,600,000,000
currency in circulation. To adopt this plan would, therefore, reduce the circulating medium from $1,600,000,000 to
$900,000,000. Such a reduction could not be effected with-
out plunging the country into deeper distress than even

now prevails. It would increase the available assets of the treasury, theoretically at least, but not in such assets as could be used except at the option of those who desired to exchange their treasury notes for gold and silver. There is already, under present laws, a large stock of such useless assets stored up in the treasury vaults in the $500,-000,000 of silver now on hand.

THE THIRD QUERY.

The Baltimore and Carlisle-Springer plan, our present national bank plan, or any other form of legislation which confers upon individuals or corporations the right to issue so-called money, is class legislation of the worst form.

Both these plans contemplate the retirement of all money except gold and silver issued by the Government. The greenbacks they propose shall be refunded by the issue of interest-bearing bonds. This alone would impose upon the people in favor of the bondholders and bankers an additional burden of $17,500,000 a year in interest. The greenbacks are practically a loan to the Government without interest.

The banks and bondholders are exceedingly covetous of that $17,500,000, hence every plan for currency reform, as they choose to call it, contemplates the retirement of this best money of the people, to be replaced by bank issues on which they would make another handsome profit.

The framers of the Constitution intended that the central Government only should issue money. Hence they forbade the States the right to "coin money or issue bills of credit." Anything a bank may issue is not money, although it may be called such and for the time being pass as such, but lacking the essential qualities of legal tender no one is obliged to accept it in payment of debts or accounts unless he chooses to do so.

That is real money only which possesses full legal tender power for the payment of all debts and dues both public and private. It makes but little difference out of what material such money is made so long as it is durable and not easily counterfeited. It must, however, be issued by the Government, as Congress alone can make it real money by making it a legal tender and has no right to delegate its powers.

Class legislation, as we understand it, is a species of legislation which benefits the few at the expense of the many, or that which selects out a few for special benefits while not extending like privileges to the many. On this basis, while depriving the people of the right to issue their own money and giving that privilege into the hands of the few bankers for their private gain is class legislation, I cannot see how the same rule will apply to the free coinage of silver.

Those people take a very narrow view of this great question and do not grasp its magnitude and importance who view it only from the point of view of the advantage such legislation would be to the miners of silver. The class legislation in favor of gold has resulted greatly to the advantage of gold miners and practically ruined the silver mining industry. To reverse this legislation and restore silver to its former mintage privileges, it is true, would reduce the profits of gold mining and restore the silver industry.

Thus far it may be called to a certain extent class legislation but not altogether of an illegitimate character, since it restores an industry which has been greatly wronged, while it only deprives the gold mining interest of certain special favors given it at the expense of the silver producers.

Its favorable or unfavorable effect on the various mining interests is a very insignificant factor as compared with the great reduction in the price of all the products of labor and consequent industrial depression which has been the direct result of the abandonment of the bimetallic and the substitution of the single gold standard.

Where the silver miner has lost thousands through the depreciation of the price of his products the farmer and other producers have lost millions. Likewise where the silver miner will gain thousands by the restoration of the bimetallic standard with free coinage the other producers will gain millions. It is not what the miner gains or loses but what the people have lost and have to gain by such legislation that most interests us.

As has been fully explained in previous chapters of this book, the abandonment of bimetallism and the substitution of the narrower gold standard, making gold alone primary money, has doubled the purchasing power of all money, to the gain of the fund and bond holding classes and the serious loss of the producing classes. The restoration of genuine bimetallism on the ratio of sixteen to one, will restore the purchasing power of money to its former normal condition, which is only another way of saying the price of products would be restored to a fair basis, so that debts, bonded and otherwise, can be paid in the same priced money as that in which they were contracted. The free coinage of both metals is essential to a perfect system of bimetallism, and as the restoration of bimetallism is essential to the prosperity of all the great wealth-producing classes and would only result to the disadvantage of the money lenders, if such indeed is class legislation it is a legitimate and necessary kind.

It is next to impossible to enact any legislation which shall not adversely affect somebody's interests. The greatest good to the greatest number is the only safe rule legislators can go by in making laws.

The better plan   if we must adhere to the

principle of convertibility, would be to coin both gold and silver on the ratio of sixteen to one, each having free mintage privileges-at this ratio, making both legal tender for the payment of all debts and dues both public and private, then issue for each coined dollar a paper dollar, which shall be convertible into coin at the option of the holder, said paper money to also possess the qualities of full legal tender. Then let both go into circulation, retaining about twenty-five per cent of the coin in the treasury for redemption money.

This would give the people what they want, paper money of full legal tender, out of which the banks have made no profit. It would also give the banks coin for their reserve and for foreign exchanges.

Such a currency would be above suspicion as to its security, safety and stability. It would also be as elastic as any currency which could be devised. The plan would immediately increase the circulating medium and we could depend upon our prolific mines to supply more money to keep pace with the requirements of business.

The former ratio of gold and silver bullion, sixteen to one, would be restored, and as the demand would always be greater than the supply the ratio of price would not vary, leaving no margin for speculation.

Under such a sound, flexible financial system we would enter into and maintain an era of prosperity such as, as a nation, we have never before experienced.

QUESTION NO. 11.—AMERICAN SILVER ONLY.

What objection, if any, would you urge against the policy advocated by many of opening the mints to the free coinage of American silver coupled with an import duty on the foreign article high enough to be prohibitive?

F. R. LEWIS, Indiana.

Those who advocate such a policy are more patriotic than politic and do not grasp the breadth of this question. What bimetallists seek to accomplish is to restore the

ratio of price between the two metals, not in this country
only, but in the world. The proposed discrimination in
favor of American silver would defeat this purpose. The
prices of our chief exports, grain, cotton, provisions, etc.,
are made in Liverpool. If we can raise the price of
silver, or to speak scientifically, depreciate the price of
gold in England, we shall correspondingly raise the price
of these our chief exports, and with them all the other
primary products of labor. To open our mints to the free
and unlimited coinage of both gold and silver on the ratio
of sixteen to one on the plan proposed in answer to question No. 4 (see page 183) will surely accomplish this result. This would restore prosperity to the great wealth-
producing classes. The hum of the lathe, the spindle, the
hammer, the anvil and the trowel would also again be
heard throughout the whole of our country, and the independence of self-conscious manhood which prosperity
ever inspires would again assert itself.

QUESTION NO. 12.

I am more than delighted with your clear, logical explanation of the cause of hard times. You are indeed a public
benefactor. I hope you will devise ways and means to give
your book the widest possible circulation. A few million
copies distributed among the producers of the country would
carry the election for bimetallism "without a string to it"
in 1896. To make a beginning towards distributing these
millions I will take 100 copies as soon as the book is completed.

I would like to ask what is the nature of that fearful
calamity which the goldite press and writers uniformly assume would befall the country should we be forced to a silver basis as they assume we shall if the bimetallic standard is
re-adopted? I have never yet seen it explained. Perhaps
you can enlighten me and others interested.

So far as the welfare of the nation as a whole is concerned the direful calamity begins and ends with the as-
sumption. It is a spectre of the imagination, nevertheless real to those who believe in it. That is: the fear of
the calamity which these writers designedly inspire, the

nature of which is not clear, becomes a real factor in guiding the actions, speech and votes of those who are led to believe in it. They are influenced to act as if the danger was real and clearly discerned.

The ghost of the imagination of a superstitious person is just as real to him and inspires just as much terror as if it really existed.

The restoration of bimetallism does not mean that the nation will be forced to a silver basis, as the goldite writers either ignorantly or hypocritically assume. With our prolific gold mines yielding their treasures to the extent of $40,000,000 a year, and our large exports of products calling for gold from gold standard countries, it would be an impossibility to force us to a silver basis more than temporarily as was fully explained in answer to question No. 7. With silver restored we can well afford to loan Europe our gold. It would only be loaning her the vehicle with which to convey back our prosperity, consequently we have much to gain and nothing to lose, even though we should for the time being be forced to use only silver as redemption coin.

Whether individually it would be a calamity or not depends on the point of view. A bondholder might consider it a calamity because it would undoubtedly reduce the exchangeable value of his bonds, and the annual interest they yield as measured by the products of labor. In fact, this is the end sought by means of bimetallism. The security-holding class, as has been before explained, have for the past thirty years been actively manipulating legislation in their own interest. By so doing they have succeeded in doubling and in some instances quadrupling the purchasing power of their holdings and of the annual interest their securities yield.

From the point of view of a producer he has nothing to ose but much to gain by the restoration of the bimetallic

standard even though it should for the time being compel
the treasury to pay its obligations in silver. For example,
the goldite Philadelphia Press in an editorial on the recent
rapid depletion of the gold reserve in the treasury, said
that the nation had a narrow escape from being forced to
a silver basis, meaning that the treasury exhausted of its
gold coin would be compelled to redeem its paper in silver
coin. This, it further said, would have meant the reduction of the value of debts one-half. Not a bad result to
contemplate from the standpoint of the producer, especially in view of the fact that the policy of exclusive gold
payments looking towards absolute gold monometallism
has doubled the value of debts. Another and plainer way
of stating the case is that being forced to a silver basis
would have doubled the debt, interest and tax paying
value of products.

Senator Sherman, who more than any other man is responsible for the legislation in behalf of security-holders
which has brought the country to its present deplorable
condition, in his Akron, Ohio, speech during the late campaign admitted that the free coinage of silver would double
the price of farm products.

Secretary of Agriculture Morton, one of the most rabid
goldities, in an article in the North American Review for
February, 1895, tacitly admits the same thing. In fact, I
believe it is generally admitted, and that no spokesman
for the security-holders will deny it. It is the one and
the only thing in bimetallism which they fear. Senator
Sherman and all the rest on the contrary try to show that
it will be of no particular advantage to the producer to
thus receive double the prevailing prices for his products
because the same agency would also advance the prices
of the articles he has to buy so that while handling more
money he would gain nothing.

These zealous advocates of the interests of the parasites

willingly overlook the fact that the products of the wealth-producing classes of the United States are practically mortgaged through our secured interest bearing indebtedness to the amount of, in round numbers twenty-five thousand million dollars, which with the annual interest thereon, the wealth producers must pay, and that doubling the price of the products of labor reduces the burden of this debt in like ratio.

This is the end bimetallists are seeking and it must be accomplished or the producers of the nation are ruined.

The security-holder is practically a parasite and stands for the death principle. With his interest he feeds on the vitality of national life and if allowed his own way, as has been the case for the past thirty years, he will reduce the wealth-producing classes to lower and lower levels of practical bondage, until the vital spirit of liberty and progressive independence is sunk into the degradation of dependent slavery.

On the other hand the wealth-producing classes are the life principle, the vitality, energy and creative force of national life. Their prosperity means national health and progress. Their degradation means national decay. It ought not to take long for a patriotic statesman to decide which of these two classes should be most favored in legislation. The restoration of bimetallism means no calamity but prosperity to the producing classes, and with them we include the manufacturing and mercantile classes. Gold monometallism on the contrary means slavery for the producing classes and with it national decay.

QUESTION NO. 13.

I do not understand how the Government by passing a law can add to the price of any commodity. The price of silver has fallen under the operation of the natural law of supply and demand. I cannot see how the Government can raise its price simply by enacting a statutory law saying the price shall be so much   ALBERT K. WILSON, Minnesota.

Suppose Congress should enact a law making it mandatory on the Secretary of the Treasury to buy all the wheat
that might be offered at $1 a bushel and the Secretary had
the means at hand to carry the law into effect, wheat
would at once advance to $1 a bushel and remain fixed at
that price. The reason would be found in the unlimited
demand. On the same principle the law restoring the
bimetallic standard and opening the mints to the free
coinage of both gold and silver at the fixed ratio of sixteen to one would at once restore the relative price of
these two metals, because an unlimited demand would be
created for the metals at the ratio fixed by statutory law.
As long as any person can take his bullion to the mint and
receive therefor coined dollars or their equivalent in treasury notes of full legal tender power exchangeable for
taxes, debts, or other commodities, the price cannot fall
because the demand exceeds the supply.

It was statutory law which maintained the relative
prices of silver and gold for centuries up to 1873 until the
bimetallic standard was abandoned and the law discrimi-
nating against silver enacted.*

QUESTION NO. 14.—FIAT MONEY.
What do you understand by fiat money?

GEORGE GRAHAM, Illinois.

All money is fiat. It is the fiat of Government which
makes it money. The Government stamps a piece of gold
or silver or prints a piece of paper and calls it a dollar,
or five or ten dollars as the case may be, and makes it
unlawful to refuse it in payment of debts.

In common parlance, however, the term is used to de-
note what is called irredeemable paper money, money
which has no commodity value or which is not convert-

*Silver would not have fallen in price had not the prop of statutory law, the
law of free coinage, been cut from under it.

ible into commodity value money at the option of the holder.

If it was not for the use of gold and silver as money the exchangeable value of the metals would be much less than it is now. It is the fiat of Government and the unlimited demand for the metal which has the right of free mintage which gives the greater value to it.

QUESTION NO. 15.—IDEAL MONEY.

I admire your earnestness and the able way in which you champion the people against the money power, but I cannot agree with you in advocating convertible money. Inconvertible paper money with full legal tender powers is, to my mind, the ideal money. What objection can there be to it?—An Old Greenbacker.

Certainly paper money is the ideal money. It is the kind of money the people prefer. It is much more useful and convenient than either gold or silver, but, subject to the varying policy of an ever changing Congress and Government, is it safe? If we could have a constant ideal Government and wise legislation then there could be no doubt but that paper money would be best. But subject to the whims of a changing Congress with power to contract and expand it from time to time according to its changing moods or the influences which might be brought to bear, an exclusive currency of this kind would be dangerous. It is true, Congress accomplished a similar disastrous result by demonetizing silver. No great disaster would have followed this act, however, had not several others of the leading commercial nations done the same thing at the same time.

As gold and silver are recognized the world over as money, with, under restored bimetallism, a bullion value equal to their coinage value, their purchasing power would be but little affected by the acts of any one nation; while with a currency composed exclusively of irredeemable paper, the acts of Congress expanding or contracting the currency would have a disastrous effect upon the relative values of debts and commodities.

An example of this may be seen in the contraction from 1865 to 1872, resulting in the great panic of 1873. The paper money of 1865 was of this kind. The contraction which our unwise statesmen brought about at the instigation of the English bondholders resulted in terrible disaster to the nation. If we had had plenty of coin money at that time and the paper money had been convertible or credit money, its contraction would not have resulted so disastrously because it is the volume of primary money, not of credit money, which fixes its purchasing power.

We have also to defer to some extent to habits of thought and custom. The world believes that the only real money is coined money, and the world is a conservative old fogy, very slow to accept what it is not used to. For these reasons we think it the part of wisdom to approach the ideal by easy steps and get as near to it as we can. If we can restore bimetallism with dollar for dollar of paper money, both full legal tender, we should be willing to let the old fogy financial world retain its myth of convertibility.

QUESTION NO. 16.—LEGAL TENDERS DURING THE WAR.

Were the first $60,000,000 treasury notes issued during the war of secession a legal tender? Mr. Horr, editor of the New York Tribune, says they were not. I cannot place reliance on what he says, for his paper is run in the interest of the banks and monopoly. S. D. L. Ross, Idaho.

The first non interest-bearing demand notes were issued under the act of July 17, 1861. The issue was not to exceed $50,000,000. They were redeemable in coin. All notes of larger denomination than $50 were to bear interest. The law provides these notes might be paid to government employees and officials, but were not legal tender for duties. These notes were exchangeable for bonds.

The act of Aug. 5, 1861, provides for the issue of demand

notes to the extent of $50,000,000. They were made receivable for "public dues," but what dues was not stated. At first the law was construed to exclude them from the custom house. For this reason at first they went to a discount. But later the Secretary of the Treasury ordered them received for duties, when they immediately went to par with gold, although they were not, by law, made legal tender at that time.

Wm. A. Birkey, in his book entitled "The Money Question," says of these notes:

These notes were receivable for all public dues, duties on imports included, and were subsequently made a legal tender for private debts, and the result was they commanded the same premium over the ordinary greenbacks that gold did, and went up with gold step by step to the enormous premium of 285. Could any better evidence than this be required to prove that a greenback, made full legal tender would circulate at par, or nearly so with gold? The demand notes were, of course, very obnoxious to bullionists, because they gave the lie to their theories of paper money, and accordingly they were got out of the way at the earliest moment possible - all but about $75,000, which were probably lost, and, if so, constitute a gain to the people at large.

It is ever memorable that these notes were not at par because they were payable in coin, but for the reason that they were receivable for duties on imports and all other debts due the government, and a legal tender for private debts. So long as they were not so receivable they were at a discount, though payable in coin.

The full legal tender act passed the House Feb. 6, 1862, and the Senate Feb. 12, 1862. These acts made the above notes full legal tender. This act adds $10,000,000 more to the issue of the demand notes, making the total issue of this denomination $60,000,000 full legal tender notes.

From these facts we leave the reader to decide whether Mr. Horr was right or wrong.

Feb. 25, 1862, the act first authorizing the greenback with its restricted legal tender as we have it to-day was passed. It authorized the issue of $150,000,000 legal tender notes, made legal tender for everything except "duties on imports and interest on the public debt." These notes under this act were made redeemable for "bonds the same as coin." Otherwise the notes were inconvertible. The bonds a¹so issued under this act were payable in lawful money of the United States meaning these legal tender notes.

Had the greenbacks been made a full legal tender they would have remained at par and at least $1,000,000,000 have been saved to the public which subsequently went into the pockets of the bondholders, banks, and Wall street gamblers, who were responsible for this restrictive clause.

It was during the fierce debate over this restrictive clause in the Senate that the Great Commoner, Thad Stevens uttered these memorable words:

I have a melancholy foreboding that we are about to consummate a cunningly devised scheme, which will carry great injury and loss to all classes of people throughout this Union. * * * * There was a doleful sound came up from the caverns of the bullion brokers, and from the saloons of the associated banks. * * * It now creates money; and by its very terms declares it a depreciated currency. It makes two classes of money—one for the banks and brokers—another for the people.

Senator Henry Wilson, afterwards Vice President said:

I believe that no measure that can be passed by Congress unless it be a bill to provide revenue to support the Government will be received with so much joy as the passage of this bill, with the legal tender clause. In my judgment if you strike out legal tender clause, you will have every curb stone broker in the country, the bulls and bears of the stock exchange and all that class of men who fatten on public calamity and the wants and necessities of the people, using their influence to depreciate the credit of this government and break down the value of demand notes.

The motive which actuated the associated banks and bondholding class in fighting for non or restricted legal tender notes throughout the many fierce money wars of this and a later period may be understood by consulting the Hazard circular (page 157) and the letter of Hippolyte Grenier (page 160).

It was the same enemies of the producing classes

actuated by the same motives which secured the insertion of the restrictive clause in the legal tender of the present silver dollar and silver certificate which makes these forms of money full legal tender except when otherwise stipulated by contract. It is on account of this permissive clause that bonds and mortgages and many other forms of contract are made payable in gold.

It was designed with satanic inhumanity to depreciate silver and paper money and measure the purchasing power of money on a narrow gold basis, thus to place the debtor more completely within the power of the lender; the producers in the power of the bond and fund holding classes; the workers in the power of the idlers or parasites.

I cannot urge too strongly upon the producers of the United States the necessity that the first step in the restoration of bimetallism should be the removal of this restrictive clause.

This is all important. A law restoring free coinage to silver, without full legal tender, would be disastrous to the principles of bimetallism, whose keystone is legal tender. Such a law would only result in sending gold to a premium, and compelling the payment of all gold mortgages and bonds with gold bought at a premium, and further, to give the Wall street gamblers another opportunity to play football with our finances as they did with gold and restricted legal tender greenbacks during the war.

Let us not, therefore, fight in the dark, or allow the enemy to catch us napping again, but shoulder to shoulder intelligently strike, first for full legal tender then for free coinage on the ratio of 16 to 1.

We are not living in barbarous times when on account of toppling governments the one essential in money was intrinsic value, but under a stable government in an intelligent age in which we have learned, both by experience and the higher economic laws, that it is not the material out of which it is made that makes money, but the fiat of government—the law of legal tender.

QUESTION NO. 17.—SOUND MONEY, HONEST MONEY, CHEAP MONEY?

Why do so many of the papers always speak of gold as sound money, honest money, etc., and of silver and paper money as cheap money, etc. GEORGE SAND, Ohio.

They either do so in ignorance which in a public journalist is inexcusable or with deliberate hypocritical intent to deceive and prejudice the people against a portion of the money of the United States with intent to bring it into discredit that those who control the gold of the world may extort more of the products of labor from the workers of the world.

These idolatrous worshipers of the golden calf are only doing the bidding of the bondholders, curb stone brokers, bulls and bears and gamblers on the stock exchange of Wall and Lombard streets. "That class of men who fatten on public calamity and the wants and necessities of the people," who are using their influence as Senator Henry Wilson in his speech in the Senate on the legal tender act said they would "to depreciate the credit of the Government and break down the value of the demand notes," only in this case it is silver, the silver certificate and greenback.

Such conduct on their part is unpatriotic amounting almost to treason.

Any legal tender money issued by the United States Government by the authority of an act of Congress is both sound and honest money whether it is made of gold, silver or paper, and any person, newspaper or other agency discrediting such money is at least unpatriotic and deserves the severe rebuke of all patriotic, honest people.

The only suspicion of unsoundness in other forms of money than gold is the clause in the greenbacks which voids its legal tender in the payment of duties on imports and the interest on the public debt and that in the silver dollar, treasury note and silver certificate which places it in the power of the money lender to make void their legal tender by special contract.   The people should see to it that this suspicion of unsoundness is removed without delay.

The cry of "cheap money" comes from the same source and is inspired by the same desire and intent to blindly prejudice the people.   It is usually accompanied by the rank Pecksniffian statement that the depreciated dollar always finds its way into the poor man's pocket; that the rich man will keep the best money himself and pay wages with the depreciated money, etc., all of which is designed to deceive, frighten and prejudice the working people so that they can be used on election days as cat's paws to rake out the golden chestnuts for these pseudo champions of the workingman.   Pretty champions these. There is not one chord of harmony in their gold hardened hearts which vibrates in sympathy with the honest workingman.

If our inquiring friend was better posted on the controlling influences which dictate the policy of the great newspapers of to-day, and the insignificant power the editor—whose power is supposed to be so potent—wields, he would hardly need to ask why so many papers uphold the goldite party against the interest of the producers of the country.

First, the great metropolitan journals are in almost all cases run by corporations whose stock is in the hands of the fund holding classes.   Those of the east are largely owned by non-residents living in Europe.   The controlling interest in the Chicago Tribune is also said to be owned in England.   Two of the other leading papers of Chicago, the Herald and Post, were, up to February, 1895, owned by John R. Walsh, president of the Chicago National Bank.

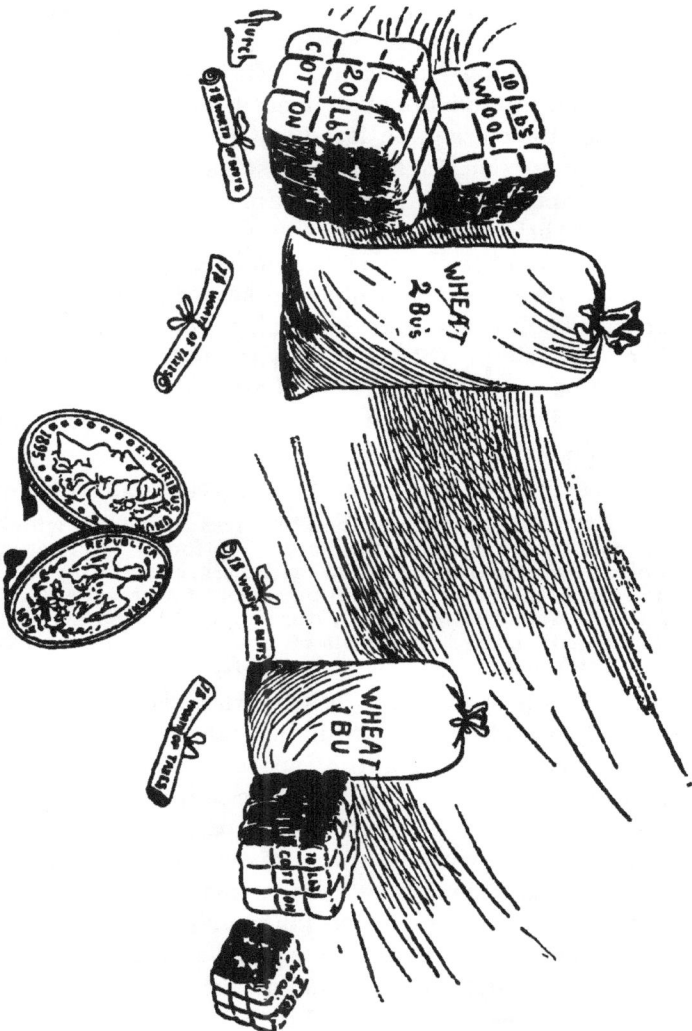

THE MEXICAN VS. AMERICAN SILVER DOLLAR.

Illustrating how the purchasing power of the latter has grown while its debt-paying power remained stationary. See page 270.

They have since been sold together with the Times, the latter the only outspoken silver paper in the city, to a syndicate of Chicago capitalists. Through this sale of the Times the capitalists have silenced another of the papers that had the courage to stand by the people.

The editors on the staff of these papers are mere hired men compelled to write as they are told to write regardless of what their own opinions may be. At the present time we know at least three editors on Chicago dailies who personally were in favor of bimetallism with free coinage who in their editorials were upholding gold monometallism. They are simply hired advocates and no more weight should be given such editorial dictum than to the pleading of a hired attorney at the bar, who often pleads a case he knows is wrong.

QUESTION NO. 18.—MEXICAN VS. AMERICAN DOLLARS.

For the past year I have had business in Mexico which frequently took me across the border. I found that across the line an American silver dollar, although containing the same amount of silver only, would buy about twice as much as the Mexican dollar, whereas on returning to El Paso my Mexican dollar only passed for about 50 cents. How do you explain this difference?   K. L. ANDREWS, Texas.

Mexico is on a silver basis. Her silver dollar is her unit of account or price, while we are on a gold basis the gold dollar being our unit of account. Twenty-five years ago when the silver dollar was the unit of account in this country also, the Mexican dollar passed current in this country at par with our own money. The Mexican dollar has not changed in value. Its exchangeable value for the products of the Mexican workingman's labor is just about the same as it was twenty-five years ago, and the Mexican farmer gets just as many dollars for the same quantity of products as he formerly did. For this reason also it takes no more of his products to pay his taxes and debts than formerly.

With us it is different. We changed our unit from silver to gold and abolished the former bimetallic standard. As other nations did the same thing about the same time the demand for gold was greatly augmented as has been fully explained in previous chapters. This greatly increased, in fact, doubled its exchangeable value. The gold dollar of a fixed number of grains being the unit, as it increased in exchange value it carried up with it all other forms of money and all forms of indebtedness. As a consequence, while the Mexican dollar has remained stationary, our dollar has doubled in purchasing power. The Mexican across the border accepts our silver dollar at the relative value which we put upon it at home, the same value as a gold dollar, while we accept the Mexican's dollar at his own home valuation, which is that of silver bullion.

It will be readily seen that this change of standard is very greatly to the disadvantage of the producers of this country. The Mexican farmer pays his debts and taxes on the old basis with the same quantity of his products while the American farmer has to produce and sell twice as much in order to buy dollars with which to pay his taxes and cancel his indebtedness.

QUESTION NO. 19.—TO MAINTAIN THE PARITY.

The President and Secretary of the Treasury maintain that in order to maintain the parity between our different forms of money so that one dollar shall be just as good as any other dollar it is necessary for the Government to use gold exclusively as redemption money. Whereas, the law says paper money is redeemable and bonds payable in coin, meaning either gold or silver. Why do they assume this necessity?
GEORGE GORDON, Massachusetts.

They assume this necessity because they are either unwittingly the catspaw of the bondholders or hand and glove with them. The reader can draw his own conclusions. This policy has been a very expensive one to the people of the United States. With $500,000,000 of coin in the treasury vaults which the Government had a right under law to use for redemption money, the producers of the country have been put under further bondage to the extent of $162,000,000. This is only a trifle, however, compared with the further losses sustained in the depression of prices of products resulting from these repeated bond sales.

This policy has placed the Government completely at the mercy of the gold clique as is witnessed by the last sale of $62,000,000 of bonds which the President through his mouthpiece in the Senate claims he was compelled by those who control the gold to sell at about $1.04 when they were worth $1.20 and were quickly resold by the gold clique at that price.

One other financial truth, demonstrated by the experience of the past few months, is this: Gold that does not come to us in the course of trade will not stay here when bought with bonds. The outflow of gold could be stopped at once, and the necessity for more bonds be removed, if the Secretary would stand by the legal tender qualities of silver and reserve the right to pay in coin of his choice rather than transfer the option of the Government, expressly set forth in the promise to pay, to the creditor.

The only correct way to make one dollar forever as good as another dollar is to make all dollars full legal tender for all debts and dues, both public and private. And the only correct way to keep the two metallic dollars at a parity is to restore full fledged bimetallism. France, with more silver in her coined money than we, has had no trouble to maintain the parity between her gold and silver money. The reason is she recognizes both as full fledged money, and the government pays in either at its own option.

The only correct way to restore and maintain the former relative value between gold and silver bullion at a fixed ratio is to open the mints to unlimited coinage without discrimination. Bimetallism, with free coinage, would surely restore prosperity, while every move the Government makes in line with its present policy tends to further depress the price of labor products.

PRESIDENT ANDREWS ANSWERS QUESTIONS.

In line with the question and answer part of this series of articles nothing more instructive can be given than to republish a portion of a lecture delivered by President E. B. Andrews, of Brown University, delivered at Meadville, Pa., December 20, 1894.

President Andrews was one of the delegates appointed by the United States Government to the International Monetary Conference held at Brussels in 1892. He has, perhaps, given more attention to this topic from an educational standpoint than any other living man. Unlike many professors of political economy in other institutions, his tongue is not tied by the interests of some millionaire founder, or compelled by the conditions of his hire to dance and sing to the piping of the capitalist supporters of the college.

The interrogations were propounded by monometallists. In the course of his lecture President Andrews said:

ABOUT THE PRICE OF WHEAT.

With reference to the question of wheat I think the cause of the fall in the price is misconceived. The cause of the fall in wheat is not, in my judgment, to any extent set forth when you talk about the cheapening of cost of production and transportation. The great overplus market where prices are fixed is Liverpool, or, generally speaking, London. Before the price of silver had fallen, a man from America or India or Argentina could trade with one just as well as another. But now silver is demonetized and instead of the silver in the silver dollar being worth the gold in a gold dollar it is worth in a little while only 90 cents in gold. The old amount of silver will buy just as much wheat in India as before, but the old amount of gold will get a great deal more silver than before. The seller from India is in condition to say to the buyer in London, give me your whole trade and I will do five cents better than I did before, more or less. The American farmer has got to raise wheat and he has got to sell it. Therefore he is obliged to follow down the Indian merchant. And when silver goes down to eighty cents the American has got to go down to eighty cents, and to seventy cents and to sixty cents in turn. He has got to do it or starve. And that, ladies and gentlemen, is the philosophy of the low prices of wheat in the United States of America.

If you will take the gold price list of wheat and compare it with the gold price list of silver bullion you will find that the wheat has followed the silver as the shadow follows the man. I know that certain gentlemen have "monkeyed" with that, some by taking very brief periods and particular months when the price of wheat might be for a time for local reasons going up or down a little; but generally, taking considerable periods two or three or five-year periods, you will find that most remarkable parallel. I consider it nonsense to talk of the cause of the fall in the price of wheat as the cheapening of the cost of production and transportation. The railroads have been compelled to follow the price of wheat just as the farmer has and for the same reason. Rather than give up the traffic in wheat altogether the railroads put a little extra tariff on some things, as the local freight traffic, and put the transportation of wheat down to the very lowest figure, even perhaps a little below cost.

Q. Is it not true that the price of wheat has fallen in Argentina, a silver-using country, just as much as it has in England, a gold-using country? A. The gold price of wheat has certainly fallen in Argentina, as it has fallen all over the world, as I have already pointed out. But the general price has not fallen in India or Argentina or China or anywhere, but on the contrary there has been a slight tendency in India at least, which has been the great competitor of the United States of America, for wheat to go up in terms of silver.

This statement of Prof. Andrews is well authenticated. It is not only true as to wheat, but as to other export products of these countries. In the standard money of those countries their products have not depreciated in price. On the contrary, the price of their commodities have really appreciated on account of the greater demand to supplant the products of the United States. Thus whether we will or no the price of our products is fixed by the price of silver, while we are compelled to pay our taxes and debts, and for many of the necessities of life

AN ANCIENT STORY WITH A MODERN MORAL. SEE PAGE 366.

with gold or its equivalent.   This is what monometallism
does for the American farmer.   If we had retained the
bimetallic standard there is no reason why wheat should
not now be selling for as much as it did fifteen or twenty
years ago—for its natural price—a dollar a bushel.
Equally, the restoration of bimetallism with free coinage
of both metals on the basis of 16 to 1 will restore prices
and prosperity.   There is no question about it.   This is
not the mere talk of "silver cranks," but is admitted by
the foremost goldites.

Continuing Prof. Andrews was asked concerning

MAINTAINING THE PARITY.

Q. Is it not true that from the beginning of this century
down to the time the mints of the leading commercial nations
were closed to silver, all attempts to maintain the two metals
at parity failed, the price of one or the other rising or falling
alternately, and did this result in great confusion, in the repeated disappearance of one metal, then the other, and that
the closing of the mints to silver was to avoid this great and
long-standing evil, which constantly kept prices fluctuating?
A. No, it is not true at all. The fact is quite the contrary,
that from 1803 to 1873, every year but one, large sums of gold
and silver both were brought to be coined at the French mint
at the ratio of 15½ to 1. Therefore, that relation was maintained at the French mint absolutely, that mint being ready
at any time to take any amount of silver or any amount of
gold at that ratio, that ratio being departed from only in
localities considerably remote from the mint, and then in
only very slight degree to very slight extent, the variation in
all those seventy years being less than the variation between
certified checks and gold in New York City during 1873. And
yet certified checks and gold were supposed to be on a parity
one with another.

Some gentlemen, like Mr. Edward Atkinson, have scraped
together in different countries these instances of a slight
premium of gold over silver, or silver over gold, and they have
said that before 1848 gold passed out of circulation, and that
after 1848 until 1870 silver passed out, etc., but these statements, I assure you from a most careful examination of the
figures, are quite untrue. Gold and silver both were constantly brought to the mint in great sums. Let any one explain that in conjunction with the allegation that either
metal departed from circulation.

That wonderful fact of maintenance of gold at a parity with silver and silver at a parity with gold at 15½ to 1 through those seventy years in the face of changes in the relative production of these two metals far greater than any that have taken place since 1873, is another thing that the friends of gold monometallism will never let the public know if they can help it, because it is absolute death to their theory. It can not be explained in any other way than that governments, a sufficient number proceeding with due discretion, can maintain those metals together for a very long time easily, so that a given amount of one will have the value of a given amount of the other.

Another very remarkable fact is that the parity of those metals was kept up during all those years substantially by France alone down to 1865: After 1865 to 1873 France had a little help from Belgium, Switzerland and Italy. Now, if all of that wonderful parity, under difficulties greater than have existed since 1873, could be kept up practically by one nation alone through seventy years, I ask you who are accustomed to reason whether the Latin League, together with the United States of America, Great Britain, the German Empire, Austria, Russia and Scandinavia together could not so tie these two metals together that they would never become parted?

If the reader will refer to Chart No. 9, page 111, he will, in the tables there published, find a full confirmation of the Professor's statements, the fall in the price of silver is not due to variations of production, as so often claimed, but is due to taking out from under it the law of legal tender and free mintage. We must impress this fact, strongly upon the public intelligence. Had the French mints or the mints of the United States remained open the former parity of value would surely have been maintained. Likewise the restoration of bimetallism with free coinage will restore the parity. The gain to the producers of the country which will follow such restoration, we have frequently pointed out in these articles. With the restoration of silver to its former gold value will come the restoration of the prices of all farm and other products of labor, and, consequently, restoration of prosperity to the laborers.

WAS IT A CONSPIRACY?

Q. Is there any evidence that the closing of our mints to free coinage in 1873 was done in pursuance of any conspiracy. or that those who voted for the new coinage act of that year were animated by any corrupt or dishonest motive? A. To this last part of this question, that those who voted for the new coinage act of that year were animated by any corrupt or dishonest motive, I answer, no. I do not believe that there is any evidence that any of them acted from any corrupt or dishonest motive. The only thing for which they can be blamed is for allowing the legislation to go through silently without any discussion upon it by themselves or by the country. That was more their ignorance in not knowing that they were taking hold of a tremendous power. They were ignorant, and I think they were to a certain extent to blame for that, but I do not think they were corrupt. With reference to the first part of the question I think a somewhat different answer must be given. I believe there are bankers and gold owners in London and Berlin and New York and perhaps elsewhere who knew perfectly well the result of the demonetization of silver, who knew that it would instantly put a new value into every pound sterling of their holdings, and that those men used influences unknown to the men over whom they used it, at least so far as this country is concerned used that influence to bring that legislation to pass.

WILL RESTORING SILVER DIMINISH TRADE?

Q. Is it not true that all or nearly all the poorer nations of the world use the silver standard exclusively? Is not their trade and commerce, taking out India, which is a British province, as nothing compared with the trade and commerce of the gold-standard nations? A. I think few, very few, silver nations are worse off than poor Portugal. Still, in general, it is true that the poorer nations use the gold standard. As to the trade of the silver nations, for America it is very important. That trade has made England rich. We trade comparatively little with gold nations of Europe except it be in agricultural produce. Now, the manufacturing interests of this country have become so immense either they must have an immensely larger home market or they must have a foreign market. Suppose by free coinage or in any other way we could get hold of the trade of the silver-using countries? The result would be unparalleled prosperity, such a boom in American manufacturing interests as has never taken place since we had a national being. China, for instance, is about to open the grandest market for cotton goods that ever was. England is there waiting for it. If we had silver back so there could be facile trade and money communication between China and Japan on the one hand and America on the other, we would have a better chance than England. The trade of the silver-using countries is not a bagatelle by any means.

Suppose the manufacturing industries were to boom as I have suggested, what would be the result on farming communities of this country? Why, you would have a home market such as you never could have under any other policy. I think if we could command the markets of the silver-using countries, or a very large part of it, the manufacturing plants in this country would double in from fifteen to twenty-five years.

We refer the reader to previous articles for a full confirmation of what Prof. Andrews here says. There is no doubt about both the honest, though not blameless ignorance, and the venial corruption. One of those at least upon whom the shadow of guilt rests heavily, is still helping shape the financial legislation of this nation. It is unnecessary to say that for the past twenty-five years on every occasion he has interposed his satanic cunning to intercept any financial legislation which was designed to benefit the producing classes.

Unfortunately, the ignorance still largely prevails, both among legislators and the people. This ignorance, which the worshipers at the shrine of the golden calf are ever laboring to intensify, is the one great bar to the undoing of the great and venial wrong. How shall we undo it except every one who has become enlightened to the truth shall become a beacon and let his light shine?

I believe this statement to be incontrovertible. The chief reason England closed the mints of India was because the English manufacturers had become jealous of the rapid increase of manufacturing establishments in India and the immense growth of trade between that country and China and other eastern countries. The English manufacturers well knew that this trade was due to the facile relations growing out of the fact that both countries were on a silver basis.

Q. If the double standard is impossible; if we must choose between gold or the silver standard, is not gold the better? A. I think so for the present, but would not undertake to say that would be the best policy always. If we alone had to make an everlasting choice I would say choose silver, for the reason that ultimately the trade of the silver-using world· would be more important to us than what trade we could have with England, Germany, France, and other gold-using countries.

We do not like the term "double standard." It conveys a wrong impression, which monometallists are not slow to use to the disadvantage of bimetallists. It is not a double, but a two metal, or bimetallic standard. Two metals constituting one standard, one acting against the o her to maintain the equilibrium of price, on the same principle that a bimetallic pendulum maintains standard time. We do not call it two pendulums, but one composed of two different metals. While gaining the trade of these other nations, there is no reason to believe that we shall lose any of the trade of the gold standard countries by returning to a bimetallic basis.

REAL VS. CREDIT MONEY.

Q. Since 1873, when the new coinage act was adopted, there has been added to the currency in circulation under the operations of the Bland-Allison and Sherman acts $827,000,-000 of silver coin and silver certificates, which now exceed the gold by over $200,000,000, and raising the amount of money in circulation per capita from $18.94 to $23.80. This enormous addition of silver to our circulation, constituting now nearly one-half of the whole, has taken place while the fall of general prices has been going on. Does not your remedy of still more silver, an unlimited quantity of it, in fact, seem a strange one in view of the circumstances?

A. If you reinstate silver with the co-operation of a number of nations, you enlarge the basis of fundamental money, and that is what tells on prices. This is a fact that Dr. Griffith, an ardent monometallist, has not made clear. He has shown that any amount of change or subsidiary coinage, coinage that had to ride upon the back of some other form of money, will never raise prices. That is true. So prices have not been much affected by the amount of silver we have coined in this country, because it has not been free coinage of that silver, and had to ride upon the back of gold. Until within a little over a year the amount of gold available for the purposes of money has been falling off, absolutely a little, and relatively a great deal, to the demand for general money. Therefore, your coinage of silver, large as it has been under the Bland-Allison act, and under the Sherman act, has affected the price of commodities, perhaps not at all, and, certainly, very little. If the law now before Congress (the Carlisle Banking law) to put a great amount of paper money into circulation should go into effect, I think that you would find, except locally, prices would be very slightly changed; because all that money, if it had any basis at all, would have a gold basis, and gold, though perhaps increasing a little this year because of the great output of South Africa, is decreasing in proportion to the amount of it needed for money.

This fully confirms what we have repeatedly stated in these articles, that it is not the volume of credit money, but the volume of primary money, or the money of final redemption, which fixes prices. Primary money is full legal tender money, which is incontrovertible, the value of which is not maintained because it is redeemed in something else. Gold is the only primary money in gold standard countries, silver, with paper, being only credit money, whose value is maintained because it is convertible at the option of the holder into gold money. For this reason the exchangeable value of gold fixes the exchangeable value of all other forms of money in the relation they bear to commodities. In studying this great financial question, this important fact must not be overlooked.

WAGE-WORKERS NOT BENEFITED.

Q. If wages, owing to whatever cause, monopoly of trades unionism, if you please, have been increased or even remained stationary, and other prices have fallen owing to demonetization of silver, isn't the wage earner benefited by this condition, which increases the purchasing power of his wages, whether the rest of us are benefited or not? A. No; the wage receiver is the most hard beset in the long run of any of us in this matter. If you could have all the work possible for the laboring population under a different system of money, and also have the purchasing power of your dollar paid

for wages increased as it has since 1873, then, of course,
the wage receiver would be better off by that system. The
rest of us would be worse off. But that is just the state of things
that you can not have. You can not multiply industry, you
you can not provide labor for the wage receiver to do, and,
therefore, the highest and most disciplined classes of labor,
even in the long run, must submit to a curtailment of wages,
as they have. It is a very great mistake to suppose that the
wages of labor have, as a whole, kept up until 1890. The
wages of skilled labor, at least of many kinds, did keep up
till about that time. But the wages of wage receivers, class-
ing all together, have been steadily falling since 1873. And
that must always take place when prices are falling. In
other words, while the mere increase of purchasing power of
a dollar in wages is a good thing for labor, yet if you introduce a state of affairs which means paralysis of industry, the
cessation of a great deal of industry, a great many failures in
industry, it is impossible that the laborer should keep on in
his old line of prosperity. Since 1873 you have had more
strikes in this country than in all the history of the country
before; you have had more in England, more in France. It
has been one of the phenomena of the period. Say what you
please, it means that the laboring classes, take them as a
whole, have not been as well off during these years as they
were before.

The only class benefited are those who have fixed incomes, such as the bond and other interest bearing debt
holders, Government officials, etc., always providing the
depression does not become so great as to compel repudiation, or, per force, the reduction of taxes and salaries.

CHAPTER VIII.

WHAT THE AUTHORITIES SAY.

In this chapter it is my purpose to quote liberally from the writings and speeches of eminent men residing both in our own and foreign countries whose position and attainments qualify them to be considered as authorities. My object is not only to support the position taken in these articles as explaining the reason why times are hard, but to enlighten the reader on every possible phase of this subject so that should he choose to let his light shine as he must he can not only speak authoritatively but for the benefit of those who want authorities he can quote the most weighty in the world as supporting his facts.

The high priests of the shrine of the golden calf, like to have the public believe that the bimetallists constitute a few miners out west who want to enhance the value of their silver mines and some erratic "silver cranks" and "calamity howlers," among western Populists. That such is not the case is manifest by the many authorities already quoted and those who shall speak through this chapter.

BIMETALLISM IN GERMANY.

Unlike our own Congress in which the great agricultural interests have scarcely a representative, the Agrarian or farmers' party constitutes a strong minority in the German Parliament, a party which has frequently to be consulted and reckoned with in shaping the policy of the empire.

This farmers' party is fully alive to the importance of bimetallism to the interests of the producing classes of the empire and are tireless in their efforts to bring it to the front.

It succeeded in having a commission appointed in January, 1894 to consider the silver question. This commission held its first session February 22, 1894 and continued untill June 6 the same year.

The following is a translation of Mr. Arthur Raffolovich's version of the president's summary of the arguments of bimetallists, extracted from the Economiste Francais of October 27, 1894. We cannot make a better beginning to this chapter than by quoting it here:

The bimetallists alleged that since the introduction of the gold standard, the price of silver has fallen more than fifty per cent. They did not find the cause of this phenomenon in the increase of production, for if, with respect to the comparative conditions of the production of gold and silver, we go back to the year 1850, that is, to a period anterior to the Californian discoveries, we find that the production of gold increased in much larger proportions than that of silver, and that notwithstanding the price of the yellow metal never fell perceptibly at any time. Bimetallists find the causes of the depreciation of silver in governmental measures exclusively, that is, in the demonetization of silver and the closing of the mints to its free coinage.

The bimetallists maintain that there is an unlimited demand for silver, and in support of this, cite the fact that all the silver produced immediately finds a purchaser and that there is no silver on the market in excess of the demand for it. They find the effects of the demonetization of silver, first of all in the increasing purchasing power of gold, and they then infer that, as at present it is necessary to give for the same amount of gold a greater amount of merchandise or of labor than in the past, the gold standard has caused the price of commodities to fall. In order to show the effects of the standard on the prices of the principal articles of consumption, the bimetallists rely on the well-known tables of Mr. Augustus Sauerbeck, on those of the London Economist, and on a whole series of statistical data.

The bimetallists see in this decline of the prices of commodities, not only the cause of the economic crisis, and, consequently, of an economical evil, but they infer that this business depression is attended by disastrous political consequences, and that it may be said that the development of revolutionary socialism, and even that of German Anti-Semitism, depends in a certain measure on business depression. They see in the introduction of bimetallism the remedy for actual economic and political evils; they maintain that

there is not sufficient gold at present for the countries that
have the gold standard already; if these countries maintain
their monetary system, the other states, which still have the
silver standard will be forced by the general conditions of
trade to adopt the gold standard, and from the adoption of
that standard there would result a still greater scarcity of
gold, in consequence of which there would be a new decline
of prices. The bimetallists declare that geological research
shows that there is a great probability that, in the future,
and even in the near future, the auriferous beds of the world
will be exhausted, and that their exhaustion will be followed
by an aggravation of existing evils.

The bimetallists, therefore, demand a legal tender power
of silver equal to that of gold, and they desire to attain that
equality for silver by means of free coinage of the white
metal; from which they expect a greater circulation of the
media of payment, and, as a consequence of the latter, a rise
in prices, and, therefore, the termination of the actual present business depression.

The representatives of bimetallism have besides declared
that the ratio between gold and silver, so far as they are concerned, is a secondary consideration. They say, however,
that the restoration of the old ratio of one to fifteen and one-
half is an end worthy of attainment, and they do not consider
it a condition sine qua non in bimetallic negotiations. They
even believe that the ratio between the two metals may be
the object of a compromise. They allege that from the moment when the demonetization of silver ceased, when the
situation which existed before the adoption of the gold
standard has been restored, the old ratio will become established of itself, and that silver will stand to gold in the ratio
of one to fifteen and one-half. Lastly, they affirm that the
charge made by the monometallists that the bimetallists desire to meet their obligations in a depreciated money or one
of less value is unjust, and this because as soon as, in consequence of the legal introduction of bimetallism, silver has
obtained the same payment power as gold, the payments of
debts may just as well be made in the white metal, whose intrinsic value will be equal to that of gold.

AN ENGLISH VIEW.

The English people are by no means unanimous in favor
of the gold standard, in fact, her agriculturists and productive industries are suffering, perhaps not to a like extent,
but to a great extent, as our own in consequence of this gold
idolatry. In this connection a report of a special commit-

tee appointed by the Liverpool Chamber of Commerce,
February 24, 1879, under the following resolution, in the
light which it sheds on this question from an English
standpoint, makes good and interesting reading:

That the question as to remedial measures for the continued mercantile and manufacturing distress, as being
largely caused and intensified by the discrediting of silver as
money, be referred for consideration to a special committee,
with power to add to their number and report.

The special committee so appointed, reported as follows:

To THE PRESIDENT AND COUNCIL OF THE INCORPORATED
CHAMBER OF COMMERCE, LIVERPOOL. GENTLEMEN:—Your special committee, appointed by the council on February 24 last,
to consider if any and what remedial measures might be
taken for the amelioration of the present mercantile and
manufacturing distress, in so far as it may be caused and
intensified by the discrediting of silver as money, have now
to submit the following report:

In the discharge of the duties devolving upon them your
committee have throughout been impressed by a deep sense
of the important nature of the investigations confided to
them.   In the presence of the extremely depressed state of
trade, and of the long continuance of the depression, the
committee considered their first duty to arrive at the truth
regarding the adverse influence which the recent demonetization of silver in Europe is alleged to be exercising over trade
and commerce throughout the world.   They, therefore, determined to prosecute their inquiries under separate branches,
and they took as the first branch of inquiry the effects of the
discrediting of silver on our commerce and industries, and
after full deliberation and discussion the following conclusions were unanimously arrived at:

EFFECTS OF DISCREDITING SILVER.

1.   That the recent shrinkage in value of the world's silver
money, measured in gold, is very large, and there is every
reason to fear that with the prospect before us the depreciation will continue to increase.

2.   That there has, besides, been much diminution in the
values of investments of English capital in the public funds,
railways, etc., of silver using countries.

3.   That we are now compelled to look upon the silver of
the world as, in large measure, cut off from its previous
sphere of usefulness as one of the two agents for the liquida-
tion of international indebtedness.

4.   That the serious diminution of the world's money,

caused by the disuse of silver, may, in the future, lead to frequent panics, through the inadequate supply of gold for the world's wants.

5.   That the uncertainty regarding the cause of exchanges in the future largely prevents the further investment of English capital in the public funds of silver using countries, or in railways, industrial enterprises and commercial credits.

6.   That the friction and harassment now attending business with silver using countries as India, China, Java, Austria, Chili, Mexico and others, naturally lead merchants to curtail their operations in the export of our manufactured goods, and to restrict the employment of English capital in such business.

7.   That this is a most serious question for India, which many believe to be so impoverished as not to be able to bear increased taxation.

8.   That the depreciation of silver seriously affects the power of silver using states to purchase English manufactures and leads to increased taxation, thus further curtailing the trade which has hitherto been carried on in English commodities.

FACTS CONCERNING PRODUCTION.

Having arrived at conclusions so serious, bearing so directly on the present mercantile distress, your committee next resolved to take into consideration the main facts regarding the production of the two precious metals during the present century.

And they arrived at the following conclusions thereon:

1.   That early in the present century the supply of silver from the mines of the world greatly predominated, being in the proportion of three of silver to one of gold.

2.   That, on the other hand, from the year 1848 and for twenty years thereafter the supply of gold greatly augmented and largely exceeded that of silver.

3.   That during recent years the supply of gold has fallen off very much, viz., from about £33,000,000 in 1852 to £19,-000,000 per annum at the present time, while the supply of silver has augmented considerably.

4.   That at the present time, however, the supply of silver does not equal that of gold, the yield being about £14,000.000 of silver to less than £19,000,000 of gold.

Your committee, consequently, became impressed with the conviction that the recent fall of silver cannot be attributed to excessive production. After further mature deliberation they adopted the following resolution:

That the recent fall in the price of silver is principally to be attributed to the suspension of its free mintage in France and the states of the Latin Union, consequent upon the adverse action of Germany in demonetizing silver. To this resolution there was one dissentient.

At this stage of the inquiry it seemed to be incumbent on your committee to ascertain and put on record their conclusions as to the means by which silver had, for so long a period previous to the year 1874, been kept, with very unimportant oscillations, in such a relation to gold as to make it possible to speak of a par of exchange between the two metals, and the following resolution was adopted by them as expressing the result of their deliberations under this head:

That the bimetallic system of France and the other states of the Latin Union, in conjunction with free mintage prior to 1875, tended to produce an equilibrium between the two metals and to give stability to all exchanges between silver using countries and England.

Your committee having thus arrived at clear and strong convictions as to the magnitude of the evil and the serious consequences to our commerce and industries resulting from the discrediting of silver by the nations of Europe; having ascertained, also, what they believe to be the real cause which has brought about the discrediting of silver as money; and, having recognized the beneficial action of the French bimetallic system, so long as it was in operation, they then proceeded to the consideration of the last, but most important branch of the inquiry, viz.:

THE REMEDIES SUGGESTED.

What remedial measures ought now to be adopted so that silver may again perform, internationally, its proper function as money.

The following resolutions contain the result of their deliberations under this head, and it is especially to these, in their important bearing on the present state of the monetary question and to their effect on Indian finance and on the trade of England that the committee desires to call the attention of the council:

1. That a freed ratio between gold and silver, in conjunction with unlimited freedom of mintage and the recognition of the two metals as full legal tender money, would, if adopted by a majority of the leading monetary powers, including England and India, be adequate to restore silver to its former international value as money.

2. That it is desirable that the government should adopt measures for securing an international agreement by which silver may be restored to its legitimate share in providing metallic currency sufficient for the wants of the world.

Your committee would, in conclusion, refer to the fact that nearly all the members of your special committee attended

the meetings with regularity and were deeply impressed with a sense of the great importance of this inquiry. They desire, also, to place on record the almost unanimity with which resolutions so weighty have been adopted. At the commencement of these investigations much aversion was manifested against adopting conclusions which so directly impugn the wisdom of our monetary legislation of 1816, by which gold was made sole legal tender money in England. If the free mintage system of France had not been suspended, and if monetary legislation on the continent of Europe had not been made, like our own, directly adverse to the use of silver as money in the world, your committee would not have been called on to consider the wisdom or unwisdom of our own position. STEPHEN WILLIAMSON,
Chairman and Vice President of the Chamber.

AN AUSTRIAN VIEW.

Eduard Suess, professor of geology at the University of Vienna, Vice-President of the Imperial Academy of Science, and member of the Austrian Parliament, in his work on "The Future of Silver," written in 1893, says:

For a number of years, on the basis of geologic experience, the world has been warned that its entire monetary system is drifting toward an abyss. During the past year we have approached close to its edge.

As compared with gold, silver is depreciated to an extent without precedent in modern times.

Now, there are short-sighted persons who regard this circumstance as a permanent success for those governments that are in possession of a gold currency; and the complete defeat of silver, and the impossibility of its ever regaining the full dignity of a medium of commerce, especially in Europe, are looked upon as demonstrated.

But this verdict is based on but a small portion of the multitude of facts bearing on the subject. It overlooks the fact that for millenniums the two metals, gold and silver, owing to certain properties by which one became the complement of the other, shared between them the solution of one of the greatest of economic problems; that in recent decades, with the enhancement of material well-being and commerce, this problem has become enormously extended and absorbs constantly increasing quantities of metal; and that the mistake by which the bond of union between the two metals was arbitrarily severed can not become more ominously manifest, for the world's economy and for peaceful progress, than by the divergence of the values of the two metals.

This divergence, moreover, is the very contrary of those

assumptions under which some years ago the introduction of the gold standard was proposed and later on defended.

All commerce proceeded without disturbance as long as gold and silver stood to each other in a relation of value established partly by law and partly by usage. The first impulse toward unsettling this relation was given by the large shipments of gold that came to Europe from California and Australia after the year 1849. The world was startled; gold came in such abundance that it began to fall in value; voices were heard in Paris proposing the complete demonetization of the metal, so unreliable in its production.

The possibility of an international agreement unfortunately recedes more and more in the face of accumulating difficulties. The conditions of production, both in agriculture and in industry in regions with falling standard, depart more and more from the conditions in regions with rising standard. The steady increase and improvement in all the means of mental and physical intercourse has brought about a solidarity of all advanced nations, which comprises not only their modes of thinking, but also a large share of their interests. If, in consequence of withdrawal of gold deposits, the Bank of England raises its rate of discount, every great market of the earth knows it on the same day. The constant silver purchases of the American Treasury determine the level of hydrostatic equilibrium of the price of silver all over the earth. They influence the price of wheat in India, of silk in China, of the sugar that leaves Hawaii. And, as at times an epidemic sweeps over a continent and attacks all nations without regard to political boundaries, so we have seen economic crises spread with invisible power over whole continents, and a single state stand helpless in the presence of the destroying forces.

With the divergence of the values of the two metals the world's commerce approaches a great crisis.

Nature has bounded man's life on earth by certain conditions, to which even the richest nation and the most powerful government must conform.

The present development of the conditions of currency in Europe is in contradiction with the geologic conditions under which the metals occur. The warnings remain unheard. Let us now attempt to trace out some features of this unnatural development of things.

*   *   *   *   *   *   *   *   *   *   *

Speaking of the period succeeding the American Civil War:

In March, 1863, large issues of paper money began to be made, and the mean rate of gold (100—par) is 146. In July,

1864, it reaches 285; about that time the Government debt has already risen to $1,740,000,000, aside from all emissions of the South. In April, 1865, at last the decisive victories of the North take place, while the debt has risen to $2,700,000,000; very slowly the rate of gold sinks, and in 1870 it is still 115.

But this very high rate of gold becomes a premium on the exportation of the wheat, which begins already during the war under peculiar circumstances—that is to say, the premium on gold has raised the price of wheat for the farmer of that part of the country eightfold.

* * * * * * * * * * *

But in order to obtain a correct view of the very complicated and instructive relations which, in the course of that decade, influenced the outflow and inflow of gold, we must, first of all, go back a little and cast a deeper glance into the development of the economic conditions of the country.

At the time of the war, and of the great issues of paper money, high prices for the products of agriculture prevailed; at that time the farmer extended his enterprises and contracted mortgage debts at a rate of interest of ten per cent, and much more. When the value of the dollar rose, the producer's premium disappeared. But at the same time the heavy mortgage debt remained. The great Government debt has dwindled; the mortgage debt has risen by this time to $3,000,000,000. All these circumstances acted all the more oppressively because India, America's competitor in the market of the world, being a silver country, retained its premium.

* * * * * * * * * * *

Thus, in the same year, 1889, there were also exported considerable amounts of silver; the purchase of the higher amount of 54,000,000 ounces per year, that is to say about $70,000,000, by the Treasury, had begun only in autumn of 1890, whereas formerly the amount had been only 24,000,000 ounces per year. The drainage of gold, however, increased, and the Director of the Mint, Mr. Leech, has published accurate records concerning the outflow from New York for the period from February 13 to July 24, 1891, during which this outflow amounted to seventy millions.

"An examination of the above table," says Mr. Leech, "discloses the very singular fact that, of this large amount, all but $9,300,000 was shipped when the rate of sterling exchange was below the point (about $4.886) at which gold shipments can be made without loss. The movement, therefore, must have been artificially stimulated by banks and bankers in Europe paying a premium on gold, or making discounts to bill drawers for cash remittances. This was the result of a condition of affairs very unusual in the mercantile world."

    *   *   *   *   *   *   *   *   *   *

LAW AND NATURE AT VARIANCE.

So long as present conditions continue the difference of the reciprocal value of the two metals will increase from year to year. In other words, nature offers too little gold for present demands, while she offers silver in abundance. Thus the present legislative institutions are at variance with the conditions established by nature. Let us continue the supposition of an unchanged state of legislation. The figures show how quickly, especially since 1885, the value relation has changed, and how slight the influence of the American purchases has been. Even now agriculture, and in part industry in Europe are sorely at disadvantage against silver countries, such as India and Mexico. The most striking proof of this is the development of the Indian cotton-spinning mills at the expense of Lancashire. The advantage of this situation accrues in England to the holders of interest-bearing notes, the productive value of which increases with the growing scarcity of gold.

Under these circumstances it is not surprising that already, in April, 1890, the parliamentary debates on this subject assumed temporarily the embittered character of a struggle of labor against capital, in which the employers and workingmen alike demanded the restoration of the value of silver.

ENGLISH WORKERS KNOW WHERE THE SHOE PINCHES.

The former president of the Chamber of Commerce of Liverpool, S. Smith, submitted 140 petitions, with 60,000 signatures, asking for the re-establishment of the bimetallic system. He described the losses which labor was suffering by the one-sided enhancement of the purchasing power of gold. That, he said, was a tax which the drones of society levied on the working bees. It could not promote the welfare of society if the income of the idle, non-producing class was raised at the expense of the toiling masses. One-half of this new burden was derived from the demonetization of silver. He called the attempt to depreciate silver a huge fraud on civilization. The contraction of the currency was merely in the interest of the rich, and was opposed to the interest of the whole nation.

Sir Houldsworth, a cotton-spinner from Manchester, declared that it was incorrect that the wage worker found indemnification in the fall of the prices of the means of living for the loss in work or wages. That equalization either did not take place at all or at most very late, and for that reason the wage workers were so heartily in favor of this petition, since they regarded these conditions as the root of the long years of losses. Mr. T. H. Sidebottom, a cotton-spinner from Cheshire, lamented the pitiable condition of all debtors in the country, who had assumed burdens under entirely different conditions. The producers were, at this day, the victims of a monetary vivisection. It was said that England is a land of creditors. But who had made her such if not the inventive talent and the industry of her inhabitants?

To this Sir Lyon Playfair replies that the participation in a bimetallic congress means that England, the great creditor of the world, is to invite the debtor nations to deliberate whether the debts contracted in gold since 1816 might hereafter be liquidated in depreciated silver. The new Latin Union would last just so long as England was willing to remain in the union, in order to be shorn like a gentle sheep by the debtor nations.

* * * * * * * * *

SPEAKING OF MEXICAN PROSPERITY.

Aided by this premium on exportation, exports are rising from year to year, wealth flows into the country, and the textile industry begins to improve. "Silver demonetized by Europe," says Struck, "will retaliate in so far as the great industrial countries of Europe, owing to the depreciated value of the white metal caused by the action of these very countries, will never again supply cotton goods of extensive consumption to the Mexican and probably to other markets."

Still more vividly, however, is the shifting of the situation to the disadvantage of Europe expressed by the circumstance that Mexico has utilized this prosperous time for great and permanent investments, which guarantees its productive power for the future and have assured President Porfirio Diaz an undisputed position in this land, formerly disturbed. In his address to Congress in April, 1891, he was able to point out that there are now in operation over 10,000 kilometers of railways and 31,700 kilometers of telegraph lines; that since the preceding August (1890) some 606 new mine concessions had been applied for, that the furnaces of Monterey and San Luis de Potosi had been completed and others were in course of construction; that a public-school law was being elaborated. In a second address, September 16, 1891, the President announced the progress of vine culture and silk culture. Since 1893 the number of pieces sent by mail had risen from 5,000,000 to 125,000,000. Six new steamship lines had been conceded. The customs receipts in four years had risen 9,000,000 pesos.

It might be expected that the great exportation of precious metal would check the development of other kinds of exportation, but this is in nowise the case. While the average exportation of other products of the country in the preceding five years was 49,700,000 pesos, it rose in the last two years to 62,500,000 and 63,100,000 pesos.

The loss which Mexico suffers by the payment of interest on gold debt now amounts to about 2,000,000 pesos a year.

In this way Mexico repeats the same phenomena which were exhibited by the other silver lard, India, to wit, unchanged purchasing power of silver in the country itself, hence premium to the advantage of the producer against gold lands, general economic advance, permanent opening of the country, but on the other hand difficulties of the financial administration due to foreign debt in gold.

WHAT RESULTS WOULD FOLLOW FREE COINAGE.

Let us suppose, therefore, that the United States decide upon the free coinage of silver. Silver rises in value. Perhaps European governments, despite Windom's prediction may succeed on that occasion to get hold of some fraction of the greatly overestimated gold circulation of America, even though it be at the increased price of silver, and thus to offer some transient relief to the gold market in Europe. The prices of the two metals converge. Silver is relieved of a part of the loss which it thus far suffered through lack of esteem, but it does not rise to fifteen and one-half. This result is indicated by the ratio of production, the consumption of gold, and the experience of the slight effect of previous silver purchases on the price of the metal. A premium remains for silver countries, all the more because the causes continue which promote the scarcity of gold.

A pan-American standard may be established on the basis of silver alone. Not without reason does the silver party adhere to Mr. Blaine.

But the outcome of such a movement must be the partition of the earth.

* * * * * * * * * * *

In fact a silver land finds it very difficult to buy of a gold land, and will always prefer to seek its necessaries in a land having the same standard.

In Bolton, near Manchester, the cotton manufacturers have just decided to work only four days in the week and to lie idle for three days. And while in Europe there is thus taking place a displacement of the conditions of production, for which comfort is vainly sought in the cheapening of a few of the means of living, a cheapening which for the most part, vanishes in the retail trade, the Chamber of Commerce of Bengal at the same time passed a resolution which likewise complains bitterly of the present state of things. The confidence in the silver rupee is said to have sunk in business circles. No European capital is said to go any longer to India; the relations between the East and the West are said to be stagnant. The Indian Government would either have to make a move toward international agreement, or, if that be unattainable, it would have to introduce the gold standard into India at once.

Thus the tension is increased, and both parties suffer.

The utterances of the Bengal Chamber of Commerce leads us from the commercial to the financial relations. Indebtedness in gold, especially when it rests on a silver land, manifestly rises from year to year with the divergence of values. While any economic gain due to the premium in the silver land is distributed among thousands of hands, in the figure of interest which is due in gold, the burden finds concentrated expression, and it increases with every fraction by which the ratio rises. Many a statesman of an honestly toiling, upward-striving land watches with anxiety this figure which withdraws from his country undeservedly and inexorably a part of the fruits of its industry, and conveys to the bondholder unearned and unexpected gain. The crises of recent times have furnished abundant examples in which the paying capacity of a debtor country was exceeded and a good part of the capital was lost along with the interest.

Here I would like to return to a word of Balfour's. Money is said to be also the measure of value of deferred payments. The longer the period of deferment the graver must be under present circumstances the consequences of the progressive divergence of the values of gold and silver. The silver land is loth to buy in the gold land but it must be yet far more careful not to incur longtime gold debt. The almost complete cessation of the emission of foreign loans in London in 1891 is a consequence of the experiences in South America, which, however, have become as instructive to all other debtors as they are to the creditors who have to bear the loss. That, and not the success of the gold regime, is at this day the reason of the cheapness of loan money.

* * * * * * * * * * *

Hence any international agreement, though urgently to be recommended will at this day much more than in former years, after the bond, unfortunately, has been prematurely severed, bear the marks of a transition measure. The object of this measure would be to prevent the partition of the earth till the moment, perhaps distant, perhaps near at hand, when Asia shall be more opened up, or when the world shall be ready to dispense entirely with the monetary service of gold.

Europe, I fear, is laboring under a grave delusion. The economy of the world cannot be arbitrarily carried on in the mere hope that somewhere a new California and at the same time a new Australia may be found, as in 1849-52, whose alluvial land may again give relief for a decade. The present

small undulations in the figure of production, however, are
without any further significance for the grand process.

Under these circumstances it might indeed happen that the
results foreseen by Lexis would ensue, to wit, that even with
a very high ratio within a bimetallic union a premium on
gold would grow up in the course of years, called forth not
by the demand for gold for exportation but by the demand
for gold within the area of the league itself.

But any condition is better than the present one, in which
we are drifting on toward the partition of the earth into two
trade areas.

*   *   *   *   *   *   *   *   *   *

We assume the case that the United States, despite all
warnings, establishes the free coinage of silver. At
one blow the Pan-American standard is established.
All Asia joins in. The gold standard is limited to Europe
and the English colonies, but without India. That, we
said, is the partition of the earth. This idea of a partition
of the earth into a silver sphere and a gold sphere has already
come forward repeatedly.

WOULD DENUDE THE EARTH.

In the gold area, too, there would at first be improvement,
but soon there must ensue more and more contraction, fall of
prices, injury to labor.

All obstacles now thrown in the way of commerce by tariffs
would dwindle into insignificance compared to the barrier
that would be erected by the partition of the earth into two
solid areas of different money standards.

As the silver area comprises all zones, all natural products,
and. in the United States, also all industries, a great independent economic unit would be constituted by the silver
area. Exportation from the gold area would be rendered
difficult. and yet the gold area would be dependent on the
other for many products, as is proved by the balance of
goods, already passive in a high degree even to-day, of Great
Britain, Germany and France. Silver capital would grow up
in the silver area, and silver lands would borrow only silver
capital. At the same time, however, in the whole silver
area industry would continue as hitherto, consuming gold.
That is the "walling-in of Europe."

Whether the United States will make this or some other
choice is not known, but in any case some deductions arise
from the present situation.

First of all, it is certain that Europe, in case of refusal to
enter into an international agreement, leaves America's hand
free to enact measures which must exert the most profound
influences on all commerce and on the money affairs of Europe
herself.

Furthermore, it is certain that gold alone can never become the standard of the whole earth, but that, on the contrary, a time will come when it will have been entirely absorbed by industry. Let us not forget Soethbeer's results, according to which the entire monetary stock óf the earth is smaller by almost one-third than the production of the last forty years.

From this it follows, furthermore, that, assuming that the system of metallic coinage continues to exist (and I see as yet no practical substitute), silver will become the standard metal of the earth.

* * * * * * * * * *

When Buckle wrote that famous chapter of his history of civilization in England which treats of the influence exerted by the laws of nature on the institutions of human society, he could not yet have foreseen that it would be possible from the data given by nature to establish a prognosis for perfectly definite economic questions. He took into consideration the distribution of climates and the variety of the external conditions of life. But the comparisons change as soon as man employs a definite substance whose occurrence is subject to definite laws, and as soon as one is able to take into account the limits of occurrence of this substance, the parallax of quantity as it were, albeit within ever so wide confines. Gold is not the rarest metal, but it is too rare for the task which some would like to impose on it.

Delmar, the Chief of the Bureau of Statistics of the United States, put forth the view "that the probable exhaustion of all the great gold-bearing alluviums of the world and the number and the possible wealth of the silver mines, through the effect of quantity and aside from other circumstances, would tend to widen the relation of value between the two metals, and in this way to render gold dearer and dearer, and silver cheaper and cheaper.

The same result was reached at the same time through studies in Europe. Experience since then has confirmed them. The governments to whom belongs the leadership in these things may now ask themselves whether they have the strength and the will to draw the logical conclusions, or whether they will continue to judge a subject which concerns the whole earth merely from the standpoint of the immediate interest of their States; whether, in particular, in England the interest of the Government creditors is to remain the ruling interest.

China was able through thousands of years to draw upon itself for its requirements and to continue in isolation. Europe will not bear isolation from the other continents. The question is no longer whether silver will again become a full-value coinage metal over the whole earth, but what are to be the trials through which Europe is to reach that goal.

CHAPTER IX.

WHAT THE FUTURE PROMISES.

The question most frequently asked, and which greatly concerns producers and business men of all classes, is, "Have we touched bottom?" "Has the terrible financial and commercial depression reached its limit, and may we now look for better things, or at least stability?" Or will the complete legal adoption of the single gold standard tend to further appreciate the exchange value of gold and further depress prices?

The reader must bear in mind that, while practically on a gold basis, the United States has not yet fully adopted the single gold standard. We have made the gold dollar the sole unit of value and relegated silver to the commodities by closing the mints to its free coinage. We have also discredited silver by limiting its legal tender, but as yet the bonds of the nation and all public dues are payable in coin, meaning either coined gold or silver, at the ratio of sixteen to one.

Legal or paper money also is redeemable in silver. It is not the law, but the misguided practice of the President and Secretary of the Treasury which has forced the nation practically onto a gold basis. It is not because they have to, but because they choose to, that paper money is being redeemed in gold only instead of coin. It was not because they were compelled to do so by law that the gold in the treasury was paid out in exchange for greenbacks and bonds issued and sold to replenish the stock of treasury gold to further the purposes of the gang of conspirators in New York and London, but because they chose to do so.

The reader is familiar with the efforts made by President Cleveland and Secretary Carlisle to persuade or coerce Congress into authorizing the issue of gold bonds. The intent was to still further fasten the gold standard upon the country. While there was but little to admire in the LIVth Congress, credit should be given it for refusing to sanction this act. It started in badly by repealing the purchasing clause of the Sherman act without an adequate substitute, thereby greatly intensifying the industrial depression; but it seems at the last end to have awakened to the knowledge that it had been made a catspaw of by the fund-holding classes and refused longer to become a party to the conspiracy to enslave the producing classes.

We are not, therefore, legally on a gold basis, nor is the world at large, but only approaching it. What the consequences would be should the bondholders and other worshipers at the shrine of the golden calf be allowed to accomplish what they are so persistently and cunningly seeking can only be surmised and measured by what we have already suffered in taking the initial steps.

On this subject a noted and clear-headed financial writer, Mr. John A. Grier, says in an article in the Chicago Post:

We sometimes say that we are now on a gold basis. It is a serious error. We are only approaching a gold basis and will not get there until the world utterly discards silver. This is what the gold monometallists, led by Mr. Cleveland and Senator Sherman, are blindly demanding, notwithstanding their protests and denials. Should we ever reach the gold basis, then the present will be referred to as an era of good times and high prices, compared with the times and prices of the promised golden era.

I have already abundantly shown that the fall in prices is not due to the lessening of the exchangeable value of commodities in relation to each other, but to the appreciation of the exchangeable value of gold. It follows, therefore, as a logical conclusion that the nearer we approach the universal gold standard the greater will be the demand for gold, and, as a natural consequence, the higher its exchangeable value in its relation to other products will become. As under the single gold standard it measures prices, the effect is seen in lower prices. The present condition under which we and the entire commercial world are suffering was distinctly foretold more than a quarter of a century ago, and by eminent and far-sighted statesmen since. We were told by these far-sighted financiers that if the great commercial nations demonetized silver these dire results would follow. This advice was not heeded, and we are now suffering the consequences.

Conditions have not materially changed. The commercial nations have not changed their system of finance. It follows, therefore, that the same effects, so plainly foretold, will still follow the same causes.

Water still obeys the law of gravitation the same as it did twenty-five years ago; so also the law that dear money makes cheap products is still in force. It follows, therefore, as an absolute certainty that there can be no substantial return of prosperity as long as this gold craze continues. If it is intensified, if we fully adopt the gold standard or other bimetallic or silver standard nations change to gold, in like degree the prices of labor's products will become lower and the hard times intensified.

I have already called attention to how every step taken by the present administration looking toward the gold standard has tended to depress prices and thus add another link to the galling chain. The first act in calling Congress in special session for the express purpose of repealing the Sherman act was immediately followed by a big fall in the prices of commodities. The next step was the repealing of the act without a substitute recognizing silver. This was followed by another big slump in prices.

Then each bond sale to buy gold was followed by further depression. Then the last special message to Congress asking that body to authorize the issue of a large amount of gold bonds was answered by a drop of four cents a bushel in the price of wheat. As soon as it became certain that Congress would not comply with the President's wishes a reaction took place and prices went up again. When it was found that the Senate had a strong silver majority prices advanced another notch, and have since remained firmer. This barometer of the markets is a sure indication of the pulsation of prosperity, and those who want to get at a true solution of this question will do well to study it carefully.

EFFECTS OF FALLING PRICES.

The effects of a continuation of the gold policy as it now exists, to say nothing of extending it, will result disastrously to at least four out of five farmers who have mortgages on their farms. Under the present conditions, with the present prices of farm products, it will be an utter impossibility for a farmer to live, pay the annual interest and taxes and pay off the mortgage. It means for him ruin; that whatever accumulation he has made and invested in his farm will eventually be absorbed by the mortgagee and he himself relegated to the large and rapidly increasing body of renters.

Of the baleful influence of falling prices on agriculture Senator Jones, in his speech before the International Monetary Conference at Brussels in 1892, said:

Under the baleful influence of falling prices, agriculture ceases to be profitable. In the case of leased farms, the rent, which was just and equitable when fixed, becomes, with the progress of time, unjust and inequitable, the payment requiring from year to year a constantly increasing proportion of the product, till nothing is left for the tenant but the hardest and barest existence. * * * Very few working farmers own their own farms free. The mortgage that, at the beginning, was equivalent to but one-half the value of the farm, soon, owing to the fall of prices of the product and consequent reduction of value of the property, becomes worth three-fourths and ultimately, in many cases, upon the maturity of the mortgage, the farmer finds himself compelled to yield up his entire farm to the mortgagee in satisfaction of the incumbrance. Thus, by reason of a fall of prices, owing to an increase in the value of the money unit, agriculturists are reduced from comparative comfort to absolute penury.

In looking for bodies of land for colonies I have encountered many object-lessons showing how, under the present condition, the banks and money-lenders are rapidly absorbing the landed as well as other wealth of the country. In California we examined tract after tract of land varying in size from 2,000 to 80,000 acres, which had either been absorbed by the banks or money-lenders, or which the owner, on account of the depressed condition of agriculture, must sell or lose his all to the mortgagee.

We were offered one lot of land comprising 80,000 acres, all of which had been absorbed by one San Francisco bank for less than half its value under trust deeds. It was offered us at about $200,000 advance over what it had cost the bank, and this was considered cheap.

In Mississippi I was offered 60,000 acres in small farms, all of which had been absorbed by one Jewish money-lender. He was anxious we should help him turn these farms into money so that he could still further spread his nets.

These are but large instances. Every reader of this who is a farmer can recall minor ones in his own neighborhood, or perhaps is himself a living example.

While those who have mortgaged farms have thus seen their accumulations vanish, and find themselves reduced to penury and the slavery of renters, those who own their farms find values have greatly depreciated. Farms which a few years ago they valued at from $50 to $100 an acre, and could have sold at that price, cannot now be sold at half that money. Congressman Sibley, in his speech in

Congress January 8, 1895, aptly illustrates this. He says:

Nothing more clearly illustrates the increasing value of money than an example the force of which must be apparent to the dullest intellect. If a man had sold his farm for $30,000 in 1873 and buried his money deep into the earth, or, as men do, placed it at interest at six per cent, in addition to his interest, with one-third of his $30,000 he can to-day repurchase the same farm. If this man has gained $20,000 and the interest on $30,000 for twenty years, then certainly the man who purchased the farm has lost $20,000 of his purchase money and the interest on $30,000. If a farmer had sold $10,000 worth of horses in 1874 he could purchase others, their equal to-day, for $2,000. If he had sold his beef cattle from off his farm for $6,000, he could buy back to-day an equal or greater weight of beef cattle for $2,000. Money has been magnified; sources and profits of industry have been minimized. If the man who sold the farm for $30,000 in 1873 had placed it at interest at six per cent it would amount to more than $100,000, in 1894, with interest annually added to principal. If the one man has gained through appreciation of money and interest more than $90,000 net, the man who purchased has certainly lost an equal sum. By vicious legislation money has been made a monarch, while industry and production have become beggars on the face of the earth.

Let the reader bear in mind that while farms and the holdings of the producing classes have been thus depreciating in price the bonds, mortgages and similar possessions of the fund-holding classes have been increasing in purchasing power in like ratio. The annual interest which you pay on your mortgage, or the interest which the bondholder draws, and which you pay through your taxes, railroad freights, or on the article you buy, will now buy twice as much of your land and products as formerly.

THE DECADENCE OF HOME OWNERSHIP.

In the American Magazine of Civics Mr. J. A. Collins discusses the question of the rapid absorption of the farms and homes of the people of the moneyed class, as shown by the rapid increase of renters. In considering the extracts from this article given below the reader should bear in mind that they are based on the decade be-

tween 1880 and 1890, during a period of supposed prosperity.   In all probability could a census be taken now it
would show results that would be more appalling.   Mr.
Collins says:

In Massachusetts, in 1880, only 8.18 per cent of farms were
occupied by tenants; in 1890, 15.06 per cent were so occupied,
and 25.07 per cent were mortgaged; showing 40.93 per cent of
her farm population virtually tenants—a diminution of 32.75
per cent.   In towns 67.28 per cent hire their homes, and 12.78
per cent are mortgaged, making 80.15 per cent of the urban
population virtually tenants.   Averaging town homes and
farms together, hired and mortgaged, 77.32 per cent of the
entire population are tenants.   *   *   *
In Rhode Island, in 1880, only 19.88 per cent of the farms
were hired; in 1890, 25 per cent were hired and 14.29 per cent
mortgaged, showing 39.29 per cent of her farm families virtually tenants, a diminution of free owners of 19.41 per cent.
Of her urban population, 79.26 per cent are tenants and 7.88
per cent mortgaged, making 87.14 per cent virtually tenants.
In Vermont, in 1880, 13.41 per cent of the farms were hired;
in 1890, 17.62 per cent were hired and 36.53 per cent mortgaged, making 54.15 per cent virtually tenants, a diminution
in free owners of 40.74 per cent.   Of the city homes, 54.39 per
cent are hired and 16.82 per cent mortgaged, total virtually
tenants 71.21 per cent.

Turning to the South and West, Mr. Collins finds these
results:

In the South the conditions are shown to be no better than
in New England, although land mortgages are not so common, the lender preferring a lien on the cotton crop as security, cotton being much more readily turned into money.
For this reason the bulk of the debt in the South is represented by crop liens and chattel mortgages.   In Georgia, in
1880, 44.85 per cent of the farms were occupied by tenants; in
1890, 58.10 per cent were so held and 1.42 per cent were mortgaged, showing 59.52 per cent of the farmers to be virtually
tenants; a diminution of 14.67 per cent in ten years.   In cities
80.26 per cent hired their homes in 1890 and 1.08 per cent were
mortgaged, showing 81.34 per cent to be virtually tenants.
In Tennessee, in 1880, 34.53 per cent of the farmers were tenants; in 1890, 41.88 per cent hired their farms and 1.87 per
cent were mortgaged; 43.75 per cent tenants.   Of homes in
towns 79.72 per cent are hired and 1.73 per cent mortgaged;
81.45 per cent of the urban population tenants.   In South
Carolina, in 1880, 50.31 per cent of the farms were hired; in
1890, 61.49 per cent were hired and 3.08 per cent mortgaged;

64.57 per cent of the farm population tenants. The general average of farms and city homes is 71.03 per cent ▮▮▮ ▮▮▮ 2.17 per cent mortgaged.

The figures for the Western States show them ▮▮ ▮▮▮▮▮▮ ing steadily and surely to the condition of the older ▮▮▮▮▮ ▮▮ the East. In Wisconsin, in 1880, 9.05 per cent of the farms were hired; in 1890, 13.10 per cent were hired and 37.45 per cent were mortgaged, showing 50.34 per cent of the farmers to be virtually tenants, a diminution of over forty per cent in free owners. * * * In Minnesota, in 1880, of her farm population 9.15 per cent were tenants; in 1890, 15.25 per cent were tenants and 39.31 per cent were mortgaged, making 54.56 per cent virtually tenants. This is a fair index for the West.

Emphasizing the fact that the evil is not due to local causes, and is not confined to any one section, Mr. Collins next offers a striking comparison of the proportion of tenants in the United States with that of the same class in other countries, and he finds that this country shows a greater proportion of tenant families than any other nation with the exception of Great Britain. Here is the table (in which, however, the figures for Great Britain are not given):

Country.	Percentage of Tenants.
Australia	10.17
Belgium	33.02
Denmark	66.09
France	28.94
Holland	39.60
Portugal	28.17
Sweden	17.32
Canada	12.01
Germany	84.31
Italy	55.19
Norway	81.82
South Africa	55.00
United States	(over) 70.00

Mr. Collins concludes his article with these words:

Is it not startling that in the greatest republic on earth, whose free institutions and free homes have been its boast for a hundred years, the percentage of its dependent population should be greater than even in the monarchies of Europe? This startling diminution of the number of free home-owners is an indication that points to a dark future for our country unless something is done to stay the tide of landlordism, and curb the greed of speculation that like an octopus has wound its deadly tentacles about the American home.

This does not speak well for Republican institutions. It must be traced, however, directly to following English financial policy.

"If America adopts our system of finance," said Pitt at the close of the Revolution of 1776, "her boasted liberties will be but a phantom." We are following English gold policy, and the above statistics, together with the other matter given in this book, show what is becoming of our liberties.

There is a rift in the cloud horizon. The silver lining is beginning to appear. The people are getting their eyes open, and with the awakening will come a reaction. The silver Moses is descending from the mount. With him is the power which will destroy the idol of the golden calf and rebuke its priests and worshipers.

Let everyone who has the light in him let it shine, and the darkness and inhuman heartlessness of this gold idolatry will quickly vanish. Hold aloft the banner of "bimetallism and prosperity," which is the symbol of honor, humanity, patriotism and national progress, and fight this fight as you would do battle for your homes and firesides, and right will surely triumph in the end. Remember your weapon is an intelligent vote for a candidate irrespective of party affiliations, who is an honest bimetallist, with the courage of his conviction, and that the duty of the hour is to educate as many such votes as possible before the election of 1896.